# A Sociosemiotic Theory
of Theatre

# A Sociosemiotic Theory of Theatre

**Jean Alter**

*upp*

UNIVERSITY OF PENNSYLVANIA PRESS    Philadelphia

Copyright © 1990 by the University of Pennsylvania Press
Printed in the United States of America

Library of Congress Cataloging-in-Publication Data

Alter, Jean.
    A sociosemiotic theory of theatre / Jean Alter.
       p.    cm.
    Includes bibliographical references and index.
    ISBN 0-8122-3054-X
    1. Theater—Semiotics.   2. Semiotics—Social aspects.   I. Title.
PN2041.S45A48   1991
792'.014—dc20                          90-41885
                                             CIP

Pour Elles
    Celle qui n'est plus
    Celle qui m'épaule
    Celle qui marche vers l'avenir

# Contents

# Preface

This book is certainly ambitious: it dares to propose a "theory." It is also somewhat provocative: some of its postulates run counter to widely accepted notions about theatre and semiotics. My initial intentions were more modest. I started to write this book, about a dozen years ago, in order to explore the newly rediscovered field of semiotics of theatre. Within a short time, however, it was thoroughly mapped in several major studies and hundreds of articles. There was no point in duplicating that work. I discarded my early project and, like many others, focused my research on a few discrete theoretical problems.

Meantime semiotics of theatre has become a dynamic discipline. A newsletter I was publishing could barely keep up with announcements of new books, articles, and colloquia. But this vitality had a price: a growing dispersion of research, and a certain complacency. It seems today that a tacit agreement on the general nature of theatre semiotics is masking considerable disagreements, that even the most dedicated scholars are reluctant to reexamine, or revise, fundamental concepts that generate misunderstandings. It may be too late to try to reconcile their diverging theories. But the time is right, I believe, to go back to basic notions about theatre and semiotics, clarify their problematic concepts, and propose a new theory that would strictly keep to its theoretical foundations, without concessions to prevailing opinions.

Hence this ambitious and provocative book. It has five parts. The Introduction provides the foundations of the theory. It discusses the nature of traditional theatre, and offers a theoretical outline of socio-criticism and semiotics that determine my approach. Part I deals with a basic duality of theatre which, at the same time, proposes a show on the stage and a story in an imaginary space, creating a tension between its referential and performant functions. Part II develops a formal grammar of theatre signs, articulating the mechanism of their referential operations in any given performance. Part III proposes a transformational theory of theatre as a total process, defining the text-to-stage transition as a series of production/reception transformations. Finally, Part IV analyzes various factors, including social conditions, that influence the attitude and production of authors, directors, and actors.

# Introduction: Foundations

## 1. What Theatre?

A future historian of theatre, impressed by recent pronouncements on the state of drama and stage, might call the past two decades, give or take a few years, the Time of Great Experiments. Or, the Age of Transition, during which theatre, as it has been known in the West since the ancient Greeks, finally changed into something different that still might be named theatre, but then might not. This future historian would point out that, at least in the West, we have witnessed a widespread and multiform subversion of theatrical traditions on a scope unparalleled in the past. Indeed, today's onslaught of new forms appears not only to threaten some of the most venerable features of theatre, such as the central role of the Word, but to undermine the entire traditional concept of theatrical activity. The avant-garde no longer simply attempts, as it always must, to carry out transformations within an inherited medium; it claims it is creating a medium of its own, sometimes retaining the old name of theatre, sometimes preferring others: spectacle, show, performance. With the vanishing Word, we are told, dialogues must disappear from the stage together with characters supporting the dialogues; and without characters, there can be no plot built on a story. Traditional plays are replaced by a variety of public events, from discontinuous tableaux to spontaneous happenings, calling for a variety of media, from the human body to electronic effects, and inviting a variety of audience participation.

With hindsight wisdom, the future historian might explain what all these new experiments have in common, what new type of theatre they are nurturing, if any. Our present vision, however, is still too fragmented and disoriented to yield any credible forecast of things to come. Only one observation can be made safely: Whatever its profound nature, and its outcome, the current negation of the past theatrical practice endows it with an identity that was not clearly perceived before. Paradoxically, as it is questioned and undermined with increasing violence, theatre as we know it increasingly coalesces into a distinct and closed genre, born in Greece a couple of millennia ago, regenerated several times, and possibly coming to an end in our times.

No doubt similar claims could have been made at various moments in the past. Western theatre has lived through many crises, transgressions of traditions, inventions of new forms. Atellan farces in Rome developed apart from the Greek dramatic heritage; liturgical dramas in the Middle Ages, then mysteries and Fools' plays, emerged when the classical theatre faded away; processional plays, commedia dell'arte, court masques, penny gaffs, musical melodramas offered new and subversive forms. Barely a century and a half ago, when he belatedly discovered "le drame" in France, Victor Hugo thought that he had done away with the French traditional theatre. In the twentieth century, comparable hopes were formulated by the futurists for their Variety Theatre or the Teatro dello Stupore, by the Bauhaus group for the Theatre of Totality, by Brecht for the Epic Theatre, and so forth. Yet few of these breaks involved a clear and conscious rejection of the Western theatrical tradition, entailing its closure as a genre. Some new forms evolved when the tradition was absent but waned with its (re)appearance; others thrived only on its fringes; still others eventually merged into it; and most contributed to its enrichment, development, and, hence, strengthening. Even prophets who, like Artaud, prayed for a total overthrow of traditional theatre, castigating it as a dead genre with fixed rules, inspired its rejuvenation rather than its burial.

The present situation is different. For never before, it would seem, the proliferation of new theatrical forms has benefited from a comparable license unchecked by normative concepts of what theatre must be. In the absence of rules, whether to be followed or broken, anything goes or may go as theatre as long as it is asserted to be theatre. No authority sets limits; and no one can predict what could be presented and accepted as theatre. Because of its open-ended nature, the process of theatrical creation thus displays a ludic freedom, contrasting with the constraints of a tradition that required a deliberate transgression to bring about any dramatic change.

Exploiting that freedom, diverse recent experiments are generating an unprecedented atomization of theatrical forms. Previously, even the most innovative periods rarely produced more than a couple of alternate styles; and those which survived their cultural isolation usually matured into new traditions. Today, the effervescence of theatrical experimentation transcends social and temporal boundaries. The entire world supplies theatre practitioners with an incredibly varied choice of inspiration: No, Kabuki, Kathakali exotic models, early ritual or shamanist ceremonies, African dances, Balinese mimes, reconstructed medieval mysteries, adaptations of commedia dell'arte, rediscovered classics of ancient foreign traditions. At the same time, modern technology is creating wonders on the stage that far surpass the impact of mechanical or electrical contrivances of the boldest designers in the past: Again, there seems to be no limit to what can be done with electronic inventions.

Furthermore, as soon as an experiment achieves a breakthrough, visual media are spreading it throughout the Western theatre community, stimulating interaction and new research. Additionally, never before have so many theatre people traveled around, and never so rapidly; never have so many festivals brought together so many groups from distant countries, each learning from the others. As a result, the avant-garde theatre displays, as in a kaleidoscope, a rapid succession of changing forms, combining and recombining the old and the new, and rarely maintaining one pattern long enough to let it be fixed into a tradition. It evokes an exuberant jungle where strange shapes flash suddenly, disappear, reappear elsewhere, disappear again; sometimes similar despite differences, sometimes quite surprising, fascinating, and frustrating in their ephemeral mobility. In comparison, any traditional theatre resembles a well laid out French garden that, with separate beds assigned to different varieties of flowers, presents a unified scheme despite the heterogeneity of its vegetation.

A parallel revolution is taking place in the normative area of theatre theory. Authoritative concepts are progressively replaced with individual approaches that stress relativity. True, from Aristotle to Brecht, theoreticians never ceased to advocate new theories about what theatre is or should be; but each claimed in his time that his theory had a universal validity. Some derived that authority from the observation of the dominant theatrical practice, others justified it by ethical or social ideals that demanded transformations of that practice. Whichever the case, past theories were always bound to a tradition, either given as a source and upheld as a model, or proposed as a future goal. Both types of tradition, actual or potential, influenced in their turn the ongoing creative activity, ensuring cohesion between canonical theory and praxis.

The present avant-garde theories have no such normative implications, no universal justifications. On the contrary, in the spirit of the fashionable polyphonic approach to art, theoreticians now assert their right to redefine theatre in their own individual way; and, as they do not lay claims to general validity, a single theatrical event suffices to support any single theory. Even theories that prophesy the end of theatre are validated by that logic, albeit temporarily, since some theatre groups, like the Living Theatre, have indeed carried out the predicted self-immolation. And theatre critics, echoing the Babel of discordant theoretical voices and the fragmentation of avant-garde practices, have been chasing after each new fad, fueling rather than dispelling the confusion.

The future historian's scenario of an Age of Transition is thus grounded in an unique upheaval in the theatre world. Yet, it is not the only possible scenario. It is persuasive as long as one views the theatre from the perspective of the avant-garde, but it loses much of its relevance when one looks at the total theatrical picture, focusing on the mainstream theatre. That larger perspective yields indeed a different scenario, minimizing the long-term impact of the subversion of traditional forms. For tradition is still alive and strong in theatre, and its capacity to assimilate the boldest innovations has not yet been fully tested. Nor can one assess its ability to survive the competition of the avant-garde, to resist its revolutionary thrust. But, whether it is coming to an end or not, traditional theatre still dominates the Western stage, manifesting a relatively sound constitution. It may not be as dynamic as at some glorious moments in the past, nor as exciting as the avant-garde, but it is not moribund either. In fact, it still draws most of theatre audiences and makes the most money.

One may deplore this popular appeal of traditional theatre. Obviously, it rests on a strategy that aims to please the largest number of spectators rather than to explore new theatrical forms. But this strategy does not entail a stubborn rejection of change. Theatrical taste evolves under the pressure of cultural, social, and technological developments, and theatre always responds to new demands. By osmosis, furthered by media, successful experiments of the avant-garde spill over on the commercial stage, even rejuvenate Broadway musicals. Overall, traditional theatre today may appear iconoclastic by the standards that prevailed a few decades ago. But it is a slow transformation, a cautious adaptation of new forms tested on the fringe of tradition. Traditional theatre innovates very little on its own. And even its boldest changes are smoothly integrated with the traditional features that the avant-garde has been questioning. However stunning the staging, the most tenuous plots still tell a story, performances still use a text, and actors still speak words. One may claim that the vitality of theatre thus results from a parasitic ability to feed on change without risking a change, to accept transformations without losing identity, to undergo evolution but no metamorphosis.

It is therefore possible that the future historian, instead of recording a mutation of theatre in our times, will rather refer to a new renaissance of theatrical tradition, comparable to the many rebirths it had experienced before as a condition of its survival. In that version, far from withering, traditional theatre would demonstrate once again the amazing flexibility of its nature, assimilating modernity and displaying a renewed vigor. Avant-garde experiments, which inspired this renaissance but did not directly participate in it, would be relegated to a brief chapter acknowledging their influence and their rapid exhaustion. In that scenario, their seminal outburst of subversion would end in a wild marginality, as happened to Dada. Or perhaps, in a third scenario, they would be described as early manifestations of a new distinct genre, spun off by theatre but separated from it by the regenerated prestige of tradition: a genre that would also include other performance events such as one-man shows, beauty queen pageants, Cristo's exploits, son-et-lumière spectaculars, or live versions of video clips.

Visibly, among the various possible scenarios, only one shows a future theatre that breaks with all traditions and yet is still identified as theatre. A theory of theatre oriented by that uncertain outcome would be highly speculative. Granted, speculation of this sort has its rewards: satisfaction of matching tradition and subversion, bridging past and future, designing a universal model that could encompass all future types of theatrical activity. Some theatre scholars have yielded to the temptation and evolved theories that, in the words of Bernard Beckerman, could equally apply to "traditional European plays, less familiar non-Western drama, and the inchoate forms emerging from the present state of theatrical chaos."[1] Under the catchword of "theatre," the same writer groups, together with drama, such varied events as circuses, dances, and sport games. For other scholars, theatrical activity covers all types of ritual performances.[2] The insights thus gained are often valuable; they are not at issue. But the reliability of a theory founded on speculation must be questioned. In the last analysis, a universal theatrical activity that accounts for all public events that could be designed as theatre opens on a tautology: any example will demonstrate a theory that is tailored to accept any possible example. The vast horizons of speculation do not offer precise notions; they lead to teleological guesswork.

It is much sounder and safer to stay with given data, that is, a well-established theatre corpus, and to propose a theory that derives from both old and new traditions of that corpus. Aristotle's *Poetics* remains exemplary of that approach. True, Aristotle does not entirely avoid speculation, notably when he postulates, at the source of theatre, a universal instinct of mimesis. But most of his specific theatrical theory clearly refers to what was the theatrical practice in his times—to Greek stage from the moment when "tragedy, after various changes, reposed at length in the completion of its proper form."[3] He has some definite ideas about ways of improving that theatre, but offers no speculation about its future transformations, "a question that belongs not to this place."[4] The influence exerted by his *Poetics* for so many centuries and the prestige it still commands testify to the power of a theory rooted in a fixed corpus and yet flexible enough to accommodate many variations within its basic schemes.

Contemporary theoreticians do not have Aristotle's advantage of dealing with a relatively limited corpus. But recourse to open-ended universals, fascinating and fashionable as they may be, is not inevitable. As we have noted, the systematic assault on basic forms of today's theatre is now defining a much greater but equally well-delineated corpus: the theatrical tradition negated by the extreme avant-garde. Until recently, there was no convenient distance from which to survey all that had happened to Western theatre since Aristotle. Within its long tradition, differences appeared to be more significant than shared features, and shared features were taken for granted. The body of theatre, as it can be now assembled, seemed to present no unified pattern. Today, however, when they are questioned, the shared features of that complex tradition are dramatically emerging as its fundamental structures, and differences are reduced to the status of temporary variations. Theatre that used to be, and still overwhelmingly is, can be deconstructed into a small number of structural elements that are indispensable for its survival. On the basis of these features, it is then possible to formulate a theory of the living theatre. It may not account for all past theatrical manifestations, because not all of them have followed the main lines of tradition, but the exceptions are marginal. Some avant-garde experiments may also be expected to fall outside such a theory when they deliberately seek to negate all tradition. But it is not certain. Many traditional forms, as we shall see, contaminate even those new forms that flout tradition or that tradition did not anticipate.

*    *    *

The actual number of theatrical practices that are subverted by the avant-garde is surprisingly small. Disregarding individual variations, one can reduce them to five basic features. Perhaps the most fundamental, and allegedly the most endangered, is the reliance of theatre performance on a prior verbal text. Yet that text plays an essential role in theatre. Its existence ensures that at least one stage in the theatrical process can remain stable. Like scores in music, fixed texts are expected to generate, by a series of transformations, an unpredictable number of ephemeral performances, sometimes similar one to another and sometimes quite different. Thanks to the texts, theatrical events can thus combine the old and the new, build up the new on the old, revive the old through the new. Furthermore, preserved verbal texts offer us the best records of past performances. Our ideas about Greek, Elizabethan, or French romantic theatre are mainly based on our familiarity with drama by Sophocles, Shakespeare, or Hugo. Without such texts, however minute our research of secondary sources, it would be hard to reconstruct past stage events, compare performances of the same play at different times, propose a history of theatre, establish a theatrical tradition.

The verbal text can be oral or written, or both. In the Western tradition, few oral texts have been preserved without having been recorded in writing at some time. Like many improvised performances, most purely oral texts are gone forever. Secondary sources mention them, but we cannot know what they were exactly. Our familiarity with past performances of the commedia dell'arte benefits from the existence of written indications, or bits of dialogues, upon which some of them were based. Written texts, in contrast, largely conserve their verbal integrity despite linguistic changes. And, since Gutenberg, they have become widely available. For the last centuries, printed drama has thus provided the standard for the verbal text, the basic theatrical document for scholars and directors dealing with the problematic relation between text and performance.

The current vulnerability of the prior text as an essential feature of theatre may have been partly caused by subversion carried out by avant-garde experiments. But a much greater threat lies in the potential of video recording. Theoretically, with the invention of motion pictures at the turn of the century, the written text lost its status as the only permanent document of the theatrical process: it could be replaced by a film. However, for technical or economic reasons, very few movies have provided reliable records of performances. Even today, despite the wide availability of cheap videocassettes, with plays prerecorded or recorded from television shows, there are few serious performance libraries, and only very successful performances are made available to the public on video. But the potential exists. Of course, even the best video recording does not replace a live performance; but neither does the written text. And both serve equally well as generators of future performances. It could be claimed that no one expects to see new performances based on a recorded Planchon's staging of *Tartuffe*, while many expect to see new performances of Molière's *Tartuffe*. But why not? Surely a film could inspire as many transformations as a text. In fact, performances are now called "performance texts," or "testo spettaculare," and it would be logical if Planchon's *Tartuffe*, recorded on video, were to be restaged with various subtle or dramatic transformations. Cinema has shown the way with remakes or alterations of its classics. The question is whether a theatre relying on prior performance texts rather than on purely verbal texts could still qualify as theatre. Obviously, the nature of the "author" would be different. But a text is a text, and the sequence text-performance would not change. Perhaps the ascendance of video recordings as basic theatrical texts would rejuvenate traditional practices instead of signifying their end.

A second feature of theatre now under attack is the story. Traditionally, theatre always tells a story. It may be a story about historical characters or imaginary characters, individuals with names or anonymous types, personified animals or animated objects, social groups or ideologies, emotions and aesthetics. Some stories may even be absurd or contradictory. But all must be stories; that is, they must articulate a certain number of events that are related in a specific pattern and carried out by one or more characters. This means in turn that theatre must respect the laws of causality associated with any storytelling. It has been claimed that ideas, or even simple stories, can be presented on the stage with juxtaposed or repeated static scenes rather than with causally related actions; and some avant-garde experiments of the Living Theatre attempted to demonstrate it. But most theatrical practices eschew static scenes and, when they present a series of discontinuous tableaux, "vivants" or animated, they connect them logically one to another or topically to the general theme of the story.

The central issue is the survival of the story, whatever the way of telling it. As long as there is a story, it can be told with a linear chronology or with flashbacks, continuously or with gaps, in a realistic or symbolic style, in an open or closed space, with or without explicit commentary, clearly or obscurely, economically or with redundancy, stressing verbal or physical expression, appealing to reason or emotions, and so forth. The resilience of traditional forms of theatre owes much to the flexibility of its narrative strategies, enabling it to assimilate avant-garde experiments that offer new ways of telling a story but do not question storytelling as such. As a result, some of the boldest performances of modern plays, for example the staging of *Waiting for Godot* on the roofs of an industrial city, clearly belong to a traditional concept of theatre, enhancing its appeal with a surface rejuvenation.

Third feature: action must be carried out by human beings, that is, actors. This tradition is so essential to theatre that few avant-garde practitioners advocate getting rid of all live actors. Yet various attempts have been made to minimize their dominant role. In some plays, say by

Beckett or Handke, they are deprived of physical presence. Their disembodied voices provide the only action on the stage, sometimes telling a story taking place elsewhere, sometimes carrying the story by their mere presence. Or, again as in Beckett, their bodies act and carry a story, but they are totally silent. In the same spirit, recent theoreticians have tried to expand the notion of theatre so as to include puppet shows, especially when visible puppeteers supply the puppets' voices.[5] But are puppets really theatre? One notes that, for most people, puppets stand for human beings. Granting them the symbolic status of live actors, one could place them within the limits of theatrical tradition.

This does not mean that all action must be performed by actors. Mechanical devices have always been used when nonhuman characters play a role in the story: gods, supernatural powers, animals, machines, or animated objects. When they are made to talk, of course, their live voices evoke a human agency. But vocal or silent, they do not substitute for actors who retain the central position in the story and on the stage. The only real subversion of tradition occurs when, as in some musicals, the appeal of glamorous mechanical devices preempts the interest in human stories. But such cases are marginal despite the growing role played by technological wonders in musicals as well as in avant-garde theatre. A more significant threat to the centrality of actors lies rather in the ever more widespread use of nontheatrical media on the stage. Films, video clips, and written texts projected on vertical surfaces can be made to contribute much to both the action and story of a play. Yet this trend, begun by Piscator in the early twentieth century, has failed to reach its full potential development. And traditional theatre has smoothly integrated its mildest forms, making them serve the actors rather than compete with them.

Whether actors are professionals or amateurs has little relevance in that context. They can even be drawn from the audience. But they must truly perform as actors, that is, act out the characters in the story. One hears frequent calls for a theatre where "actors play themselves."[6] As such, the formula is doubly misleading. In the first place, in order to play oneself, one always must see oneself as an other, and hence play an other. In the second place, all actors in that sense always play themselves as actors after the opening night of a performance. But these equivocations should not hide the real meaning of the demand, which is that actors should act their own story produced by them at the time of the performance. A few experiments carried out in that spirit collapsed rapidly; for theatre has always demanded that actors play characters that they are not, tell a story that is not their own. In that sense, both characters and story are fictions for the actors as well as for the audience. Even historical figures have a fictional status on the stage because they never appear there themselves, nor perform their own actions. To the extent that it always tells an imaginary story, theatre thus always offers fiction.

The next feature, recently much discussed by defenders and de-tractors of conventional theatrical practices, posits a strict autonomy of the performance space. Whatever its specific form, this area is taken to be reserved for actors, while a precise boundary separates it from another area assigned to the audience. Various avant-garde perfor-mances have sought to break that boundary and, by the same token, to destroy the very notion that theatrical activity must take place in a special, distinct, and closed space. Performances were staged in the street, in public squares, in factories, in private houses and apartments, on country roads—in short, in any location that, in contrast with traditional practices, could not be experienced as an autonomous stage area.

Yet one should not overestimate the novelty of these subversions. Nor, which comes to the same, the role that a special performance space played in traditional theatre. True, most of its past perfor-mances, from the Greeks to off-off-Broadway, were presented in spaces specifically designed for that purpose. But many also took place in ad hoc locations, inside or in front of churches, on pageant wagons travel-ing the highways, in drawing rooms or in taverns. While certainly favoring a stage, theatre does not seem to be bound to any particular type of stage; it has long demonstrated its ability to turn any space into a stage.

More significant appears to be the symbolic barrier that, whatever the actual performance area, separates actors from spectators. Perhaps because it always tells a fiction, theatre postulates a discontinuity be-tween the real world of the public and the fictional world of the characters evoked on the stage. To enforce the separation between the two worlds, actors are expected not to enter the space of the spectators and vice versa. It is this convention that *Dionysius in 69*, and other manifestations of audience participation, transgressed with notable effects. Here again, however, one must observe that such transgres-sions are not really new. The barrier between the two worlds was already breached when a "maître de jeu" evolved among actors of medieval church plays, just as it is now when Kantor directs on the stage the performance of his Krakow theatre. Similarly, the public and comedians mingled on the seventeenth-century French stage, penny gaffs performers interacted with tavern customers, and all sorts of addresses were made by actors to the public, from Shakespeare to T. S. Eliot. Perhaps the entire notion of two separate worlds embodied in two separate spaces needs to be revised. Perhaps spatial and symbolic barriers must both be respected as a rule and transgressed for specific reasons. A closer examination of concrete theatrical practice could help to clarify that point. At this time, it suffices to note that an autonomous performance area, despite derogations, still operates as a traditional theatrical space. In other terms, that theatrical practice still postulates the presence of some "stage," that is, a distinct space reserved for the staging of a text.

The last feature involves the much debated centrality of the Word, especially in the form of dialogues. It is a crucial matter, linked to the role of the text as a permanent core of theatre. Of course, no dramatic text is exclusively composed of dialogues; it may minimize them while expanding stage directions or commentary. There is no doubt, however, that traditional dramatic texts have overwhelmingly favored dialogues. From the time when Aristotle credited Aeschylus with establishing the dialogue as "the principal part of tragedy,"[7] little has changed in that area until the recent calls to remove the word from the stage, or at least to downplay its function. This movement away from a verbal theatre has affected the staging of many traditional plays, classical as well as modern. In Planchon's *Tartuffe*, in Mesguich's *Hamlet*, in all performances of *Waiting for Godot*, body language and costumes of actors, and all sorts of visual stage business, have been competing with the dialogue, sometimes dampening or transforming its message. But none of these experiments tampered with the written text. By and large, theatre still identifies dialogue as the only stable source of changing performances: everything can be attempted onstage but dialogue must be preserved.

I am not suggesting that the presence of dialogue suffices to define a properly theatrical practice, nor that theatrical action, largely carried out by dialogues, should be interpreted in terms of the linguistic speech act theory. Theatre has always told its story not only with dialogues but also with a variety of other means: other forms of verbal expression, such as singing or recitation; other systems of signs such as body language; performing activities such as dancing, acrobatics, mime, or music; and diverse signals projected by sets, props, and mechanical contrivances. But none of these means have marked theatre with the same constancy as did the dialogue. In fact, most of them are mentioned very briefly in dramatic texts, if at all; and new stagings of old texts normally disregard their textual indications, substituting new choices. In other terms, while they form a part of any performance, these various signs have no stable influence on the total theatrical process. In contrast, the respect for the integrity of the word, that is, the dialogue, has always been enforced.

The exact nature of the dialogue, of course, is determined by the specific words of each text. And the importance attributed to these words by particular performances can vary, verging sometimes on subversion. Both past and modern theatrical events thus raise thorny questions when they preserve the dialogue but minimize its impact. English court masques or French melodramas in the eighteenth century clearly focused on the appeal of actors, costumes, music, and mechanical devices. Were they true theatre? What about musicals today? What about plays where only one character speaks or is present on the stage? And what about a speechless performance? Are they real theatre? For plays reduced to monologues the answer is relatively easy since, in most cases, these monologues disguise a concealed dialogue, external or internal. Cocteau's *La voix humaine* and Beckett's *Happy Days* are in fact very traditional: they favor the word. Beckett's "play" *Acts Without Words*, however, has no words at all. It could be staged like a pantomime, leaving the field of theatre, but it could also be performed realistically, as if it were a traditional play with a totally silent character. Either way, a marginal case. Theatre admits many such gray areas at its boundaries, and their undecided character must be accepted.

*    *    *

The overall picture is now sufficiently clear. It ought to be quite familiar. Indeed, as defined by its five main features, my theatrical corpus closely corresponds to the public events experienced by the vast majority of Western audiences under the name of "theatre" or its equivalent in other languages. To sum it up, as economically as possible, we shall posit therefore that, in our tradition, theatre stands for *the set of past, present, and perhaps future public performances that are based on fixed verbal texts essentially composed by dialogues, and during which live actors present the actions of characters involved in a fictional story.* The theory that I am proposing will be limited to that theatre, discounting deviant or alien forms, or discussing them only in their relation to the tradition.

## 2. What Sociosemiotics?

In contrast to theatre, practiced and studied in its various manifestations for many centuries, the notion of "sociosemiotics" may be unfamiliar. The term itself is rather awkward, but it conveniently suggests the general nature of its meaning. It has been fashioned by analogy with the better known "sociocriticism" and, like the latter, it conveys the idea of a certain social or sociological orientation. It also announces that this orientation is applied to semiotics, that is, a relatively new discipline that is defined as the science of signs. To that extent, a sociosemiotic theory of theatre clearly implies a socially oriented examination of signs in theatre. However, both the "socio" and the "semiotic" components cover today a diversity of concepts proposed by individual theoreticians or theoretical movements. Furthermore, none of these variations fully accounts for the precise sense of "sociosemiotics" in this study. A double clarification is therefore needed in order to permit a more exact understanding of the theory.

\* \* \*

First, the social orientation. It partly refers to sociology of semiotics, that is, to the manner in which a given society organizes the production, distribution, and reception of all sorts of signs. In a similar sense, sociology of literature focuses today on general networks of production, distribution, and reception of all sorts of literary works. In the past, however, sociology of literature was rather expected to investigate the social generation of particular literary works, revealing how their specific themes and forms are influenced by historically determined social factors. This critical survey of the content of books rather than of their circulation is now usually called "sociocriticism." In the same spirit, "sociosemiotics" will then refer here not only to a general sociology of signs but also, and mainly, to the survey of social factors that determine historical changes in the function, nature, and meaning of particular sets of signs. And these particular sets of signs, in this case, will be sets of signs that operate in theatre.

In other words, I shall examine here the impact of social factors on those features of theatre that involve semiotics: production of fixed verbal signs, transition between text and stage, production of stage signs, codes and references of signs, actors as signs, reception of signs by the audience, and so forth. Ideally, such an examination ought to bear on a large number of theatrical events throughout history, outlining a diachronic evolution of theatre under the influence of changing social factors. Or, it could offer a detailed analysis of one concrete example, demonstrating how various synchronic social factors combine to determine the specificity of a single event. A number of recent studies have followed either of these two directions, or both.[8] By and large, however, sociosemiotics of theatre is still in the stage of theoretical unrest and, despite some remarkable achievements, needs an exact theory more than historical applications. No theory, of course, can be totally abstract. I shall provide a number of illustrations, either to justify a theoretical statement or to demonstrate its practical consequences. But theory will remain my central concern, and illustrations will be largely limited to a clarifying function.

From such a theoretical perspective, the first question that must be answered is: Why am I focusing on social determination of theatre signs? At least two other sources of influence should be acknowledged: individual inspiration and formal interaction. Theatrical activity, in all its forms, always manifests some desires or needs of individuals, expresses some personal problems. Since Freud, we know that psychic pulsions, especially on the subconscious level, have a determining impact on the production (and reception) of art. Fiction in particular— that is, the special type of communication that postulates a degree of gratuitousness—opens wide the door to disguised phantasms, and perhaps serves to liberate them. We know that fiction offers no true information, has no practical value. But it enables us to formulate, in unconscious disguises, our unconscious problems, and to solve them unconsciously, as in a dream. And theatre has a high level of fictionality, marking both its signs and the meanings that the signs convey. Author, director, actor, spectator, all contribute to the elaboration of the theatrical story, and all may be expected to project on it their unconscious problems. Not always, to be sure, since routine and repetition, professional and financial interests, social pressure and other "objective" reasons motivate many theatrical activities. But individual inspiration remains at the source of original theatre, bringing change within its tradition.

By that logic, a study of factors that generate creative theatre should start with the psychoanalysis of individuals involved in theatre. True, one cannot totally dismiss luck, talent, opportunities, cultural background, family traditions, or other chance factors that determine why these individuals chose theatre over other types of fiction in order to work out their unconscious problems. But the actual reasons for that choice are difficult to ascertain. Besides, such factors determine only the surface features of theatrical production. In theory, the primacy of the psychoanalytical approach can be little affected by such circumstantial influence. Practically, however, psychoanalyzing theatre people raises unsurmountable problems. We have learned how to look for unconscious sources of theatrical texts and performances,[9] but we have no way of verifying our findings. Most "authors" are dead; directors, actors, and spectators are rarely available for analysis; and most theatrical events originate in too many individual psyches to allow for a breakdown of their separate contributions. Of course we may speculate, and construct fascinating hypotheses, such as Green's on *Hamlet*, but it is safer to admit, once and for all, that unconscious personal sources of theatre cannot be known. A sane theory of theatre must accept that some questions cannot be answered satisfactorily, that some sources of the theatrical event cannot be grasped concretely even when their theoretical nature is identified.

Formal interaction as a mainspring of change in theatre poses different problems. In contrast with personal inspiration, theatrical forms, past and present, can be easily surveyed. Also, much is known about their relation to other art forms and various cultural features. It is tempting therefore to seek, in the interaction of formal factors, the source of variations in theatre styles and individual works. In this spirit, through development, antithesis, or contact with newly discovered alien forms, classicism begets romanticism, romanticism begets symbolism, symbolism begets naturalism, and so forth. More specifically, Hugo's creation of French *drame* in the nineteenth century could be explained by the growing influence of the Shakespearean tradition in France; Ionesco's "absurd" dialogue in *The Bald Soprano* by the popularity of the Assimil method of teaching English; and Mnouchkine's Kabuki staging of *Richard II* by a deliberate borrowing from an oriental exoticism. Sometimes encouraged by playwrights and directors themselves, such a formal analysis is particularly suited for historical studies, where it could be carried out in a semiotic spirit.

One notes, however, that a formal evolution attributed to interaction between forms concerns more the "how" than the "why" of theatrical innovation. The formal approach, in its descriptive function, can offer a precise account of diachronic changes in theatre, but it does not elucidate their ultimate reasons. Indeed, no interaction of forms can ever be assumed to be necessary or inevitable, no contact automatically ensures influence, and no observable relationship exhausts all the potential relationships. There is always an element of choice, and that choice demands explanations that reach outside the field of forms. Why did the French wait till Hugo in order to adapt English drama, and why did they do it then? Why did Ionesco want to imitate the Assimil dialogues? What attracted Mnouchkine to the Kabuki style, and why at the time it did? These are not unanswerable questions, but they require a consideration of social factors. In a similar manner, fashion's alternation between long and short skirts, traditionally explained by an alternation of styles, has been traced to changes in economic conditions and resulting psychological attitudes. In short, there is nothing wrong with a formal approach to theatre; it is both practical and theoretically satisfying; but it falls short as an explanation of real sources of theatrical innovation.

The recourse to social factors to explain theatre thus partly results from the inadequacy of other approaches. Partly it also reflects the highly social nature of theatrical activity. Any performance involves an act of communication between two social groups; and theatre as an institution depends on a close support and control by society. Other performing arts have similar social involvements, but their place in society has been historically more secure. Musicians and dancers did not suffer from the opprobrium long attached to comedians. A social approach to theatre, thus, is a "natural." But the main reason for the "socio" in sociosemiotics is not limited to the special situation of theatre. It reflects a more general conviction that social factors exert a determinant influence on the evolution of all forms of symbolic behavior, including theatre. In particular, I am postulating here that theatre, like other arts, manifests a certain tension between a changing social reality and a lagging adjustment of ideology.

The overall notion of a social determination of values is not new. It reached its maturity in the nineteenth century, inspired by a growing acknowledgment of the role of group relations in social life. The advent of sociology as a science and Marxism as a philosophy of history led to the wide acceptance of a strong association between social problems and ideological postulates. The exact nature of that association, and its consequences for art, have been debated ever since. Among all the schemes, Marxism has long retained a privileged position, partly because of the scope and consistency of its system. The sequence of changes: new tools, new modes of production, new social organization, new dialectics of embattled classes, new ideologies, new content and forms of art, still has much appeal. However, many features of that system have been now declared to be obsolete, or too simplistic, and even avowed Marxists have sought to revise Marxist theory.

Some of these revisions, offering variants of modern "sociocriticism," deal with relations between social factors, ideology and art, raising issues pertinent to sociosemiotics of theatre. I am chiefly referring to the theories of Lukàcs, Adorno, Goldmann, Benjamin, Althusser, and Jameson. It is significant that, with respect to fictional works, they have been progressively moving away from the idea that fiction directly mirrors society, that social problems find their way into literature by a spontaneous process of reflection, without modification by the author. Lukàcs's *totalization*, that is, the constraint of overall coherence; Goldmann's mediation through a *worldview*, an analogical screen of beliefs inserted between real problems of social groups and structures of their literature; Jameson's *ideologems*, units of ideology that, appearing both in society and in novels, link problematic social values with fictional issues—all three notions attribute a distorting effect to the activity of the writer. They assume, in other words, that writing operates a transformation of raw social material into an autonomous fictional work.

These strategies of modern sociocriticism visibly try to overcome the resistance that concrete fictional works put forth to earlier Marxist approaches. At the same time, they testify to a growing interest in "creative" criticism. Instead of showing parallels between equally obvious aspects of History and Fiction, they seek to produce original readings that enrich the understanding of literature. In some of these theories, one can also detect a defensive reaction against those recent intellectual trends that, undermining ideological premises of sociocriticism, Marxist or near-Marxist, have been turning away from any involvement with History. Hence Jameson's attempt to enlist structuralism, psychoanalysis, semantics, and feminism in his historically oriented theory of the political unconscious. But this is not enough.

For most sociocritics still fail to explain why fiction is produced at all: that is, why writers, whatever their social situation, bother to communicate fictional information about it. What is, indeed, the point of telling stories that have no truth value? Psychoanalytical theory, as we have seen, justifies the production of fiction by the need to solve personal problems. A fictional work, freed from the constraints of truth value, allows for an unconscious solution of unconscious conflicts projected in unconsciously disguised forms. The reception of fiction obviously satisfies other needs with which we shall deal later. For the individual writer, at any rate, fiction thus has a therapeutic function. But are all producers of fiction afflicted with Freudian blocks? Unconscious problems are not only personal in nature. Our individual notions about ourselves, society, and the world are largely formed by the ideology of our group: normative beliefs about metaphysical issues, human nature, social reality, values, and so forth. We must expect that, as a result of obscure ideological tensions between these beliefs, unconscious conflicts will develop in individuals who share these group notions, creating problems that are not perceived consciously. The creation of a fictional world, like a dream, will serve in that case to express these problems in unconscious disguises, unconsciously seeking to solve them. Such is my working hypothesis.

I am positing that, with various degrees of intensity, sensitive individuals are perturbed by social problems that neither they nor their society have as yet clearly identified. To be sure, not all such intuitive perceptions generate strong ideological tensions, not all tensions demand fictional solutions, and not all fictional solutions are tried out in theatre. Social circumstances play here an important role. They must be taken into account if we want to explain why given writers, directors, and/or actors are particularly perturbed by given ideological tensions, and what leads them to use theatre for fictional solutions. However, these explanations can be only offered a posteriori; they have no predictive value. In that sense, they are as problematic as psychoanalytical explanations of deep personal problems. But they have one great advantage: they can be checked against our knowledge of past or present social conditions. Similarly, in contrast with unconscious personal problems, many social problems that could not be consciously identified in the past can be identified and verified today, thanks to historical hindsight.

Not all fiction lends itself to sociocritical analysis carried out in this spirit. When, however, a concealed social tension can be detected under the surface of the fictional story, one may expect not only that it expresses a real social tension but also that, as an unconscious mainspring of the fiction, it informs most of its specific features. In that sense, fiction does not offer a mediated or distorted picture of a state of affairs acknowledged by the artist to be true, as many sociocritics would have it, but a disguised picture of a state of affairs that has not yet been acknowledged to be true. To that extent, the function of fiction is indeed to provide a vehicle for communicating information about History that historical discourse has not yet diagnosed. And that information primarily concerns those changes in society that are perceived in their discrete manifestations and often are found to be scandalous, but elude prevailing ideological categories and hence cannot be clearly understood.

A brief example to illustrate this point. We know today that many changes in the French ancien régime were related to the progress of the bourgeoisie at the expense of the nobility. And indeed many contemporary accounts expose individual bourgeois rising above their status, and some attribute that scandal to the perverting power of money. But there was no clear identification of these changes as manifestations of a general transformation of feudalism into a bourgeois society. By and large, ideology preserved fundamental feudal values and signs, so that even the richest bourgeois continued to believe in an innate superiority of nobility and sought titles instead of power. With historical hindsight, we can thus detect a double tension in that period: one, the social promotion of the bourgeoisie as a class; and two, a growing gap between a changing reality and an obsolete ideology.

Most sociocritics have been focusing on the first tension, showing, say, why and how Molière, in *Le Bourgeois gentilhomme*, reflected or mediated the class struggle between the bourgeoisie and the nobility. However, even the best contributions of that type, while revealing how fiction represents history and suggesting new readings of fiction, rely on a knowledge of history essentially drawn from seventeenth-century historical texts. In contrast, the existence of tensions of the second type, that is, conflicts between reality and ideology, cannot be directly derived from information contained in historical texts. The authors of these texts perceive society through their own ideological bias and, exerting a tight control over a factual material, shape their view of reality so that it can fit ideology instead of conflicting with it. Fiction, however, because of the unbridled nature of its stories, allows for all sorts of departures from the prevailing ideology. Structural flaws, hidden contradictions, disguised incoherences reveal, under the smooth surface of the fictional logic, surprising gaps between what the author attempts to show and what he actually does show: an unconscious conflict between the ideological bias of the text and the reality that it seeks to reflect. Analysis of such tensions yields little new about the underlying ideology, usually stated in explicit terms. But it can unearth fragments of History that history could not yet identify and hence did not record: a reality that might elude even modern historians who restrict their sources to historical texts.

A sociocriticism focusing on this type of tension will not disregard social problems represented in fiction, but it will posit that they could be misrepresented, concealing different problems in the historical reality. In that sense, for example, the conflict between bourgeoisie and nobility in Molière plays might be shown to disguise a more general conflict between the fixed values of seventeenth-century society and its economic, social, and political evolution. One may even hypothesize that the social group with which Molière unconsciously identifies is neither bourgeoisie nor nobility but a still nameless conglomerate of people falling somewhere between the normative categories of status: some bourgeois living like nobles, some nobles living like bourgeois, intellectuals and artists, and all sorts of marginal individuals. In his plays, Molière expresses a malaise that these people experience directly, but that many others may also feel, that is, the failure of traditional class distinctions to provide them with a clear self-identification.

The sociosemiotic approach I am adopting here generalizes this hypothesis. It postulates that the tension between ideology and reality and the resulting unconscious malaise usually testify to an obsolescence of the society's system of signs. Such a semiotic malaise no doubt affected language in Molière's time so that some of its signs—words such as "bourgeois" or "noble"—while still understood as references to status at birth, no longer could refer in that sense to many segments of a changing population. Similarly, specific signs of nobility, such as swords, uniformed lackeys, or royal service titles, although notoriously no longer reliable, preserved their value till the French Revolution and disturbed the perception of social order. More important, occurrences of such a semiotic malaise, spread by osmosis throughout society, also affect the depiction of reality in fiction, especially in theatre that stresses the display of visual signs. By the same logic, even fiction's forms, including theatrical styles, when they operate as fixed signs— that is, become artistic conventions resisting change—encounter the perils of obsolescence and risk creating their own semiotic malaise. As for all semiotic malaises, such risks are obviously greater when social and cultural changes occur at a particularly rapid pace, leaving behind the much slower adjustment of ideology, values, or art forms.

\*   \*   \*

As a key to the social "why" of fiction, synchronic or diachronic, the notion of a semiotic malaise is thus particularly suited to detect tensions between ideology and reality, suggesting historical conditions of creative change. By the same token, sociosemiotics lays the claim to be a variant of sociocriticism that is particularly apt to deal with fictional works. There is, however, another reason for adopting a sociosemiotic approach for the study of theatre: an unprecedented possibility of dealing from a single perspective with the totality of the theatrical process, from the production of the text to the reception of the performance.

Indeed, thanks to semiotics, we now can understand not only the "why" of the total theatre process but also the "how" of all its successive transformations. Some progress in that direction was made when structuralism, narratology, linguistics, and poetics led to the formulation of various "grammars" of fiction, some of which were adapted to theatre. However, even the most insightful, or most specifically oriented toward theatrical activity, were essentially restricted to the analysis of the verbal text.[10] At the same time but separately, a number of theoretical statements and practical analyses have centered on performance problems, stressing philosophies, techniques, and responsibilities of directors and actors. The methodological and topical divergence of these two approaches made it difficult to grasp the entire theatrical activity in the form of a continuous process. From the perspective of semiotics, however, there needs to be no dichotomy between a verbal text and a live performance. Both these manifestations of theatre, as well as other aspects of theatrical activity, can be viewed as stages in a communication of a story by the means of signs. True, textual signs, that is, mainly words, rely on the single system of natural language, whereas performances display a variety of stage signs that belong to many systems: natural language in dialogues, but also body language, intonations, colors, facial expressions, sounds, costumes, and so forth. But, despite the disparities between their specific systems, all these signs operate according to the same general semiotic laws and contribute to the storytelling. On this common ground, they combine, interact, and continuously transform their joint project. In that sense, the full theatrical cycle can be defined as a series of semiotic transformations of a story (with its specific ideas and emotions), first told with words and then watched on the stage: a unified process that accounts not only for theatre signs but also for all other theatre features related to the operations of signs.

In that spirit, resuming the pioneer research of the Prague Circle in the 1930s, various contemporary semioticians have recently proposed new "grammars" of theatre.[11] All of them share the belief in the central role of signs in theatrical activity and, taken together, they illustrate the stimulating variety of semiotic approaches to theatre. But, because of their variations, they fail to add to an integrated scheme that can be embraced as a whole. Furthermore, even the most ambitious of these "grammars," offering systematic descriptions of theatre signs, are rarely grounded in a clearly perceived theory of semiotics. They either stick closely to descriptive goals or, when they move beyond, take various positions that do not serve the purposes of strict sociosemiotics. As a result, I find I must formulate my own "grammar." To a large degree, of course, it relies on existing theories of systems of signs; no personal theory can be very original. My "grammar" innovates very little by stressing those features of theatre signs that manifest the influence of social factors. However, its special contribution, I should like to think, lies in a new and rigorous reformulation of a theory of semiotics that can be applied to theatre.

\*   \*   \*

Modern semiotics, indeed, means many different and confused notions to many different people. Its very name furthers the confusion; it has at least two main variants, "semiotics" and "semiology," generated respectively by the American philosopher Charles Saunders Peirce and the Swiss linguist Ferdinand de Saussure. Furthermore, under either name, or the French "sémiotique," it can also refer to a certain brand of structural semantics,[12] the study of prerational impulses by Julia Kristeva, or an all-encompassing "production of meaning in society."[13] No doubt all these areas involve some types of signs, but these signs are not always understood in the same way, nor with sufficient precision, which leads to sterile debates over concepts such as natural signs, signals, zero signs, and so forth. Besides, the very notion of signs has been undermined by deconstruction theories. While, in its strictest meaning, semiotics is still conceived to be the science of signs, it has been torn by internal disputes about the ways to interpret signs. In order to deal firmly with semiotics, I have, therefore, to redefine a basic terminology and demonstrate that it serves a coherent semiotic theory. I shall thus clearly establish where I stand on the most confused and/or controversial issues.

Such an undertaking would ideally require a lengthy discussion of major semiotic theories, past and present, acknowledging what I borrowed and what I rejected, and what were my reasons. But my sources are of little interest, and it would not be very convenient to provide their exact list. Most semiotic notions have been long floating around, and I would be at loss to state where I encountered them for the first time, or when I explored them in detail. In fact, perhaps the most influential work on my views on semiotics has been Ogden and Richards's *The Meaning of Meaning*, which doesn't claim to be semiotic at all. Some other sources will be found in the selective bibliography at the end of this study.

Nor would it be convenient to offer here an extensive summary of my general theory of semiotics. Only a limited number of its basic concepts have a direct impact on the semiotics of theatre and hence need to be introduced at this point. They can be usefully presented in the form of five propositions, involving half a dozen central semiotic terms: sign, signifier, signified, referent, concretization, iconicity.

## Signs Do Not Refer to Themselves

From now on the sign will be understood as *something that stands for, or refers to, something else that it is not*.

In theatre, the words of the verbal text are signs that refer to states of affairs that are *not* these words. When the text is read as *literature*, words refer to places, people, actions, emotions that are located in the space of the story. The dialogue refers to words spoken in that space and hence not to words that one reads. When the text is read as *theatre*, that is, as source of a future performance, words refer to the space of a stage on which actors move around and talk; and again, the words that these actors speak are not exactly the same as the words we read in the text.

Similarly, anything perceptible on the stage during a performance operates as a sign when it refers to something that it is not. Sets are signs referring to a story space outside the stage, actors are signs standing for characters in the story, words spoken by actors stand for words spoken by characters, stage furniture are signs that refer to fictional furniture in the story world, and so forth.

It is important to keep in mind this basic difference between signs and what they stand for. Since signs cannot refer to themselves, actors in their function as signs cannot be their own signs, cannot play themselves as they are at the time of the performance. As a rule, then, the performing artist in a one-man show is not operating as a sign, as would a theatre actor, unless the show consists of imitating someone else. By the same logic, a chair on the stage cannot refer to itself. And when a character in the story uses verbal or body signs that seem to refer to that chair, in fact he or she is referring not to the chair on the stage but to a different chair in the space of the story.

However, everything on the stage may be *desemiotized*, that is, stripped from its function as a sign. In that case, sets, actors, and furniture are perceived and appreciated for what they are: sets, actors, furniture. But they do not refer to anything in the story space. No doubt actors as human beings, perceived in their professional or private status, can communicate from the stage with the audience and use signs, such as gestures or facial expressions, to refer to their feelings toward spectators as human beings. In that process, however, they trigger or reinforce the desemiotization of the performance, and draw the attention from the story space to the stage space.

## Signs Are Intentional, Not Products of Causality

Signs are produced and received in the process of a communication based on a shared convention. Thus they are always taken to be intentional, though the intentions of the producers can be misinterpreted by the receivers. When we perceive what could be a sign on the stage, the theatre convention requires us to assume that it is intended as a sign referring to the fictional story. When an actor stumbles, for example, we trust that the stumble is an intentional sign standing for a stumble by the character played by the actor. But what if we have good reasons to believe that the stumble *was* unintentional? In that case, we no longer see it as a sign. We no longer see the actor as a sign of a character but as an actor on the stage. In short, we desemiotize that segment of the performance, switching from the story space to the stage space, from a process of communication to a directly experienced reality.

If we take the stumble to be an accident rather than a sign, we still may wonder why the actor stumbled. Or, if we interpreted the actor's stumble as an intentional sign for the character's stumble in the story, we may in turn wonder why the story character was made to stumble. In either case, the explanation will involve some sort of causality: the actor (or character) stumbled because of poor health, bad sight, too many drinks, bad luck, and so forth. Our answer will depend on what we believe, by experience or by hearsay, to be the natural cause of stumbles. Our conclusion will be as valid as the causality on which it is based. But it would involve no semiotic intentions, no communication. Logically, then, we should not say that the actor's (character's) stumble was a *sign* of physical impairment, alcohol, or chance, but that it resulted naturally from any of these causes. By the same logic, we should not say that smoke is a sign of fire, but that it is caused by fire. In all such instances, the perceptible happening, stumble, smoke, or any other natural result of a cause is not intended to communicate information about its cause; that is, it is not intentional, and it is not a sign even though some semioticians call such events "natural signs." In theory, then, natural signs are not true signs, but the term offers an easy reference to results of causality.

This split between intentional signs and events ruled by causality has a special relevance to those story characters who are expressing unconscious emotions through their words or gestures. Their strange behavior is communicated intentionally by the actors in order to inform us about some psychic disorder of the characters; and we have no trouble understanding these intentions of stage signs. But, in the story space, that strange behavior is not communicated consciously by the characters, and hence is not conveyed by their intentional signs. In order to understand the psychic disorder of a character, we must therefore have recourse to causality, that is, to our knowledge of natural psychological laws that operate in our world or in the fictional story world.

## Signs Associate Signifiers and Signifieds

In order to be perceived, a sign must have a distinct material form, hereafter called the *signifier*. That distinct signifier is conventionally associated, by a specific *code*, with a certain meaning provided in its coded definition, that is, with a class of states of affairs, hereafter called the *signified*. A signifier associated with the coded signified operates as a sign.

When we know the code of a system of signs, we are able to associate the signifier with the coded signified, and vice versa, and hence to produce and receive signs belonging to that system. Most codes are generally known in a given culture, and theatre borrows from them many of its discrete signs: words, gestures, facial expressions, intonations, costumes, colors, styles, and so forth. They are easily perceived, identified, and decoded. Occasionally, however, a given text or performance introduces a new code, sometimes reduced to a single sign, by a systematic new association between distinct signifier and signifieds. For example, the color red may be associated with treason rather than with love or violence as in the general color code, so that each appearance of red on the stage is perceived as a sign of a treacherous intent. Both verbal text and performance thus create their own signs.

The materiality of the signifier plays a special role in theatre. In order to be clearly coded in its distinct form, a signifier must be reduced to a relatively small number of essential properties, mainly shapes and sounds. But these properties rarely if ever have an independent material existence; usually, they coexist with other properties that are not included in the coded definition of the signifier. In real life, we simply block out these irrelevant properties: we identify a written word, for example, by the shape and order of its letters, disregarding their size, texture, color, and so forth. In theatre, however, because it is also a show to watch on the stage, every sign invites a close scrutiny of its materiality, a potential source of aesthetic or erotic appeal. In a dialogue, we identify spoken words as signifiers by the perception of their distinctly coded sound; but, at the same time, we pay attention to the pleasant or unpleasant quality of the voice. A common signifier of a king status is a crown on the actor's head; but while acknowledging the crown as sign of royalty, we may also appreciate it as a jeweler's creation.

The noncoded properties of voice and crown, or any other similar feature on the stage, may then draw our attention away from the coded properties of the signifier, or evoke some competing different signifier, or even make us oblivious to the presence of any signifier at all, so that we forget that we are dealing with a sign. In real life, we would deplore the ensuing breaks in communication. In theatre, however, such breaks are often planned and appreciated when they lead to a welcome desemiotization. An audience bored with the story will applaud a pretty voice, crown, or, more generally, a body, a costume, a set.

In contrast, signifieds play no significant part in theatre. Whatever its coded signified, any sign on the stage, whether seen or heard, automatically conveys a specific feature of the fictional story. The sounded signifier "Hamlet," for example, is associated by code with the class of all possible Hamlets, but the sign "Hamlet" in a given performance clearly refers to the specific imaginary Hamlet evoked in that performance. When staging that specific Hamlet, a number of properties are inevitably added to the definition of the class, that is, to the signified. These additional properties determine our mental concretization of the specific Hamlet: tall or small, handsome or ugly. But the signified as such is not affected, and its contribution to our concrete semiosis is minimal.

True, one might claim that, within the story, characters sometimes discuss the operations of signs and define classes of states of affairs, that is, they deal with signifieds. However, in that unlikely case, the class definitions formulated by the characters would acquire the status of specific statements comparable to any other specific statement made in the story; they would not function as abstract signifieds of signs. One might also claim that some misunderstandings of stage signs result from a defective knowledge of codes, and hence that problematic signifieds play an important role in theatre. But the knowledge of codes must be assumed to be generally adequate. No doubt signifieds change as codes change, so that the same signifier may in time become associated with different classes of states of affairs. But such changes are gradual and, at any given moment, affect very little the shared understanding of signifieds. With a few exceptions, notably when theatre introduces its own new signs, the study of production and reception of a performance need not deal with the issue of signifieds.

## Signs Refer to Referents to be Concretized

The specific state of affairs to which the sign refers shall be called the referent. The referent is *not* a general class of states of affairs defined by the signified of a sign; it is a concrete manifestation of that class, at a given time and in a given space.

Since they are always intentional, signs always occur in an existential context, referring to specific states of affairs for some specific reasons. Any specific manifestation of a class of states of affairs can thus become the referent of a sign. In other terms, a referent can be anything about which the producer of signs may want to offer information: real or imaginary places, events, people, emotions, ideas. Even vague notions can be referents since, as they are conceived and communicated by the producer of signs, they are always concretized by the specific place, time, and source of their production. But not all systems of signs are equally suited to convey all referents. Natural language, for example, excels in communicating abstract concepts but not physical appearance; pictures, in contrast, show appearances with great efficiency but deal poorly with ideas. In theory, using many systems of signs, theatre could be expected to be able to handle almost any imaginable referent. Practically, however, because it favors actors as its signs, theatre mainly focuses on concrete people: their actions, feelings, problems. It has more trouble communicating abstract notions, although it often attempts to do so with its verbal signs.

The main problem with referents is that they are never exactly the same for the senders and for the receivers of signs. Whether the sender's referent is real or imaginary, experienced by senses or conceived mentally, does not matter much: when communicated with signs, it always undergoes a mental reduction to only a few of its properties. In that process, a specific state of affairs is identified with a class of states of affairs, that is, with the definition corresponding to a signified. That signified, associated with the coded signifier, is then produced as a sign. But the identification of the referent with its class requires a generalization that sacrifices many specific properties that are not part of the class definition. In order to recover some of these properties, the sender can multiply references and add new signs, but each one will undergo the same generalization and their totality will never convey all the lost properties. Even theatre, despite its ability to show and tell at the same time, cannot communicate complete referents: a director's complex vision of Hamlet is always simplified when he or she selects the signs with which to communicate it on the stage. That it also risks being both enriched and modified by personal properties of the actor is a different problem, resulting from the transformational nature of theatrical processes.

Communicated always imperfectly by the sender, the referent undergoes a further alteration during its decoding by the receiver of signs. The perception of signifiers leads to their coded association with signifieds, that is, with classes of states of affairs. In order to obtain specific referents from these general definitions, the receiver must supply them with enough additional properties to concretize them firmly in a specific spatial and temporal context. This *concretization* is a mental operation that relies on each receiver's individual imagination, associations of ideas, and background. The resulting referent will have at least some properties that the sender's referent did not have, that is, it will always be different. The theatre's special power to show what it tells both magnifies and minimizes the impact of such differences. It magnifies it because the spectator, perceiving anything that is *shown* on the stage as a sign, cannot easily distinguish between properties intended to be communicated and those that are displayed by concrete signifiers in excess of their coded signifieds. By the same token, however, the appearance of referents located by the spectator in the story space needs less concretization than, say, referents communicated only with verbal signs. Of course, this minimization of differences mainly concerns the visualization of characters and their actions. Emotions and ideas generally are more difficult to concretize in theatre than in literature.

## Iconic Signs Look Like Their Referents, Symbols Do Not

The material form of a sign, its signifier, may resemble the material form of the referent. Such a sign will be called an icon, or an iconic sign; and the degree of resemblance will determine its degree of iconicity. In contrast, when the signifier has no perceptible resemblance with the referent, the sign will be called a symbol, or a symbolic sign.

The formal relationship between signs and referents, or between signifiers and signifieds, is quite complex. It involves differences between the ideal form of signifiers, limited to coded properties, and their concrete form, with all excess properties; it also involves differences between signifieds, defined only by coded properties of a class, and referents that always present additional specific properties. The very notion of resemblance admits various interpretations. In order to clarify all these problems, different theories of signs have offered different classifications of formal relationships. The most complete and systematic was proposed by Peirce; unfortunately, it is also the most unwieldy. Insofar as theatre is concerned, however, only a couple of Peirce's basic notions need to be borrowed and adapted.

First, that all codes associate signifiers and signifieds on the basis of a shared convention, regardless of the origin of the convention. But the relationship between forms of signifiers and signified has no great relevance for theatre since signifieds play a minor role in theatrical processes. Second, that relationships between forms of signifiers, perceived and identified on the stage, and the forms of corresponding referents, concretized in the mental story space, are marked either by some resemblance or by an apparent lack of resemblance. If resemblance obtains, then stage signs are icons; if not, they are symbols. Of course, the degree of iconicity may vary and, when it is very low, the boundary between iconic and symbolic signs becomes uncertain. On the other hand, semiotics of theatre has no need for Peirce's third type of signs, the index; it may frequently occur in semiotic exchanges in the story space, but has little relevance as a stage sign.

Clearly, then, theatre is the most iconic of mediums. The forms of its dominant signs, that is, the actors, resemble the forms of the corresponding referents, the characters, almost to the point of identity. The signifiers perceived on the stage are human beings who stand for other human beings in the imaginary story space; their appearance, behavior, emotions are almost identical. Even the words they speak onstage stand for almost identical words spoken by the characters. No doubt, for the characters in the story space, words are symbolic signs; but, in their semiotic function on the stage, they operate as icons. That theatre also uses symbols does not detract from this fundamental iconicity. In fact, as shall be seen, the special appeal of symbols on the stage relies precisely on a transgression of the conventional iconicity of theatre. Besides, most symbolic signs are contaminated by the presence of actors who project their iconicity on everything on the stage.

*   *   *

Even thus simplified, the network of semiotic relations operating in theatre presents nevertheless various openings for the manifestation of a semiotic malaise. In the story space, contradictions may occur between notions conveyed by stage signs and notions deduced from causalities. Or: the story space may be perturbed by contradictory stage indications. Or: referents concretized by spectators may strongly differ from referents intended by performers. Or: codes may mislead, or become obsolete, and signs may fail to refer to any precise referent. Or: excessive desemiotization may tear holes in the fabric of the story, undermining its coherence. Or: symbols may be taken for icons and vice versa. A more systematic analysis of signs operating in theatre will yield further forms of potential semiotic malaise. Hence the need for a more comprehensive grammar of theatre signs. But the central purpose of sociosemiotics remains to show how all these manifestations of malaise are either generated or influenced by unconscious social tensions.

## Notes

1. Bernard Beckerman, *Dynamics of Drama. Theory and Method of Analysis* (New York: Drama Book Specialists, 1979 [1970]), p. 12.

2. For example, see Richard Schechner, *Between Theatre and Anthropology* (Philadelphia: University of Pennsylvania Press, 1985).

3. Aristotle, *Poetics*. Everyman's Library (London & New York: Dent and Dutton, 1943), p. 11.

4. Aristotle, *Poetics*, p. 11.

5. See Jiří Veltruský, "Puppetry and Acting," *Semiotica* 47¼ (1983), pp. 69–122.

6. See Judith Malina's comments on *The Connection*, performed by the Living Theatre in 1959: "The actors began to play themselves." Quoted in Pierre Biner, *The Living Theatre* (New York: Avon Books, 1973), p. 48.

7. Aristotle, *Poetics*, p. 11.

8. Among semiotically oriented studies, Erika Fischer-Lichte's *Semiotik des Theater* (Tübingen: Gunter Narr, 1983) offers a historical appraisal of the German theatre in the eighteenth-century; Michel Corvin's *Molière et ses metteurs en scène* (Lyon: Presses Universitaires de Lyon, 1985) surveys in some detail the contemporary staging of several Molière's plays (but without much attention to social factors); and Patrice Pavis's monumental *Marivaux a l'épreuve de la scène* (Paris: Publications de la Sorbonne, 1986) analyzes both synchronically and diachronically the meanings of texts and performances of Marivaux's plays.

9. See, for the text, André Green, *Hamlet et **Hamlet**. Une interprétation psychanalytique de la représentation* (Paris: Balland, 1982). Or, for the performance, Michel Corvin, "Sémiologie et spectacle: *Georges Dandin*," in *Sémiologie et théâtre. Organon 80* (Lyon: CEETC, 1980).

10. See, for example, Etienne Souriau, *Les deux cent mille situations dramatiques* (Paris: Flammarion, 1950); or Jacques Scherer, *La dramaturgie classique en France* (Paris: Nizet, 1970).

11.  After the seminal Tadeusz Kowzan, *Littérature et spectacle* (The Hague: Mouton, 1975), originally published in the 1960s, one must mention at least, in alphabetical order, Marco De Marinis, *Semiotica del teatro: l'analysi testuale dello spettacolo* (Milano: Bompiani, 1982); Fernando De Toro, *Semiotica del teatro* (Buenos Aires: Editorial Galerna, 1987); Keir Elam, *The Semiotics of Theatre and Drama* (London and New York: Methuen, 1980); Erika Fischer-Lichte, *Semiotik des Theater* (1983); André Helbo, *Les mots et les gestes* (Lille: Presses Universitaires de Lille, 1983); Patrice Pavis, *Problèmes de sémiologie théâtrale* (Montréal: Presses de l'Université du Québec, 1976); Anne Ubersfeld, *L'Ecole du spectateur* (Paris: Editions sociales, 1981).

12.  This is the case for the influential semiotic theory formulated by A. J. Greimas who, in fact, developed under that term his earlier research in *Sémantique structurale* (Paris: Larousse, 1966).

13.  See Keir Elam, *The Semiotics of Theatre and Drama*, p. 1.

# I: Reference and Performance

Theatre fulfills many functions. Some derive from its participation in social life. As a social institution, theatre offers models of behavior, conforming to prevailing norms or not; it propagates dominant or subversive ideologies; it reinforces group cohesion by bringing people together; it provides ritualized forms of entertainment; it enables theatre professionals to earn a living and investors to make money; it channels craving for public self-expression. Such functions are encouraged, tolerated, or condemned by society, and their changes reflect the influence of social changes. To that extent, a survey of these functions contributes to clarify the social "why?" of particular forms of theatre. A sociocritical *history* of theatre must thus pay close attention to its social functions. They also need to be taken into account in a sociocritical *theory* of theatre, but only as contingent factors rather than as basic features.

For society doesn't really need theatre in order to achieve the goals inherent in these functions; other institutions and other media serve them as well or better. Social functions, however important, cannot account on their own for the development of theatre, even though they have a strong influence on its evolution. Or better: they can be fulfilled by theatre only because theatre is what it is, and does what it can do, regardless of changing social conditions. In contrast, theatre always involves two other functions that define its proper and distinct nature. They are always present whenever theatre takes place, regardless of social conditions. Inseparable from all manifestations of theatre, they are experienced in the form of an inherent duality of theatrical activity: on the one hand, its reference to a story that takes place in a mental space outside the stage; on the other, its display of real performances on the stage.

When it refers to an imaginary story, theatre is involved in a process of communication; it fulfills a *referential function*, carried out with signs that aim at imparting information. From the perspective of a semiotic theory, this referential function, or referentiality, clearly constitutes the central feature of theatre. But theatre is also a public event, a spectacle or a show, attempting to please or amaze the audience by a display of exceptional stage achievements, that is, special *performances*.[1] In that sense, like sporting events or the circus, theatre serves what I shall call the *performant function*: it satisfies our natural desire to achieve or witness something extraordinary. Such *performances* are not communicated with signs; they are experienced directly; they fall outside the operations of semiosis. However, because the performant function coexists with the referential function, and interacts with it, it cannot be disregarded by a semiotic theory of theatre. Indeed, taken together, references and performances define the dual appeal of all theatre.

But coexistence doesn't means simultaneity. Referential and performant functions cannot operate at the same time; one requires focusing on the story space, the other on the space of the stage. Mutually exclusive, they compete, at any given moment, for the attention of performers and spectators. However, over the full time of a production, as they follow each other, they eventually combine their effects, and the momentary success of one compensates the failure of the other. The tension between the two functions thus ensures a permanent diversification of theatre's appeal; it could explain its survival in societies where references or *performances* fall out of favor. Yet most theories of theatre fail to do justice to this mutual support between referential and performant functions. Favoring one at the expense of the other, they tend to reduce the purpose of theatre to the fulfillment of one function only, and they justify their bias by a one-sided account of theatre's origins: either referential or performant, but rarely combined.

## 1. Origins: Referential Theories

### Mimesis: Theatre as Imitation

Aristotle's *Poetics* first firmly established imitation as the principal source of theatre. The theory is well known, though some points remain obscure.[2] It postulates that theatre, like Poetry or Art in general, manifests two universal features of human nature. One is our natural production of melody and rhythm—important elements of theatrical productions—and presumably the production of words as well, though Aristotle doesn't mention it explicitly. The second is the instinct to imitate, yielding a natural pleasure in the production and observation of imitation. Aristotle relates that instinct to an even more basic need to learn, since one learns from imitation, but *Poetics* does not elaborate that point. In fact, it appears to contradict it when it claims that a work of art, not recognized as an imitation from which something can be learned, still can offer pleasure by its formal features, "the workmanship, the colors, or some such cause."[3] By implication, Aristotle endows thus theatre with a dual nature, approaching the two functions of traditional theatre: presentation of information through imitation, and the display of aesthetic performances. As a rule, however, the text of *Poetics* rarely mentions aesthetic pleasure, and minimizes the performant function. The main purpose of theatre remains imitation.

Viewed from today's perspective, this focus on theatre as imitation has significant implications for semiotics of theatre. Imitation always presupposes a model, that is, something that is imitated. For theatre, Aristotle defines this model as "actions of men." In a world still largely unknown, teaching by imitation how men could master their environment was no doubt a most useful project; and self-imitation has always had a solipsistic appeal. More to the point, whatever Aristotle's reasons, he obviously believed that actions to be imitated in theatre had to have an earlier, actual or probable, existence in real life. Their intentional imitation on the stage could never reproduce them exactly but, at the same time, could resemble them sufficiently to be identified as their imitation and source of learning. In semiotic terms, Aristotle's main components of action, people and events, are thus imitated on the stage by the means of iconic signs: actors who stand for characters that they are not but with whom they share most of their features.

Which leads to two further observations. In the first place, Aristotle's theatre, when it imitates actions of men, intends to impart some information about them that is conceptualized by poets and performers, that is, the producers of signs. That information is assumed to be intentional by the spectators, the receivers of signs, who expect to understand it and react appropriately. To that extent, a theatre performance constitutes an act of communication, based on a shared knowledge of semiotic codes. Its referential function is fulfilled when the audience experiences the pleasure derived from the process of learning as well as from watching imitation. In the second place, to communicate its information, theatre relies principally on iconicity. All its other features, generating other types of pleasure or valuable emotional experiences, play a secondary role. However traditional and seductive, even the appeal of the performant function is only grafted on the basic referential function carried out by iconic signs.

Aristotle's main concept of theatre as a useful form of communication is flexible enough to retain today much of its power. True, many postulates of *Poetics* have become obsolete, either because they concern an obsolete theatrical form, that is, classical Greek tragedy, or because they trust in obsolete axioms, say that imitation is the basic human drive. But the general scheme still informs those modern theories that also stress referentiality. They trace theatre to different historical sources, replacing dithyrambic hymns and phallic songs with rituals or shamanist practices; they assign it different teleologies; they may even minimize iconicity and maximize the role of the performant function. However, like Aristotle, and perhaps under his influence, they place the main purpose of theatre in the communication of information intended to achieve a pragmatic goal. They can be grouped in two categories, reflecting the nature of that goal.

## Rituals and Speech Acts: Theatre as Action

Early in the century, inspired by anthropology, notably Frazier's *The Golden Bough*, modern scholars sought to place the origins of theatre in rituals performed by primitive societies. These rituals were assumed to offer a partly mimetic reenactment of a mythical event in order to bring about the actual or symbolic reoccurrence of that event. The theatrical activity inherent in such reenactment was believed to have then evolved into more advanced forms of theatre. In that theory, imitation still played a key theatrical role, but not as a source of pleasure or learning: it served to exert a magic control over forces of nature, seasonal variations, life and death cycles, powers of gods, succession of kings, rule of law, and so forth. One could claim that theatre thus started as a form of communication, whereby the entire community, performers and audience together, addressed supernatural entities.

In fact, such a ritual communication hardly fits the semiotic model. The reenactment of a mythical event may be considered to be a complex sign intended by the community to stand for that event; supernatural entities may be viewed as the receivers of the sign, expected to perceive it and act upon it. For the community these entities were shrouded in mystery and endowed with powers beyond human understanding; they could grasp ritual messages by magical means and be compelled by the same magic to bring about the reoccurrence of the desired event. But they did not share the semiotic codes of the community, did not treat the ritual as a sign to be decoded, did not engage in the processes that normally define communication. The belief in the efficiency of ritual dramatics, somewhat like the belief in the power of prayer, was essentially a matter of faith: faith in a meaningful universe and faith in supernatural goodwill. The primitive community was seeking to influence its fate through spiritual communion rather than through rational communication. Still, it somehow trusted in the referential function of the ritual which, through its theatrical activity, indeed reenacted—that is, told—the story of the desired event.

One could speculate that this faith originated in the intuition that laws of nature are based on repetition. If day must follow night because, repeatedly, days have followed nights, then a repetition of an event, even in the form of imitation, might ensure its reoccurrence by virtue of a quasi-natural law, identified with the will of supernatural entities. Or maybe theatrical rituals simply expressed an unconscious need for repetitions that Freud detected in human psyches. Either hypothesis, or both together, could explain why public rituals remain popular today although they have no messages for supernatural entities. Our theatrical homecomings, for example, may both please us by their ritual repetition and reassure us about their future reoccurrence. Yet this explanation is not totally satisfactory. In today's rituals, as no doubt also in primitive rituals, something else bonds together audience and performers: another type of communication, involving exchange of signs and shared codes.

We know that early rituals, in order to exert their magic, required the participation of the community. The audience had to understand what events were reenacted, and trust in the power of the dramatics to bring about their reoccurrence. Similarly, modern rituals best achieve their goals when the participants share the knowledge of their codes and approve their purpose. In both cases, rituals reaffirm the identity of a group, reassure it about its control of the future, and reinforce the communal cohesion through the joint participation in a semiotic exercise. In that sense, rituals as well as traditional theatre carry out a standard communication between two separate but sometimes overlapping subsets of the group: performers on the one hand, and the rest of the community on the other. As, respectively, senders and receivers of signs, they are expected to share the same codes and hence to understand each other; and communication of information provides the formal occasion that brings them together.

Theories that view theatre as an outgrowth of rituals thus always acknowledge its referential function; but they also justify drawing attention to theatre as a social activity, seeking to influence people. Again, as for Aristotle, one may discard the obsolete notion of historical origins—few scholars now see primitive rituals as an Ur-theatre; but the main thrust of the scheme continues to appeal even to avant-garde theoreticians. Jean Duvignaud's sociological theory thus claims that theatre, through the characters in its stories, serves to instruct the audience in social identities and behavioral models.[4] Through that referential process, facilitated by close contact with the public, it offers an effective medium for the propagation of ideological messages that strengthen social institutions. By its references, then, theatre may be said to participate in the political violence which, says Michel Foucault, is carried out by all texts. Actually, of course, theatre's support of the Establishment can be counteracted when its subversive activity promotes social change. Sartre's theory and practice of a "committed" theatre illustrate how the referential function can raise rebellious consciousness. Closer to rituals, "guerilla theatre" calls for a revolutionary violence, but still relies on storytelling to achieve its goals. True, not all approaches inspired by rituals focus on social issues or the referential function. Eugenio Barba's Odin Teatret, for example, stresses the phatic function of communication: its actors, favoring a style both personal and ritualistic, attempt to establish human contact with their audiences. Nevertheless, they tell a story, and rely on that story more than on dazzling *performances* in order to generate a community spirit.

The same combination of referentiality and intent to influence people marks approaches inspired by the speech act theory initially formulated by J. L. Austin. Borrowing the scheme whereby the cognitive (locutory) function of a statement cannot be disassociated from the intended and actual results of that statement (illocutory and perlocutory functions), some theatre semioticians claim that a play, as a whole or in parts, is an intentional statement made from the stage to the audience in order to elicit a response, and hence always includes a triple operation: it refers to an imaginary story, it tries to influence the spectators, and it causes reactions that do not necessarily correspond to its intentions.[5] Within that scheme, referentiality still prevails, since at least the intended results, if not the actual results, depend to a large degree on the communication of the story.

Attempts have been made to carry this approach further, minimizing or denying the referential function and stressing the will to influence. Marco De Marinis, questioning the very notion that theatre is a form of communication, defines it rather as a "strategy of manipulation and seduction" of the public, an art of "theatrical passions."[6] In theory, human contact, and all sorts of stage *performances*, could have in that sense as much importance as the content of the story; but, in fact, De Marinis focuses on the role of the story in moving people to think or to act. Even the practitioners of the "Rezeptionsaesthetik," focusing on the perlocutory function of the play, that is, on its actual results as they can be grasped in public reception, cannot help dealing with the referential story because, in reception texts, reactions to the story take at least as much place as reactions to stage *performances*.

## Shamans and Structures: Theatre as Revelation

Referentiality also marks the most recent theories that place historical origins of theatre in shamanist practices.[7] According to that view, dramatic activity began when the shaman, watched by an attentive and awed tribe, would go into a semitrance, during which he narrated and mimed his trip to the abodes of tribal divinities. He would act out his encounters with major gods who resolved problems of great importance to the tribe, but also with minor spirits that often appeared in animal shapes. At first sight, his performance might seem to resemble a primitive ritual, since it also involves a mimetic communication between humans and supernatural entities. A closer look reveals, however, at least two major differences, pointing to a different concept of theatrical function.

In the first place, the delivery of the message, although central in the shaman's mission, plays only a minimal role in his performance; it lasts the time to make a few statements, whereas the delivery of the ritual message, the reenactment of a mythical event, accounts for most of the ritual ceremony. The best part of shamanist acting refers to episodes of his journey, unrelated to the content of the message; and a space is thus opened for a dramatic activity carried out for its own sake. In fact, it is believed that shamans progressively increased their use of material figures to represent the animal spirits with which they interacted on the way to the gods; endowed with voice, these figures then became theatrical characters involved in an embryonic adventure story. By this theory, the point of the performance shifted from the communication of a message to the communication of a story.

The second difference concerns the nature of the message. In rituals, it constitutes a magic speech act with which performers influence mysterious powers. In the shamanist ceremony, the central message comes from the powers to the community, and the shaman transmits it in the same way that an actor delivers his lines. But this message is not a divine speech act designed to bring about an event. It is rather the clarification of a mystery, the revelation of a secret known only to gods. Information imparted in rituals clearly originated in a specific human need; information obtained by the shaman from gods, even though it answers specific human questions, originates in supernatural wisdom and expresses absolute truth. Centered on the message as a revelation, the referential function of the ceremony thus acquires a sacred dimension. By the same token, however, references to the shaman's anecdotal journey are downgraded in status. In that part of the performance, he merely tells the story of an individual experience, and its stock episodes lack suspense. In order to keep the audience's interest, the shaman turned into an actor must rely on the seduction of his art, offer a dazzling show, in short, play on the performant function of the theatrical event.

Whether well-founded or not, the theory of shamanist origins of theatre accounts marvelously for both referential and performing functions. It also symbolically evokes the dual nature of theatrical semiosis: a journey through signs to an absent meaning. This duality implies that theatre always reveals something, but, like the shadows in Plato's cavern, never shows it directly. In that spirit, influenced by the shamanist theory, a recent critic argues that theatre manifests the fabled "illud tempus"—a time of myths of origins and eternal archetypes: concealed in the text of a play, it is revealed in the performance, enabling us to experience "imaginative truth" in the shape of "present truth."[8] A similar though less exalted approach assumes that performances must be faithful to the playwright's intentions. In that still popular scheme, the author is assigned the authority of the shaman's god, while director and actors split between them the shaman's role in conveying the authority's message.

Surprisingly, theatre is also viewed as medium of revelation in modern structuralist theories. Writing in the 1960s, Etienne Souriau first proposed to formalize theatre stories by the means of a small number of basic action roles: Thematic Force, Desired Object, Opponent, Arbiter, Helper, and Beneficiary. All their possible combinations and distributions were to account for all past, present, and future dramatic situations: not by chance, however, nor by a structural logic, but because these functions mirror eternal tensions at work in the universe. Theatre, for Souriau, was a microcosm of the world, reflecting the true nature of human behavior. Each play, beneath its surface originality, revealed some of that truth, and author, director and actor had no greater part in this revelation than the shaman conveying the message of gods.

This approach, even more than the others, reduces theatre to its referential function. Souriau's scheme, and similar systems devised by Greimas and structural narratologists, seem to disregard contingent aspects of a story that differentiate it from an archetypal pattern; and, in that process, they clearly discount the influence of the performant function on the content as well as on the form of specific works. Few theoreticians, however, are really blind to the partial character of such an approach. Souriau and Greimas, but also Cole, De Marinis, or even Aristotle in several asides, acknowledge that they present only a theoretical model of theatre and that, within that model, they deliberately foreground only those features that they believe to be most pertinent to their theory. To the extent that their theories differ, and highlight different features of theatrical praxis, they overlap rather than contradict each other. The medieval passion plays, for example, no doubt had a ritual appeal for their religious audiences, but also, like shamanist revelations, they communicated the knowledge of truth; they were certainly intended, through the power of mimesis, to elicit pleasure and/or to purge passions; and they exerted an ideological action on the spectators, reinforcing their common faith. All of such goals obviously must rely on the magic of the performance, but, separately or together, they primarily stress the referential function of theatre. From any of these perspectives, whatever the aim, theatre operates as a form of communication, imparting information about a state of affairs. Some manifestations of the performant function are also involved and most referential theories acknowledge it; but they place them on the margin of theatrical activity. To appreciate the real role of the *performance*, one must turn to other theories, reflecting a different approach to the problem of origins of theatre.

## 2. Origins: Performant Theories

### The Game Principle: Theatre as Necessity

In most cases, communication is a serious business seeking to achieve pragmatic goals through the exchange of knowledge; it relates to the image of the human being as *Homo sapiens*. There is competing image however, that portrays the human being as *Homo ludens*, primarily oriented by the game principle. From that perspective, playing games is not an optional activity, to be enjoyed occasionally by individuals, but a necessary and integral part of social life. That concept embraces both serious and ludic games; in either case, they involve a gratuitous behavior that follows arbitrary rules. Ideally, in that sense, a game is an activity that is carried out for its own sake, and its outcome is not supposed to have a direct effect on the player's life. Admittedly, this definition needs further refining, but it will do for now.[9] In fact, each theory of game-playing understands it somewhat differently while retaining its main thrust.

For Johan Huizinga, whose *Homo Ludens* popularized by its title the notion of a "playful" man, all of human social activity originates in the game principle.[10] Theatre, as a cultural institution, belongs in his category of "higher" forms of play, but the origins of theatre can be traced to "primitive" forms that antedate even ritual dramatics. At its source, then, theatre does not involve any vital communication; it is a "natural" game. Similarly, in his study of games, Roger Caillois attributed to primitive cultures the use of *mimicry* as a source of simulation and hence drama.[11] For Caillois, theatre thus would express a clearly cultural necessity of human society rather than, as for Huizinga, the very essence of human nature.

Neither Huizinga nor Caillois was specifically interested in theatre, but their theories promoted the idea that theatrical activity is a game. Oriented by biological rather than by cultural concerns, Jean Piaget reached a comparable conclusion: human intelligence, in order to master the environment, must learn to play theatrical games.[12] Forced to structure a chaotic reality, we train our mind for that task, at no real risk, by finding structures in all sorts of simulacra of that reality. For example, when we act out roles in our imagination, or reenact them through fictitious characters, we are testing strategies needed to master the human environment. By implication, we practice theatre as a rehearsal for real life. Piaget's approach, extended to all artistic media, explains very convincingly why art always functions as a game; I shall return to it to account both for the production and the reception of fictitious stories on the stage. His argument, in fact, retains its appeal even if we believe that we have achieved a solid structuring of the environment. In such cases, indeed, we become reluctant to undertake any new restructuring, and seek to satisfy our structuring drive not in real life but in works of fiction. Besides, as Morse Peckham claims, no structured reality is totally stable, and disorder always threatens to disrupt the order we impose on the universe.[13] By this logic, our games in the form of art, always somewhat irrational, serve to prepare us to meet potential real disorders. Acting out theatre's irrational roles we obey a necessity similar to the necessity that Piaget attributed to our acting out rational roles.

For Henri Laborit, who also singles out playacting as the fundamental source of theatre, the necessary first cause lies in a biological/psychological "narcissus complex."[14] It besets us at an early stage of infancy, when we realize that we are not the totality of the world. We experience a traumatic loss of the universality of the self, and try to compensate for it by seeing the self's reflection in others; like Narcissus captivated by his estranged face reflected in the pool, we recover our unity with the *other* when we act out a role. This recaptured totality of the actor is then shared, as in a communion, by the spectators who identify, in a subliminal way, with the universal body language that, on the stage, breaks through the paralyzing constraints of verbal communication. Laborit's theory, however contrived it may seem, deserves attention because, through its reference to bionervous processes, it attempts to give a scientific reason for the necessity of playacting as a therapy. By the same token, of course, the actor becomes the prime mover of theatre.

The Freudian approach similarly views playacting as a way of solving psychological problems. However, the therapy does not involve acting out any given role, as in Laborit's scheme, but a specific role determined by the specific nature of the problem. Furthermore, the problems are clearly attributed to individual libidinal troubles rather than to the self's general loss of unity. Most followers of Freud, such as Charles Mauron and Green, applied this approach to dramatic texts and their authors.[15] But one may postulate that performers also seek in their roles, as unconsciously as authors in their texts, to express censured desires, fulfill wishful thinking, experience surrogate pleasure or punishment; and that, watching them on the stage, we enter into a specular relation with the *other*, vicariously solving our own unconscious problems.

All these theories tend to reduce theatre to the experience of role-playing. None pay much attention to the communication that takes place between the stage and the audience. The referential function of theatre, when it is acknowledged at all, has a minor part; it provides a pretext for the satisfaction of basic human drives. In contrast, the performance holds the center of attention. As such, whatever the story it tells, it has the appeal of a privileged expression of our hidden nature. Under the disguises of the role, a truth is manifested; and the reality of the stage merges magically with the fiction in which it is mirrored. The comedian is the conduit through which the theatre works that magic on the audience; and the audience is satisfied when the performance of the comedian makes it share in playacting. Seeing theatre as a necessity leads naturally to stressing its performant function, especially on the part of the actors.

## The Comedian's Theatre: Acting Out

No wonder, then, that a recent work on theatre semiotics still claims that "The comedian is all there is in theatre. A performance can do away with everything else. The actor is the flesh of the show, the pleasure of the audience."[16] With its exaggeration, since obviously no theatre performance can do away with all text and all staging, this statement belongs to an old tradition that identifies theatrical activity with acting activity, actors epitomizing theatre. Naturally, this view has always prevailed among performers, and it is fair by poetic justice: if not for the stubborn will of actors, theatre would have floundered many times in the past. As naturally, and perhaps as fairly, an opposite view has emerged among the directors who ushered a theatre renaissance at the turn of the century and agreed with Gordon Craig that the ideal actor should be a super-puppet. Yet both extreme positions are misleading. If, to return to the quote, actors were truly all there is in theatre, then theatre could not exist in its traditional form, nor perhaps in any other form either. The story of Grotowski's Wrocław Theatre Laboratory is a case in point.[17]

Initially, the Polish director's experiments stressed both communication and actors' performances. His "poor theatre" attempted to dredge rich archetypal information from the unconsciousness of actors, and to communicate it to the public. Progressively, however, inner experiences of actors delving into their psyche became the center of attention. Semiotic communication was reduced to a one-on-one exchange between an individual actor and a single spectator, then totally abandoned. In Grotowski's later secret retreat, everybody was supposed to participate in private events that, verging on happenings and psychodrama, were to encourage expanding consciousness, group communion, and collective creativity. But even that paratheatrical activity eventually died out. Grotowski moved to California in 1982, and the Theatre Laboratory was officially dissolved in 1984. There were, no doubt, political reasons why Grotowski left Poland. It is more significant that his recent "Objective Drama" project, carried out at Irvine University, focuses on research and teaching rather than on theatre performances. Participants study and learn performing techniques that are at the source of ritual dramatics; they do not act out personal roles. Grotowski's activities no longer exemplify an actors' theatre. In fact, they no longer qualify as theatre.

The notion that the actor is the prime source of theatre also presents theoretical problems. If acting expresses a basic human drive, or satisfies psychological needs of individuals, then we are all actual or potential actors; and studying theatre means studying human nature. Metaphorically, one would be justified to claim that all the world is a stage, and so forth. But metaphors must not be taken literally. Within the poetic World as Theatre we clearly distinguish a discrete theatre institution that is concrete and historical. Visibly, its existence cannot be attributed to a will for acting out shared by practically everyone: there must be some more specific reasons. Jean Duvignaud, we have seen, believes that they reflect social needs. His theory leads him to differentiate between an "acteur," an amateur actor, who likes to "express" himself through acting out, and a "comédien," a professional actor, who reserves acting out for the theatre stage. Within his scheme, we all qualify as intermittent amateur actors, indulging in personal fancies; but only professionals contribute to the goals set for theatre by society, including the mediation of social roles. As a result, Duvignaud limits the category of real actors to properly professional actors, and excludes all amateurs. Yet the history of theatre, whether traditional or avant-garde, owes many of its features to amateurs. Besides, acting out a fiction on the stage always has a ludic dimension that, like any gratuitous game, cannot help undermining the serious purpose assigned to it by society. Duvignaud's distinction between amateur and professional actors has merit, and draws attention to the influence of historical factors on the evolution of theatre. But it does not dispel objections against a concept of theatre that views actors as its primary source.

The role of actors as source of theatrical activity also fails to account for the important part that spectators play in theatre. Acting out must not necessarily involve an institutionalized audience: anyone can be the spectator for someone else, meeting exhibitionist needs. When individual acting out is channeled into a public event, that is, when theatre occurs, the relation between actors and audience fulfills a function that goes beyond acting out. More exactly, it endows it with an additional goal that turns the satisfaction of secret drives into the assertion of excellence. Assuredly, actors need to play roles, but theatre as a game undermines the interest in acting; in order to tone down the ludic nature of roles, and restore a vital seriousness to their function, actors must play them as seriously as they can, they must excel in their acting. And to achieve that goal, they need a public able to judge their performance, the theatre public that can monitor acting norms. In that sense, theatre derives not only from the actors' special need for self-expression but also from a more general human ambition to demonstrate superior achievements. Similarly, spectators expect to see excellent performances on the stage, that is, to witness superior achievements. On either side, then, the performant function is stressed.

But let us stay a while longer with the actors. When they play roles, they tell a story to the audience and ensure that some communication takes place. Their function as central figures of theatre could thus be claimed also to benefit the operation of the referential function. But not if performances were truly centered on actors. In that case, the performant function would tend to override the referential function. Indeed, a theatre serving the needs of actors would primarily seek to display their acting talents and physical attributes, to astonish and delight the audience, to keep up a ripple of laughter or applause, to consecrate personalities, to fuel the star system culminating in one-man shows; it would downplay the story. Some performances exemplify such one-sided orientation, but they are relatively rare. Traditional theatre still aims at telling stories even when it caters to its actors.

Visibly, there are more than actors at the source of theatre. And, more generally, we play not only personal but also social roles.

## Social Roles and Rules: Theatre as Life

Social roles derive from society's need to bring order to its structure. To establish and preserve that order, organized societies assign specific roles to its discrete groups and to individuals holding a special status. Expressions such as "one should stay in one's place" or "behave properly!" remind us that people fall into different categories, defined by origins, power, profession, age, sex, and so forth, but also that each category demands a different type of behavior. A king should act like a king, an old woman like an old woman, a physician like a physician, and so on. Each model constitutes a distinct social role and, in an orderly society, everybody plays the role corresponding to one's status. Of course, one can also play a role deviously, with the intention to mislead others about one's real status. In real life, such acting disturbs the social order; it is disapproved and censured. But it generates playing social roles on the stage.

That social roles can be transferred from life to theatre has been known at least since Aristotle. If, by his logic of probability, a king should act like a model king rather than like a real king, then, in the name of verisimilitude and preservation of order, an actor who plays the role of a king must also act like a model king. To that extent, the source of theatre roles lies in social roles defined by society. But if theatre were really to imitate reality, as Aristotle and his followers would have it, then social roles enacted on the stage would have no informational interest, since the spectators would know them already by their own experience. The main appeal of staged social roles could hence only reside in the art with which they are enacted, and their resulting normative power. By that logic, the performant function must then prevail over the referential function. The same observation holds for theatre roles that innovate or change social models; in order to influence the audience, they need the seduction imparted by great acting performances.

There is some substance in this theory. Roles defined by society do, indeed, find their way to the stage. But not always in the spirit of mimesis. Performances can and do transform them, either to increase their prestige or to ridicule them. Furthermore, social roles acted out in real life are rarely directed at spectators; they are rather inner-oriented. Instead of generating theatre, social roles form only one of the means that theatre uses to attain its social goals, even when these goals are commanded by social concerns. Besides, roles prescribed by social practice are not the only roles that are played in real life.

After World War II, for example, Jean-Paul Sartre's existentialism drew attention to a different type of role-playing. It held that most people choose to play "bad faith" roles: that, instead of following their "authentic" nature, they adopt certain models of behavior, usually offered ready-made by cultural ideology. Acting like, say, a patriot, a thief, or a cuckold husband is supposed to act, dispenses one from making free decisions and bearing responsibility for one's life. In contrast to actors, who know that their role-playing is a game, people who live in "bad faith" take their roles seriously. Yet the unauthentic source of their behavior disturbs them at some unconscious level; and they seek, in the eyes of *others*, the confirmation that they successfully conform to the stereotyped model. Most people, in Sartre's sense, display therefore two fundamental features of theatrical activity: they play roles distinct from their own personality, and they need a public that approves their acting.

This scheme acknowledges that cultural ready-made roles are integrated in social life. However, it explains by existential psychology why some people play these roles while others do not. In other terms, it locates the source of acting in individual choices rather than in general laws of social behavior or in an abstract human nature. By this logic, there remains that theatre would fulfill several informational functions. It would provide, as in Duvignaud's theory, stereotyped models for "bad faith" behavior. But it would also serve to expose "bad faith" by showing, on the stage, that any acting always involves roles that lack authenticity. One may well imagine, in addition, that in many spectators a ludic display of role-playing could exorcise unconscious fears about playing roles in real life.

Playing roles has a negative connotation for Sartre because it manifests "bad faith." For his contemporary Albert Camus, it rather offers a positive means of enriching one's life with imaginary experiences. In both cases, however, once it appears on the stage in the harmless form of a game, social role-playing downgrades the referential function of theatre. If dramatic characters are shown to follow the same ready-made models of behavior as real people, then a theatre performance has no information to tell the audience; its referential function is satisfied when theatrical roles are identified with stereotyped social roles: a goal of little interest. The performant function then takes over. Clearly, a superior way of enacting uninteresting roles may help to please the spectators, stimulate their passions, and enhance a play's power as exorcism or vicarious experience. At least in theory. Actual performances of Sartre's and Camus's plays did not much stress the performant function. But then their major characters, while confronting the problem of set social roles, are complex individuals who diverge from stereotyped models.

The main difficulty with social roles defined by status or behavioral models lies indeed in their very high level of generalization. Theatre surely can tell stories about stereotyped social characters, yet it rarely does. Whenever it presents individuals, especially exceptional individuals, it brutally severs its links with social roles as they are traditionally understood.

There is, however, a certain category of social roles that escape the constraints of rigid stereotypes: roles that, as Erving Goffman has shown, do not define a permanent status or nature of individuals, but only prescribe a behavior expected in special social circumstances.[18] As roles, they are assumed and discarded for short periods of time, resumed when needed, and often exchanged. Because they are flexible and mobile, they offer a rich source for theatre roles that are drawn from social praxis. These are roles we all play in many small-scale rituals of our social life: parties, family meals, professional meetings, formal exchanges at work and at home, verbal and/or physical stereotypes of lovemaking, encounters in public places, even a single person's routine of getting up, making breakfast, reading a paper or watching news, and so forth. Each of such occasions presents a limited number of variants with a limited number of appropriate roles. As we move from one occasion to another, as our fragmented day takes us from one situation to another, we move from one role to another as if we were in a series of loosely connected short plays. None of these roles is attached to a particular character, nor is linked to a single personality; on the contrary, when we behave as social actors, we play a number of disjointed roles, changing them frequently. The mini-dramas in which we are involved are inserted in a social text that we enact without questioning it. We participate in fact in society's constant drive to regulate social intercourse on the basis of smooth role-playing.

By this theory, all social life is theatre where everyone plays roles determined by rules of social behavior. Theatre proper merely frames that general activity within the conventions of the stage. To that extent, there is little difference between playing social and theatrical roles, and society's mini-dramas are a direct source of theatre performances. In other terms, theatre exists because dramatics form a natural part of social interaction. When the stage draws on reality, whether in the spirit of mimesis or transformation, real-life situations, with their roles and rules, generate theatre situations, with their own rules and roles. In that sense, whatever the story it tells, a performance always also reflects those models of social behavior that prevail in a given society.

From this perspective, theatre's referential function is limited to conveying the main events of the plot. Specific scenes, involving inter-action between characters, have no real story interest since the specta-tors, in their own social life, have experienced them in similarly dra-matic scenes. All the more important then is the conventional stage framing by which such everyday mini-dramas become theatrical games. Watching their ludic reenactment, spectators discover a mock-ing mirror image of their own status as social actors; they realize, with liberating enjoyment, that their own theatricality can be transformed into a play. But in order to achieve this type of purge, theatre must clearly affirm its nature as an artistic game; that is, it must stress the rules by which it operates as such a game. It must make clear that the stage refers to a fictional story, but also that, as part of that artistic process, actors must be appreciated as actors, and staging as an aes-thetic activity. The last two requirements strongly relate to the per-formant function of theatre, drawing attention to the reality of the stage.

Goffman's approach manifests an anthropological concern with social rituals, but, dealing with modern rites, it strips them from magic and bares their arbitrary nature as games that society forces us to play. Mini-dramas enacted in real life have no serious intention to communi-cate a message; a fortiori, when they are transported on the stage, no serious message can be expected. But ludic activities can be enjoyed when they meet the expectations of excellence. By stressing the role of the performant function, especially in the realm of aesthetics, Goff-man's approach leads to theories that consider theatre to be primarily an art.

## Aesthetic Demands: Theatre as Art

Theories that view theatre as an art, and define its nature in aesthetic terms, do not focus on its historical origins or on social or universal sources, but on special features that justify calling it an art. No doubt the notion of art raises its own problems. Obviously it involves an aesthetic dimension; in fact, aesthetics serve to define all art forms. But what is the nature of beauty? It appears to elude an essential definition so that, faced with a new form, we cannot be sure whether it is art or not. But these are theoretical problems. More pragmatically, let us assume that art is what is called art: the totality of art forms to which we attribute aesthetic quality. True, these art forms have never had a stable status because aesthetic norms, based on conventions, change in time and space. Yet most art forms have enjoyed enough stability in our culture to have generated a certain number of converging observations about their common features. Practically, we may thus agree that any given form, in this case theatre, must manifest these features in order to qualify as art. I shall limit my remarks to the implications that four such features have for theatre: representation, permanence, perceptibility, and style.

That art is representation, that is, that any art form refers to something else, has been generally accepted since Aristotle. Even music pieces, or abstract graphics, have titles that describe that which they represent.[19] One could argue that some art forms claim to be non-representational, or that others fail to communicate anything to the observers. These are debatable points but, even when conceded, they only demonstrate that aesthetic conventions are changing, and/or that representation is not always carried out successfully. By and large, art forms are still supposed to represent: to be signs standing for something that they are not. Besides, the argument does not concern traditional theatre. Its most eccentric performances continue to use signs to refer to an imaginary story. In that sense, they fully manifest representation in art. By the same token, of course, theatre as art is permanently bound to the referential function.

A second property of art is the often discussed permanence of its forms. It is irrelevant whether they are material, like painting, or immaterial, like music, or appear to have an evanescent materiality, like dance. In each case, they rely on a permanent feature that, outliving the initial production, ensures an ideally limitless number of repeated aesthetic experiences. There are theoretical objections to that notion, but they create few practical difficulties. We know that nothing lasts forever, all ending in entropy, but we also acknowledge that the Venus of Milo, Petronius's *Satiricon*, Beethoven's Fifth, even *Swan Lake* have had a long enough "life" to guarantee future survival in our culture, that is, to justify their claim to a relative permanence. That nothing ever remains identical, and that each aesthetic experience is different, even for the same beholder and for the same art form, creates no greater problems. By convention, we discount the resulting variations, postulating that we always read the same *Satiricon*; and we explain any divergence by altered conditions of perception. More significant is the difference among the ways of preserving permanence. Some arts, such as painting, sculpture, and even literature, despite changes between successive editions of its works, are always experienced in a single, permanent material form. Other arts, however, such as music, dance, and theatre, either rely on memory to perpetuate their forms, or, more generally, have two distinctly separate material forms: one form that records their permanent core, (partitions, notations, texts) and a second form in which they are actually experienced by the audience, (ephemeral performances). All arts meet the criterion of permanence, but the dual nature of performing arts opens their permanence to enriching transformations.[20]

In the case of theatre, the permanent core lies in the theoretically stable verbal text, sometimes oral, usually written, and now printed and available for mass consumption. This last development has had some unique effects on the relation between the theatre text and its performance. They will be explored in detail as a central problem of theatrical process. At this juncture it is enough to note that, because we attribute permanence to the text, we are inclined to trace manifestations of the text in all its staged performances. As a result, theatre performances are often approached as if they had two distinct functions: on the one hand, to tell a permanent story conveyed by the verbal text, on the other, to provide topical references by the means of stage signs added to the verbal signs. An audience's actual experience of theatre rarely separates the two operations. In fact, as shall be seen, verbal and stage signs interact in performances. If one holds, however, that theatre is primarily an art form, and that art forms are defined by permanence, then the permanent verbal text, with the story that has a referential function, becomes the main support of art in theatre; and all other features of the performance, lacking permanence, fulfill functions that are extraneous to theatre as art. Bound to the evanescent frame of the performance, such features elude norms of theatre as an art. Whatever they may tell or however beautiful they may be found, they are judged by their own norms, the norms of the various staging activities. They seem thus to generate the performant function of theatre, and, viewed from that perspective, appear to be a parasitic complement of art.

While it appeals to logic, such a reduction of art in theatre to the verbal text, and the resulting exclusion of performance features from the artistic nature of theatre, cannot be taken too seriously. Perhaps the notion of art is too vague, perhaps the permanence clause is too abstract, perhaps theatre is a sum of many arts, and much more besides. At any rate, a number of theoreticians, instead of advocating the primacy of the permanent verbal text, locate the artistic essence of theatre in the ephemeral features of the performance: staging in general, and acting in particular. Some, like Eugenio Barba, come close to identifying theatre with actors, but they stress the actor's work rather than psychological needs. For them, postures and motions of the body, highly stylized, have the power to create and release emotional truths; and the stories told on the stage either serve as pretexts for the celebration of the body's forms or are generated by them.[21] The reduction of theatre to a performance benefits also from the recent extension of the performance concept to a variety of artistic activities: promoted in scholarly studies by Richard Schechner and Andre Helbo, carried to an extreme in Alan Kaprow's pure art performances, this perspective obviously favors the performant function. However, such an ecumenical approach to all performing arts, losing sight of the special place that text holds in theatrical processes, denies much of theatre's specificity as an art. To that extent, the stress on the performance is as controversial as the traditional insistence on the artistic monopoly of the text.

One is on relatively safer grounds when dealing with a third property attributed to art: perceptibility of the aesthetic nature of its forms. Indeed, whatever the conditions of perception, be they physical or psychological, there is no doubt that theatre forms are first perceived in their material appearance. True, some mental concepts suggested by a performance may become objects of formal aesthetic judgments. Thus we exclaim: "What a beautiful idea!" or "What a beautiful soul!" or, while listening to a description of an absent character, we imagine how beautiful he or she must look.[22] But such mental visions are not perceived on the stage. They may influence our concretization of the story, but they lack the aesthetic power of material forms that assault our senses during the performance: lights, sounds, sets, props, costumes, and actors. The latter in particular sustain most of our aesthetic concerns, generating our expectation that we shall experience art while attending a theatre performance.

In order to discharge their aesthetic role, these material forms need first to be perceived in their function as aesthetic objects. Yet they are also signs supposed to fulfill a referential function, that is, to tell a story, and the audience's attention to that story requires a clear perception of this semiotic function of forms. A certain tension between the two types of perception thus always marks the reception of theatre as art. For that matter, all art that is expected to be both aesthetic and referential involves such a tension even when one of the two functions is stressed at the expense of the other. Thus, as we have seen, even supposedly nonreferential art always includes some references, however abstract or solipsistic. And Sartre's praise of the referentiality of prose that, in contrast to poetry, draws no attention to its signs doesn't prevent him from drawing an aesthetic pleasure from such "transparent" prose forms. In fact, as illustrated in Roman Jakobson's scheme of communication, use of signs always involves several coexistent functions; and, even when they compete for attention, none can be eliminated. A highly aesthetic text, favoring the "poetic" function, may minimize the role of its referential message but cannot do without it. A

theatre performance that stresses the aesthetic perception of stage
signs may similarly lower the interest in the story but must tell one
nevertheless. In short, the demands of theatre as art accommodate
referentiality but downgrade it in the name of a search for beauty: in
actors, in costumes, in sets, and so forth. They also encourage the
promotion of the performant function whereby actors, sets, costumes,
and all other desemiotized features of the stage are appreciated not
only for their aesthetic appeal but also for the performing skills they
manifest or for the emotions they inspire.

The last feature of theatre as art that needs to be discussed is the
matter of formal style. Theatre forms, like all art forms, are rarely
produced at random. They tend to follow conventions that determine
what we call styles. Styles change, and admit individual variations, but
even in the process of transformation they are directed by general
rules. In that sense, theatre operates like a game, perhaps because it
originates in our need to play, as some theories claim, but also because
any application of stylistic rules to a creative activity has always a ludic
dimension. Yet theatrical games, as we have seen, may be taken to be
quite serious. Whether explicit or implicit, acknowledgment of the
importance of style leads thus naturally to a heightened attention to
those theatre conventions that command, as it were, from outside, any
particular referentiality. Some govern artistic forms with rules that are
specifically formulated for theatre as art: prescriptions concerning
appearance, delivery, gestures of actors, styles of sets and props, role of
lights and sounds. Others set patterns for the interaction between the
stage and the audience: conventions defining the performance's space
and time coordinates, categories of actors and spectators, the social and
commercial status of theatre.

In both cases, when they are actually applied, there is little interest
in the intrinsic value of such rules. In contrast, much concern is shown
for the way in which they are applied, that is, for the skill displayed by
all producers of a performance who find, within the given conventions,
an inspiration for original implementations. In fact, any concrete involvement in the games of style includes the stimulating expectation
that they will be played in some exceptional way. In other terms, that
the performance as art will provide a great *performance* in the display of
a theatrical style. In that manner, the performant function, so much in
evidence in sports—physical games with simple rules—draws vitality
from the sophisticated rules of theatre.

     *   *   *

None of the approaches discussed above accounts for all features of
theatre, nor offers a full explanation of its origins. Some may be found

to be more appealing, or convenient, or convincing than others. Several raise questions that remain in suspense. There is some overlapping in various areas, or conflict, or a mixture of both. Insofar as the nature of theatre is concerned, the belief in primitive rituals as sources of early theatre yields other conclusions than the belief in modern rituals as sources of theatre today; but the focus on ritual forms yields the same conclusions as the focus on aesthetic forms. My purpose was not to dispel this confusion. Nor did I attempt to exhaust the vast library of theatre theories: many other approaches, notably from philosophical perspectives, could have been included.

I only intended, with an eclectic sample, to show that these approaches demonstrate a polarization of ways of looking at theatre, some underscoring its referential function, others the performant function. By the same token, in a circuitous manner, I have tried to come closer to understanding the nature of the performant function. It should be clear by now, for example, that it involves activities that take place on the stage, focusing on the actors, and that it operates outside the communication process whereby a story is told to the audience. But these indications drawn from theatre theories are not sufficient. The appreciation of the full impact of the performant function on theatrical practice requires a more systematic exploration of its nature. And not only as it is manifested in theatre. It will be best grasped first in other public events where it operates more openly.

## 3. Performant Function in Action

### Sports: Objective *Performances*

Performing arts are not the only public events during which an audience watches performers in action. Sporting events (and circuses) also offer achievements displayed by the performers. Obviously there are differences. Sporting events are always single events, valued precisely for their unique and hence suspenseful character. They are not performances in the sense of the word that, in theatre and circus, denotes a repeated execution of a previously established program; they are rather called "meets," "games," "matches," and so forth. Yet, within any sporting event, an action performed by an individual athlete, or by a team, is often designed as a performance, comparable to an actor's performance, and sometimes is praised as a (great) *performance*, when it manifests an exceptional achievement. Normally, the context indicates which of the three meanings of "performance" is intended. In this section, however, in order to avoid confusion, I shall set them off with distinct marks. A capitalized Performance will refer to an entire public event, a theatre or circus production, but also a sport meet; performance with a lower case initial will mean a task carried out by individuals within the framework of the Performance; and an italicized *performance* will denote such an activity when it is acknowledged to be *truly* outstanding. In that sense, whenever we attend a Performance, we always watch individual performances, but we only applaud a few *performances*. My point is that our hope to witness a *performance* constitutes an essential part of our interest in all sorts of Performances, including sporting events.

Let us consider a track and field meet and, within it, a high-jump competition. Both for performers and spectators, winning is the obvious point of the event. Each athlete tries to jump higher than the others, and supporters of a particular athlete are gratified when he or she jumps the highest. Both jumping and watching the jumps are direct experiences. As such, they need no signs to be grasped, nor do they stand for anything else. True, one could claim that all sport performances manifest a harnessed aggressiveness. But such a relation is *causal* in nature rather than semiotic: we like sports because we are aggressive and not as signs of our aggressiveness. A winning performance could be regarded with better reason as a real sign, standing for a general superiority that cannot be demonstrated by direct experience. But it is doubtful that individual athletes, when they try to jump the highest, intend to communicate any overall superiority; they rather want to show that they are the best at jumping. Besides, if winning any sport contest, or any other competition, could qualify as a sign of general superiority, the meaning of such a sign would be diluted to the point of triviality. Better then to stay with the notion that a high-jump win offers a direct rather than a semiotic gratification.

In practice, of course, many semiotic processes graft themselves onto sport competitions. Since the Greek Olympic games individual athletes have stood for particular groups: first cities, then nations and races, now also neighborhoods, schools, sport associations, commercial companies, and so forth. An individual performance, good or bad, is intensely perceived as an intentional sign referring to the performance of the entire group: all Americans feel exalted when an American wins an international high-jump contest. Furthermore, sporting events rival theatre in displaying many cultural signs that directly link participants and their groups: national flags or anthems, special designs on sweat shirts, jerseys or uniforms, partisan applause or encouragement. This parasitic semiosis, promoted by the media, is carried by supporters into the street, work places, homes. It even affects athletes who see themselves as "ambassadors" of their group, deserving compensation for their role as signs. The nostalgia for "pure" sport manifests a reaction against that growing semiotization; it also demonstrates its basic acceptance. A serious study of sport sociosemiotics is needed to assess both causes and implications of this phenomenon.

But the direct experience of a competition, and the grafted semiotic identification with a group, by no means exhaust the functions of a sporting event. After eliminating their competitors, and thus sure to win, high jumpers will nevertheless try for a greater height, even without chances at a significant record except their own. Why do they do it? No doubt because of a sport convention, but why do they follow it earnestly? To some extent, they want probably to gratify what a Polish semiotician calls the "show-off" drive, to show others how things should be done.[23] But they also seek to perform better than is expected from them, to satisfy a need for an exceptional accomplishment, to achieve what they hope to be a *performance*. Or let us take a traveling amateur of track and field who, unfamiliar with any local athletes, watches a high-jump event on his hotel room television. He is not involved in any "showing off" and has no "semiotic" reasons to grow excited as the bar reaches great heights, nearing a record. But the prospect of witnessing the setting of a new record suffices to keep him glued to the screen with the anticipation of seeing something out of the ordinary. Obviously he is motivated, as are French audiences that watch televised Wimbledon games, by the desire to see a memorable *performance*. For both athletes and spectators, sporting events thus offer, in addition to other satisfactions, the chance to participate in a ritualized celebration of excellence. To that extent, they are exemplary media for the public operation of the *performant function*.

They also permit us to grasp clearly how we determine exceptional achievements.. Obviously it is a matter of norms. These norms are levels of achievement that we *normally* expect from competent performers in any Performance. Under these levels, we place incompetent performances; above them, we situate *performances*. For most Performances, however, norms are neither stable nor clear, and any judgment involves a good deal of subjectivity. Only in sports can we apply objective norms and rely on a rational system of evaluation. As a result, the operation of the performant function in sporting events is quite transparent; it offers an ideal model that clarifies problems we have when assessing *performances* in other types of Performances.

The most striking feature of sport norms is indeed that they are quantified. As a rule, they are measured in objective units: centimeters, inches, seconds, pounds, goals, runs, or even "points." The latter, used in boxing, gymnastics, diving, or figure skating, can cause disagreement among individual judges or in the public attending concrete competitions; but, by convention, a combined opinion of judges is viewed to be as reliable as a mechanical device. In other terms, neither norms nor achievement levels depend on subjective evaluations: athletes and spectators know what standards apply.

The second special feature of sports is a clear ordering of the relative value of norms. True, all types of Performances posit that levels of competence vary with circumstantial factors: provincial actors, for example, are not expected to perform as well as actors of a prestigious big city company. But the hierarchy of competence is not evident, and no supreme norms obtain. In sports, there are two systems of norms that, taken together, allow for an objective evaluation of practically any performance. The first system measures performances on scales of quantified values. Any particular sport has several such scales, arranged in a hierarchical order: world standards and records, national standards and records, divisional standards and records, and so forth. In that sense, a high jump that breaks a world record offers an absolute *performance*, but relative *performances* can also be achieved by high jumps that reach the top of lesser scales, down to the level of a high school. This system mainly applies to individuals, though occasionally it serves to rank outstanding teams which, within their area of competition, obtain exceptional scores or win a record number of games. It has the advantage of stabilizing relativity in sport performances and, at the same time, relieving spectators from making value judgments.

The second system follows the same hierarchy of relative levels of achievement but focuses on the outcome of competition rather than on quantified performances. Olympic games and world championships are clearly on the top, then national, provincial, city, or school championships, and meets between nations or clubs. The winner of a high jump, a winning horse or soccer team, may perform poorly in terms of quantified results, but their performance will be a *performance* if they best their own record, or win against odds, or totally dominate their opponents, or decide the outcome of the entire competition. In this case too, although they are more difficult to measure, the public relies on norms of expected performances. The fact that these expectations are set in advance, and sometimes computed, mainly by experts in media, endows them with a further prestige of objectivity. As a result, just as for quantified performances, the acknowledgment of competition *performances* requires no judgment by individual spectators.

\*    \*    \*

This self-evidence of excellence, whatever the relative level of endeavor, is very gratifying in times of wavering standards. It explains the role of the performant function in sports; it may also explain why we watch sporting events as closely as possible. The celebration of excellence, its reassuring self-assertion, may indeed confirm, through an unconscious symbolic process, our racial belief in the survival of the fittest. But there is no need for such semiotic speculations. It is even more doubtful that we enjoy evidence of excellence as a vicarious demonstration of our own superiority. Not all sport spectators can identify with athletes. True, any successful effort, and, a fortiori, a successful extraordinary effort, encourages our trust in the resourcefulness of human nature, and hence in our own chances to overcome our limitations. The performant function in sports, while fulfilling other roles, caters no doubt to such a general need for self-assurance. But our culture satisfies that need in many other ways that do not involve exceptional feats. Besides, as it is manifested in *performances*, the notion of superior achievements applies not only to humans but also to animals, plants, landscapes, or manufactured products with which we rarely identify.

For there are many types of norms, and they define various types of achievement. An exceptionally performant computer, for example, excels by the speed and scope of its computations, or its versatility, or its solidity. It can also be judged in terms of its aesthetics, and admired as a *performance* in styling. Dimension can also generate norms, leading to appreciation for what is outsized or miniaturized: a mile-long hot dog, a thumb-sized dictionary, a toy poodle. In these cases, and in many instances of human *performances*, qualifying, say, obesity or erotic appeal, one can hardly speak of excellence. Perhaps, then, demonstrating excellence is not the main function of a *performance*. Perhaps the foremost appeal of an exceptional performance lies simply in its exceptional quality: the fact that it is unpredictable and unique. In that sense, a truly excellent sport record and a catastrophic plane accident, both extraordinary events deviating from the norm, exert a similar fascination. But why are we fascinated with manifestations of strangeness? What need is satisfied by *performances* that foil standard expectations?

The Freudian theory of the *unfamiliar* provides only a limited answer: neither a hoped-for sport record nor a feared accident are really unfamiliar. A much simpler if trite explanation assumes that modern existence, regulated by social and cultural norms, lacks excitement; bored with what is expected, a few individuals seek adventure in extraordinary tasks and records but the timid majority are content with a vicarious experience of such *performances*. In that view, the performant function satisfies the wish to believe that life can be exciting, that it always reserves surprises: a most convincing observation, complementing rather than superseding the other theories, but valid only for highly standardized modern cultures.

I should prefer to think that the performant function has a universal role, corresponding to a basic human drive postulated, as we have seen, by Jean Piaget: mental structuration of the world. As our structures develop, they also grow rigid, resisting the restructuration of their fundamental ordering of reality. Acknowledging and integrating change becomes increasingly painful. Deprived of its natural exercise, our structuring drive then seeks outlets in games that do not involve our life, notably in the structuration of fictional worlds offered by theatre; but it also channels its action into a relatively painless adjustment of norms that expands their boundaries without need for any radical restructuring of their measuring system. An exceptional achievement, because it is defined by a norm already structured in the given area, is integrated in that norm, expanding its coverage but not changing its structure. A new record measured in inches only adds more inches to the requirements for a future record, and a face with an outstanding aesthetic/erotic impact only makes higher demands on the aesthetic/erotic appeal of other faces with a comparably outstanding impact. It is likely therefore that we welcome, and indeed eagerly seek, all types of *performances* in order to satisfy at little expense our frustrated structuring drive; and we favor sport Performances in our search because their quantified norms require minimal restructuring. To that extent, the performant function serves to keep our notion of the world in a state of balance, using harmless *performances* to minimize the pain of adapting it to change. Such at least seems to be the most general role of the performant function, evident in sports but also prevailing in theatre. By a different strategy, but with a similar outcome, the operation of the performant function in circus enables us to substitute the authority of magic for personal restructuring of norms.

## Circus: Magic *Performances*

Circus shares with sports a dominant interest in physical accomplishments: most circus and sport performers are mainly expected to display muscular power, skills, and coordination. And, as in sports, circus *performances* concern outstanding physical achievements. But the similarity ends there. Unlike sports, circus offers no direct competition between individuals or teams, nor single events with unpredictable outcomes. It rather resembles theatre by offering runs of repeated Performances that, despite some variations, involve a repeated execution of a program rehearsed in advance. Furthermore, whereas in sports semiotic references have a parasitic, though obvious role, in circus they manifest the operation of a referential function that, again as in theatre, is fully integrated with the performant function.

True, most semiotic references in circus are not as overt as in sports or theatre. As Paul Bouissac has shown, they mainly operate on the unconscious level, certainly for the public and possibly for many performers.[24] A number of signs are openly displayed—statements, hats, or props referring to outside reality, or sound and light effects underscoring the importance of an act—but, as a rule, they are marginal, almost as parasitic as in sports: they concern clowns, who belong more properly in theatre than in circus, or convey comments that a circus director makes about acts from the outside. The real signs, in contrast, are generated by the basic structure of performances, that is, by necessary choices in the display of a skill, but they are not obvious. A "cat" tamer, for example, choosing a dangerous contact with the beast, projects different meanings depending on the choice: a kissing lioness evokes a woman in love, a knee-nuzzling lion an affectionate house pet, and so forth. Or, a tightrope walker, depending on costume and style, will be admired as a superman or derided as a bum, regardless of the displayed skill. Objects used by jugglers and magicians similarly have a semiotic power, referring to leisure or farm activities.

In each case, according to Bouissac, the act communicates an idea to spectators, and spectators appreciate the act as they unconsciously react to the communication. In that process, the performant function tends to be perturbed. In fact, Bouissac prefers not to deal with the value of a performance, disregarding the impact that demonstration of skills has on the audience. He seems to assume that the level of competence is not at stake, that circus could do without the appeal of *performances* as long as it fulfills its referential function. To that extent, while showing that circus integrates both functions, he splits apart their effects, distorting the total picture. For there is little question that the performant function always dominates in circus Performances, even while it supports referentiality. There is little doubt that the circus public always expects to see great *performances*. It is also evident that this expectation is generally satisfied. For most spectators, all circus performances are *performances*. And therein lies their specificity.

Or, more fundamentally, this specificity of circus lies in the coexistence of two separate sets of norms that are applied to its acts. One set defines the competence of a performer by parameters similar to those used by "expert" judges of acrobatic sports: smoothness, speed, originality, degree of hardship or risk. Circus professionals, directors and artists, know how to rank a performance by such norms. A circus audience, however, made of children, parents, and a few true amateurs, has no familiarity with the professional norms, cannot assess the real difficulty or quality of an act. For the average spectator, especially a child, the norm is instinctively grasped as his or her own competence, or the competence of a "normal" animal, that is, a very low level of achievement. In comparison, any circus performance, because it takes place in the circus, appears to be exceptional and sometimes monstrous; and performers are attributed abnormal powers that add to their prestige. Circus rituals further that illusion: the ringmaster introduces "the greatest artists in the world," featured acts are spotlighted or preceded by a drumroll; parades of bejeweled elephants evoke exotic, wealthy, fairyland kingdoms.

Circus artists thus always offer a double performance. For the circus people, who determine their professional career, they must reach at least the expert norm of competence, and perhaps give them a true *performance*; referentiality has no place in this sheer display of skill and daring. In contrast, performing for a naive audience only requires maintaining its trust in the extraordinary status of all acts, whatever their real quality. Often, with a semiotic sleight of hand, artists must deceive the public into believing that the most spectacular acts are also the most difficult. And that strategy requires a heavy recourse to referentiality, playing on beliefs in the mastery of man over animals, or the revenge of the underdog (or under-horse), or the superiority of beauty or brawn or brains, or the power of magic. It is this audience-oriented performance that binds together the referential and performing functions in circus.

The popularity of circus indicates that the dual system of norms is working well: partly, no doubt, because experts keep upgrading professional norms, making sure that only competent artists will perform; partly, however, because the public, rarely disappointed in its expectation of *performances*, delegates assessing performances to the producers of shows. The control of quality, exerted in sports by objective measures, is entrusted in circus to anonymous experts: a power beyond understanding, operating in mysterious ways. Like a magician's tricks, delight of children, all performances offered by circus experts, producers, and performers, are magically guaranteed to be true *performances*. And, in a circus, we trust in magic.

But, as we renounce grasping, or trying to grasp, what features of a performance are intended to surpass corresponding norms, we attribute a special status to all circus performances, excluding them, as it were, from the world we experience normally. Their magic nature sets them apart from our structures of reality; we see them as extraordinary manifestations of mystery that cannot be integrated in our knowledge, and hence require no restructuring. To that extent, circus *performances* leave intact our notions about the world. They even strengthen them as they show us that some things need not be understood. No wonder then that children prefer circus to sporting events. Still involved in early stages of structuring, they accept dark holes between structures, probably enjoy the thrill of the unknown. And they have no reasons, unlike rigid adults, to satisfy their structuring drive through a minimal restructuring of sport norms. Of course, some adults are also circus fans, perhaps because they retain a sense of wonder.

In any case, in order fully to appreciate circus events, the public must enter a pact whereby any performance will be received as a *performance*. Theatre has different conventions. Its basic pact, whereby everything on the stage is received as a sign, concerns the referential and not the performant function. Yet, even in theatre, certain spectators, increasingly numerous, prove to be also programmed, by media or word-of-mouth, to expect and applaud *performances* offered by specific actors, directors, or designers, regardless of their referential role. Like naive circus audiences, or amateurs of sports, such spectators are willing to trade their judgment for reliance on an outside authority, to give up exercising their structuring drive. But, in their case, that authority is neither objective, as in sports, nor magic, as in circus; it is partly vested in theatre experts; but it extends to makers and manipulators of social reputations, more interested in exceptional personalities than in exceptional achievements.

## Theatre: Intermittent *Performances*

### Interaction Between Referential and Performant Functions

Referential and performant functions, we noted, can interact in many ways. Both functions are exhibited in most public events but they rarely are granted an equal importance. A ballet visibly stresses the performant function even though, traditionally, it also claims to communicate some meaning. In sports, the performant function dominates more openly; but, in a symbiotic relation, it derives much of its vitality from a grafted referential function that operates through cultural signs. The resulting semiotization of sport is generally accepted although, now and then, when it perturbs an objective reception of performances, it is denounced as a perversion of sport. Circus Performances maintain a better balance between the two functions. At first sight, they seem to give priority to *performances*; in fact, they always employ referentiality to enhance their appeal. Typically, a circus program thus includes both exhibitions of skill, intended to elicit admiration for the performers, and semiotic comedy carried out by clowns. Furthermore, whatever their nature, both types of acts communicate cultural references to the audience, though often on an unconscious level. The two functions are integrated and inseparable; they operate simultaneously, supporting each other. And the public receives their impact without distinguishing between them. As a rule, however, the performant function, when it is supported by truly impressive circus *performances*, tends to monopolize the audience's attention.

Theatre follows none of these patterns. It does share with circus a basic coexistence of both functions, but, in contrast with circus, it either gives them a truly equal importance or clearly focuses on the referential function. Historically, both functions combined have always been considered to account for the total appeal of theatre. All theories of theatre, whatever their bias, from Aristotle's *Poetics* to the speech act school, assume that coexistence. And most theatre reception texts testify that the spectators, like the theoreticians, respond to both functions. Practically all accounts of theatre performances in modern press and audio-visual media, just as in letters, diaries, memoirs, or narratives of the past, evidence both an interest in referential features of plays—what story they tell and what meaning they convey—and a parallel concern for actors, staging, costumes, or designs, found to display competence, incompetence, or *performance*. This duality has significant effects on the complex problem of theatre reception and will be further explored in Part III.

But coexistence doesn't always imply a close integration. While operating together, and contributing jointly to the total appeal of a theatre performance, the referential and performant functions always potentially compete for the attention of both spectators and performers. True, this potential competition is rarely acknowledged among the producers of a play. In the ideal world of theory, playwrights, directors, actors, or technicians seek *performances* as a natural way to a better implementation of referential goals. Producing *Hamlet*, for example, they are primarily expected to tell a good Hamlet story; their *performances*, achieved by a superior telling, thus naturally combine a drive for personal accomplishment with a professional respect for referentiality. In reality, however, many performers view referentiality only as a pretext, or vehicle, for the display of their individual excellence. As a result, they pay more attention to their own performance than to the story they are supposed to tell. How many performers thus downgrade the role of the referential function is difficult to assess; their number depends on changing social and cultural conditions. One should like to believe that they are still outnumbered by "ideal" performers dedicated to both functions. Indeed, most memorable performances still manifest a concerted convergence of great *performances* and fascinating referentiality. But the temptation to promote the performant function must not be minimized. And it risks getting increasingly stronger, benefiting from conditions that, in a media-oriented society, encourage the celebration of personalities.

In fact, supported by the media, self-oriented performers often seek *performances* in areas that have little to do with the art of telling a story. On professional stages, they want to be acclaimed for their charismatic, aesthetic, or erotic appeal, originality of concepts, opulence of costumes, singing or dancing skills. In a similar spirit, amateur performances tend to focus on the talent of would-be actors, children or adults, rather than on the story of characters. Classic plays, because their stories are already well known, offer particularly suitable occasions for such a one-sided attention to the performant function; but also new plays—and not only musicals—are frequently produced for the same purpose, tailoring roles to fit special demands of famous stars. Of course, it is impossible to state to what degree a performance centered on *performances* actually does undermine the referential function. But the problem exists. And frequent contrasts made by critics between the dullness of a play's plot and the great *performance* of its actors suggests that, among the performers, the two functions do not always carry an equal weight, and that referentiality risks being damaged when the performant drive dominates.

Much more evident, and perhaps more important, is the way in which the two functions compete for the attention of the audience. For, even in theory, during the process of reception, interest in the referential story and appreciation of stage *performances* are always mutually exclusive. A spectator cannot, at the same time, watch an actor playing a role and visualize the corresponding imaginary character. Ideally, a successful staging should be transparent, permitting an unobstructed (mental) vision of the referential world. A compelling performance of *Hamlet* should, for the duration of the play, conceal the work of the director; sets should be taken to be the walls of Elsinore; and the identity of actors should dissolve into the personality of the characters. Yet such an ideal operation of the referential function would preclude a successful operation of the performant function. And vice versa, since overwhelming *performances* by director, actors, or designers, would draw the audience's attention away from Hamlet's story. In terms of a global either/or situation, the two functions can never be fully experienced at the same time.

This theoretical incompatibility leads, however, to absurd practical conclusions. By its logic, we could acknowledge the *performance* of an actor playing Hamlet only when, dazzling us with his skill on the stage, he would make us forget Hamlet in Elsinore, and thus fail in his mission as actor. Our standards of outstanding acting, derived from such *performances*, would thus be based in fact on the observation of incompetent acting. Inversely, a truly outstanding evocation of Hamlet, goal of the referential function, would prevent us from observing the skill of the actor. Fascinated by a story acted out with a truly superior talent, we would forget to pay attention to the quality of the acting, and assume that it is merely competent. But these two mutually exclusive hypothetical processes surely contradict our experience of real theatre reception, our combined response to both referential and performant functions. The theory is obviously flawed.

The flaw lies in the implied assumption that a theatre performance is experienced within a single span of attention. In reality, our attention constantly moves from the stage, which we perceive to be real, to the story space, which we concretize in our mind. The much-abused notion of theatrical "illusion," and complicated concepts such as "denegation,"[25] can be reduced to that oscillation of our attention between the perception of reality and the creation of a mental space, between our world and the referential world. We stay with Hamlet's story as long as it retains our interest; and good referentiality prolongs this interest while poor referentiality undermines it. Sooner or later, however, repeatedly and many times, we always return to the performers on the stage. As we observe them, our interest in their performance, as well as in other features of the stage, is particularly keen when they surpass our norms of competence, derived from our past theatrical experience. Yet even the most compelling performances also capture us only for a while. Superior acting, enforcing semiosis, takes us back to the referential world or, when the acting is poor, we shift there ourselves because we want to honor the theatre contract. And thus we proceed, shuttling between the experience of referential and performant functions.

This model of alternating focuses defines the general pattern of performance reception. It can be affected by a number of pragmatic factors. In the first place, it evidently works only for spectators who understand the theatre contract and, making a clear distinction between the reality of the stage and the imaginary world of the story, want to give their attention to both spaces. Second, the model postulates that the spectators have enough theatrical experience to become aware of definite norms of theatrical competence. Children and neophytes lack such bases for critical comparison and, like circus audiences, they tend either to see *performances* in all performances or only to follow the story. They are a "good" public, but their reception often deviates from the general pattern of oscillating attention. Third and foremost, the separate focusing on performance and referentiality rarely entails separate responses to the two functions. Each response rather tends to influence the other. Spectators strongly involved in the imaginary story are also inclined to find great *performances* on the stage; and inversely, great stage *performances*, while detracting from full involvement in the story, nevertheless promote interest in it. As a result, the overall impression formed at the end of a play combines the operation of the two functions, the appreciation of the story influencing the response to the performances and vice versa.

Such an interaction occurs most frequently when *performances* concern properly theatrical activities, that is, the achievements demonstrated by directors, actors, designers, even playwrights in domains directly related to theatre production: staging, acting, play writing, and so forth. A different process, which has no direct involvement with stage referentiality, characterizes nontheatrical, or cultural *performances*, received as exceptional accomplishments in fields without any binding connection to theatre: reputation or personality of performers, aesthetic appeal of sets or costumes, various forms of eroticism, and so forth. More about that later. At this point, it is only important to note that even strictly theatrical *performances* raise a series of questions about all performances on the stage and, more generally, in arts. How indeed do we determine the quality of those performances which, in contrast to sport achievements, lack clear objective norms?

## Assessing Theatrical *Performances*: Techniques and Styles

In sports and in circus, we observed, individual spectators are relieved from subjective assessing of the quality of performances; they rely on quantified measures, or on the authority of anonymous experts to whom are attributed near magic powers of seers. Theatre audiences, in sharp contrast, are always on their own. Media accounts or personal recommendations often prepare individual spectators to expect a particular *performance* on the stage, but ultimately they must judge by themselves, applying their own subjective norms. The questions we face as spectators are: What are these norms? Where do we find them? And what criteria enable us to decide that specific instances of directing and acting, or specific dialogues, sets, costumes, sound and light effects are competent, incompetent, or *performances*?

It is tempting to relate this problem to theatre's basic tension between performance and referentiality, and to derive an answer from their interaction. Visibly an audience's involvement in a theatre story depends largely on the story's content, appealing or not to individual spectators. But it also depends on the telling of the story, that is, on its staging. A successful staging ensures that spectators, whether they like or do not like the story, will visualize it mentally with clarity and intensity. And when spectators follow well the events of a story, their interest in its content remains sustained even when they are indifferent to problems it raises or when they react to them with outrage. Familiarity breeds curiosity, and negative emotions have their own hold on attention. As long as a well-staged Performance produces an overall feeling of satisfaction, whatever its sources, spectators will assume that the performers are doing a good job, that is, that they are competent. Inversely, when they feel disappointed with the story, despite its potentially appealing content, because they cannot clearly visualize it in the referential world, most spectators tend instinctively to attribute their disappointment to the failure of staging, accusing performers of incompetence. In either case, the assessment of performances needs not to be based on preexisting theatrical norms; it stems from the experience of the concrete Performance and the appreciation of its story. In theory, then, when performers succeed in promoting a clear visualization of the referential world, they also generate ad hoc norms of their own performing competence. For spectators without any theatre experience, these norms only apply to the given Performance; but it is to be expected that they will survive in individual memory as potential models for future performances.

The overwhelming majority of real spectators, of course, have always have had a certain number of theatrical experiences, resulting in many traces of such models of competence. A long familiarity with satisfying Performances reinforces, through convergence, the normative function of some of these models, endowing them with the special power of general theatrical norms. As seasoned spectators, we use these norms to assess, by comparison, whether the performers of a new Performance are competent, that is, whether their performances serve the referential function as well as did performances that we found to be competent in the past.

But we also learn that general norms involve many particular forms of competence displayed in various specific activities that make up any complex performance. Each time we return to the real stage space from the mental story space, we notice and store in our memory various ways in which the competent performers sustained our interest in the imaginary story. Consciously or unconsciously, we identify all sorts of staging or acting techniques and styles, acknowledging similarities and differences. We acquire a repertory of categories of signs, referring to complex character roles such as "a villain" as well as to precise emotions such as "a faint surprise." With each category, we associate different voice intonations, gestures, body movements, and so forth. And we expect from actors that they handle these multiple more specific signs in a way that, by experience, we have found to be competent in the past. Similarly, we build up a repertory of visual and sound staging signs that worked satisfactorily in other Performances: costumes, sets, props, lights, and so forth. As our education progresses, we group these signs in a number of theatrical styles: realistic or symbolic, contrasting or harmonious, contemporary or historical. For each category, for each style, for each sign, we develop an appropriate norm of competence. Each new Performance, when we find it satisfying, tests then these norms, occasionally enriching them with new models.

Practically, most new Performances simply conform to our normative expectations. After an exciting period of apprenticeship, we become indeed increasingly complacent about competence. Often, focusing on the referential world, we do not even notice it. Or we devaluate the competence of actors when we call them merely adequate. At best, when performances reach a high level in the range of our norms, we acknowledge them as good, very good, or flawless. In the last instance, we derive a real pleasure from a concrete manifestation of our ideal norm, an exemplary illustration of a model. To that extent, we appreciate the minimal reward offered by theatre's performant function. But it is not a striking, memorable, unique enjoyment. However pleasant and gratifying, it fails to satisfy our deeper yearning for a true *performance*—an extraordinary achievement that surpasses the norm by some unpredictable jump in quality. Satisfied with competence, we still hope that, in some future Performance, we shall experience the feeling of exhilaration that a few past *performances* have kept alive in our memory. And we want that exhilaration for its own sake, regardless of its relation to the referential function of the Performance.

The articulation between norm and *performance* is thus somewhat paradoxical. On the one hand, a *performance* is directly tied to a performance norm: the extraordinary quality of a *performance* can only be grasped in comparison with the norm of mere competence. And this performance norm in turn is directly tied to referentiality, since the competence of performers derives from their ability to tell a clear story, to evoke a convincing imaginary world. On the other hand, because it is appreciated for its own sake as a display of an exceptional achievement, a *performance* always breaks loose both from the competence norm and its ties to referentiality. Indeed, a *performance*'s gaping superiority must be demonstrated in the proper domain of staging signs, that is, techniques and styles. While it is experienced during a Performance, a *performance* is thus severed from that Performance's referential function; it only relates to general norms of techniques and styles deposited in the memory by previous Performances. In other terms, whereas competence always depends on the success of referentiality, *performance* constitutes the only pure manifestation of the performant function operating for its own sake. This doesn't mean that a *performance* has no influence on the referential function. Any theatre performance, good or bad, always affects the telling of a story; but perception and appreciation of a *performance* are independent of the success or failure of the storytelling.

Thus, in our memory of past Performances, great *performances* by actors or directors sometimes endure long after the story is lost. Although it was one of my earliest theatre experiences, I still recall quite well Laurence Olivier's extraordinary presence in a production of *Hamlet*, his entrances, his face and body, his voice, but not much else. It must have been a good show, and Olivier certainly helped it, but I no longer know how he interpreted Hamlet, nor when and where exactly I have seen him. In my memory, only the *performance* of Olivier stands out. About the same time I saw Raimu in Molière's *Le Bourgeois gentilhomme*; and I also only remember what a great actor he was. By a similar process, while I have a precise memory of the 1976 production of Marivaux's *La Dispute* by Patrice Chéreau, I clearly treasure it only for the director's *performance*, an extraordinarily bold and yet successful experimental staging of a classic.

The notion of a director's *performance* raises, however, some special problems. For the other producers of a performance, we learn progressively how to identify, classify, and rank various types of stage signs for which they are responsible. We learn to distinguish, in a total Performance, what is the proper input of playwrights and actors, costumers, set designers, light and sound technicians, and so forth. We compare their production of signs with the norms drawn from our experience in each particular field and, as the case may be, we acknowledge a competent or an extraordinary mastery of the appropriate techniques or styles. The difficulty with directors is that the exact nature of their contribution to the Performance is much harder to grasp with precision.

In most general terms, indeed, directors are responsible for the production of all signs in a Performance, including acting, designs, sound effects. In that sense, competence on their part implies that all individual performers are competent, whether they reach or not a level of *performance*. But such a general competence reserves no special technical domain for the director, no stylistic norms that could be surpassed by a director's own *performance*. It is more useful, therefore, if somewhat arbitrary, to identify the director's special contribution with the so-called interpretation of a theatrical text, that is, its transformation. Most usually, in that sense, a director demonstrates competence when the story told in the verbal text, and the related story world, are transformed, by the means of nonverbal stage signs, into different but believable story and world. As will be shown later, directors must always transform the verbal text, or a textual tradition, but can apply various strategies ranging from "faithfulness" to "perversion." Their choice depends on many factors, and, among them, there is a place for the desire to achieve a directorial *performance*. When it occurs, such a *performance* is then clearly grasped as an extraordinary transformation—a transformation strikingly different from transformations expected from merely competent directors, a transformation applauded by the spectators as an outstanding directorial feat. By analogy, such a transformation, as we shall see, may be also carried out on staged texts, including the director's own previous Performances.

But how does one appraise the extraordinary quality of a transformation? How can one grasp the level of originality that shifts a transformation from competence to *performance*? Most spectators see performances of unfamiliar texts: plays that are indeed new, or revivals of classics that they have not seen before, or performances of plays that they may have seen but that they have not read or do not remember. In all these cases they cannot detect the extent of text transformations carried out by the director's staging. They assume that no significant transformation has taken place, that the director faithfully communicates the referential world of the verbal text. Indeed, most spectators are unaware of a potential tension between verbal signs and stage signs, between references suggested by the playwright's text and references communicated by the director's Performance. On their own, that is, without outside prompting, such spectators can perceive neither the magnitude nor the novelty of a transformation, and hence cannot acknowledge any directorial *performance*. Instead, when they feel they experience an exceptional Performance, they attribute its exceptional quality to *performances* by author, actors, or stage designers.

For many other spectators, however, for all true amateurs of theatre, theatrical education involves seeing a number of "new" productions of "old" plays, plays they have seen or read before: say, *Hamlet* in English-speaking countries, and *Phèdre* or *Tartuffe* in French-speaking countries. Watching successive Performances of such classics, even their film versions, they learn how to perceive transformations, detect directorial strategies, notice original stage signs, assess the magnitude of novelty. After a number of such experiences, educated spectators also learn how to identify distinct styles and techniques, either associated with several different directors or attributed to one particular director. At this stage, they are ready to apply their training to genuinely "new" plays. Though they may not know the verbal text, they are able at least to recognize styles and techniques of stage signs, relate them to previously encountered strategies, deduce directorial intentions, evaluate the originality of the staging and, when it greatly surpasses the expected level of competence, hail the director's *performance*. Of course, as the educational process continues, standards of competence change. Each "new" production of a classic adds to the repertory of directorial transformations, makes greater demands on novelty, raises the level of potential *performances*. Well-educated spectators thus become experts in directorial performances, and their expertise, communicated by media or by personal contacts, reaches and educates other potential spectators, including those who have no real theatre experience but are willing to listen.

For example, when they were watching Planchon's *Tartuffe*, educated spectators easily identified its boldest new features: characters shown at home in intimate apparel, guards clad in nazi trooper uniforms, baroque ruins, a Christlike mannequin; none of these features had been seen before in other *Tartuffe* productions. For the educated spectators, these and other startling new signs pointed to two evident directorial strategies: on the one hand, a seventeenth-century formal comedy was transformed into a realistic portrayal of bourgeois domestic life; on the other hand, seventeenth-century concerns about devotional hypocrisy, captation of family fortunes, and rhetoric of seduction were transformed into twentieth-century concerns about totalitarian exercise of power, rise and fall of civilization, death and faith, and homosexuality. The first strategy, identified as a variation of the vast category of historical reconstitution, à la "this is the way they really dressed," was appreciated in its application to *Tartuffe* but not as a great novelty. It departed very little from past competent transformations of the play; it changed little its traditional meaning. But the second strategy, identified as a variation of "modernization," was both more striking when applied to *Tartuffe* and controversial. Some educated spectators liked it, others disliked it, but all were impressed by its radical transformation of Molière's text: unusually original, powerful and, to be sure, extremely well carried out. As a surprising "modernization," Planchon's performance was indeed a great directorial *performance*, setting a new standard, offering a new model, changing expected competence levels. And its direct influence spread far beyond the small group of well-trained amateurs of theatre. Informed by the press and television, or by more expert friends, most people who attended the show, whether in Paris or in a provincial experimental center, or who read or heard about it, no doubt received at least a basic education in the nature and importance of a director's performance.

One troubling question remains: all other things being equal, does daring novelty, or high originality, always generate the acknowledgment of a directorial *performance*? In the case of Planchon's *Tartuffe*, a near consensus obtained; but his production, while strikingly innovative in some ways, remained quite traditional in others. For Planchon's public, his transformation of Molière's text was thus well within the limits of acceptable staging of *Tartuffe*; his referential world was well within the range of possible worlds that, by convention, the public could receive as variants of the textual world. But such conventions, and hence the limits of acceptability, depend on many factors, social and/or ideological. In a less sophisticated milieu, the conventionally accepted distance between the world of the verbal text and the world of the Performance would be much smaller. Planchon's *Tartuffe*, however mild its novelty, would be found to breach the very limits of competence; it could not qualify as a directorial *performance*. Conversely, an extreme avant-garde public, dedicated to radical transformations, would certainly view it as a competent performance but too timid to be a *performance*. Both competence and the degree of originality that generates a directorial *performance* are indeed matters of expectations, and expectations are based on changing models both in mainstream theatre and in the avant-garde. Originality is a necessary condition for a *performance*, but it is neither sufficient nor reliable; it always requires judgment and manipulation.

The story of Arianne Mnouchkine's Théâtre du Soleil, based at the Paris Cartoucherie Theatre, is a case in point. While known for its collaborative staging, and excellence of its performers, it has also been long reputed for its directorial *performances*. Mnouchkine's first great hit was *1789* (1970–1971), a dazzling transformation of the historical "text" of the French Revolution. It turned a traditional story into a political message with a left-wing bias: an original but also very appropriate strategy at that time. Its transformational novelty was surprising but acceptable; it was praised as a director's *performance*. The next play, *1793* (1972–1973), further explored the same vein, had a comparable success, but was not deemed to be a directorial *performance*. The staging was still superb, but, by Mnouchkine's new standards, its transformation of the historical text followed an expected strategy; it was highly competent but not novel. Directorial *performance* was then displayed again with *L'Age d'or* (1975), a series of vignettes about the exploitation of North African immigrants in France. Mnouchkine's political commitment didn't change, but there was novelty in an original transformation of an ideological text: racial and social prejudices, working conditions, national guilt, but also stereotyped theatrical and cinematographic images. Then came Shakespeare's *Richard II* (1981), no doubt the greatest Mnouchkine *performance* to this day. It combined two daring transformations. On the one hand, it broke with Mnouchkine's own tradition, forsaking the left-wing orientation that marked her previous theatrical texts; on the other hand, it transformed Shakespeare's text into a Kabuki-style performance: a daring and novel wager that an Elizabethan drama could survive in a Japanese staging; a dramatic stylistic innovation, far removed from what could be expected both from Mnouchkine and from a Shakespearean text. We shall return to *Richard II* in Part II. Later Mnouchkine's productions, while still very successful, were less original. Two other Shakespeare texts staged in oriental style failed to elicit any surprise. And *L'histoire terrible mais inachevée de Norodom Sihanouk roi du Cambodge* (1985), while marking a return to political commitment and avant-garde staging, was found to be barely competent.

In some way, the directorial *performance* thus resembles the surrealist image which, said André Breton, must be greatly distanced from its meaning; like in a quartz lamp, the greater the distance, the brighter the bridging spark that illuminates the image. Similarly, the greater the distance between a director's new transformation of a text and the set of expected transformations of that text, the better the chances for a directorial *performance*. But there are two problems. First, like the surrealist image, even the most extraordinary transformation loses its novelty when it is repeated. A director's *performance* always expands the range of competent transformations, and requires, for an encore, a different and ever bolder achievement. Second, by moving too far away from public expectations, like an image too remote from its meaning, a new transformation risks breaking contact with the text, losing acceptance by its spectators as a credible transformation of that text. Apparently, many daring amateur directors fall into that trap, reaching for an excessive originality or overestimating the sophistication of their audience. In such cases, the directorial exploitation of the performant function misses its goal, endangers the operation of the referential function, and often brings about a collapse of the Performance.

## Nontheatrical (Cultural) *Performances*

Although theatrical *performances*, requiring appreciation of staging, acting, costumes, or sets, draw the attention from the story space to the stage space, and break the spell of referentiality, ultimately they serve both the performant and the referential function that always converge in theatre. In contrast, nontheatrical *performances* that are acknowledged as such in areas located outside the domain of theatre, say in the area of aesthetics or eroticism or cult of personality, have a disruptive impact on the total theatrical experience. True, they always take place during a Performance, and to that extent they contribute to the enjoyment of that Performance, but they neither support referentiality nor involve the appreciation of a performing achievement. They rather acknowledge the presence of an outstanding materialization of a value that is highly prized by our culture: artistic achievement, sexual appeal, public popularity, wealth, or power. In that sense, nontheatrical *performances* are always cultural in nature; they will be conveniently called *cultural performances*. The problems they raise are situated at the interface between theatre and general culture of society.

A first problem derives directly from the complex nature of our culture. There seems to be little consistency in the way that various manifestations of culture are attributed powers of seduction, then lose them. Cultural fashions are fluid and unstable, and, as a result, it is difficult to specify in any precise way what types of cultural *performances* can be acknowledged in theatre. No doubt they must be tied to some feature of the Performance, but this still leaves many possibilities. In fact, the very notion of the Performance space where the *performance* is necessarily located must be expanded to include the audience and/or the specific site of the production. The 1986 staging of the *Mahabharata* in an abandoned quarry near Avignon was hailed as a *performance*, as was Jacqueline Kennedy's presence at a Comédie Française staging of Molière in Washington. Generally, however, cultural *performances* are attributed to the same people to whom we attribute theatrical *performances*: actors, designers of sets, costumes, and lights; composers of music; sometimes directors. But the areas in which they choose to trigger a nontheatrical enthusiasm cannot be predicted. At best, one can only determine what types of cultural *performances* were most popular in the past, and suggest how cultural evolution may affect their development.

Most permanent, in that sense, has been the appeal of eroticism. Even the earliest accounts of theatrical events demonstrate that erotic seduction generates a powerful form of cultural *performances*. Already Apuleius, in *The Golden Ass*, describing a performance of Judgement of Paris in the second century A.D., made no reference to plot or acting but rhapsodized about the bodies of "a beauteous boy, naked save for the stripling's cloak that covered his left shoulder, with yellow hair, a mark for all men's eyes," and a nearly naked girl "surpassing fair and a joy to behold."[26] His focus is clear: not on aesthetics but on sexuality. In a similar vein, when René Obaldia's *Le vent souffle dans les sassafras* was performed in Paris in the late 1950s, the *performance* prize was awarded not to an excellent Michel Simon, applauded for his competence, but to Rita Renoir, a stripper just turned actress, whose display of hot sensuality seemed at that time a most provocative and daring theatre achievement. In her case, as in striptease shows, the erotic appeal involved a rather tame form of voyeurism. But in rougher times, when actors lacked respectability, especially from the seventeenth to the nineteenth century, many wealthy male patrons were reputed to be drawn to the theatre by the expectation of finding, and then meeting, exciting young actresses, notably among supporting roles.

With changes in general culture, erotic appeal has been taking on new nuances. The explosion of nudity off-Broadway in the 1960s no doubt moved many spectators to expect and/or savor erotic *performances* on the stage, but the novelty wore off rapidly; and while nudity in theatre may now shock again, it does not do so when shown on the screen. Except in pornographic shows, and perhaps some brazen video clips, it no longer connotes extreme eroticism. The progress of feminism had a different impact. With opprobrium attached to all forms of sexism, few reviewers of new plays dare today to appraise the charms of an actress, as they used to do, in terms of sexual appeal. Rather, when that appeal is indeed exceptional, they disguise its eroticism with the mask of aesthetics, drawing attention to "remarkably handsome" or "strikingly beautiful" features. But most readers interested in erotic appeal know how to read between the lines, and expect to be sexually titillated. And not only by attractive actresses but also by seductive actors since, with feminism, the power of sexuality is now more openly acknowledged by both genders. It doesn't seem then that eroticism will lose its dominant role as trigger of the performant function. It retained it in periods of sexual repression and, in a foreseeable future, it must be expected to maintain it in a culture that promotes sexuality in media and advertisement.

Genuine aesthetics have also generated many cultural *performances*. Extraordinary beauty of performers has always been singled out but, as in the account by Apuleius, such praise often has had sexual connotations, confusing beauty with erotic appeal. Real aesthetic *performances* are rather associated with theatre features that interface with other arts: architecture, painting, sculpture, music. Any seasoned spectator surely can recall loud expressions of admiration when the curtain raises on an exceptional set. In some cases, this admiration acknowledges a theatrical *performance* of the designer who, with great originality, has found a striking way of evoking a banal setting. In other cases, however, the applause celebrates the sheer pictorial or architectural beauty of the decor: colors, lines, volumes that move us in the same manner as a painting, a statue or a palace facade could do, regardless of their meaning. Yannis Kokkos, a set and light designer working in Paris, owes his outstanding reputation to such aesthetic achievements. And rightly so. Spectators drawn by his name to the 1985 performance of *Hamlet* at the Palais de Chaillot, directed by Antoine Vitez, were rewarded with the expected *performance* when a bright expanse of smooth stage floor, faintly marked with parallel lines receding in the distance, was illuminated with lateral batteries of golden lights. It was an extraordinarily beautiful vision even though its meaning was not clear. But even a small painting hung on a wall can produce a similar sensation. Taste in art no doubt always evolves, but so do technical means that create artistic effects; and thus one can expect that constant new aesthetic *performances* will keep on supporting the popularity of cultural forms of the performant function.

Related to art, and participating in its aesthetic appeal, are various forms of craftsmanship which, in any given society, have acquired a cultural value. Costumes and masks, furniture and props, manifest the presence of these crafts on the stage. As in the case of sets, they may trigger a theatrical *performance* by an outstanding originality in their contribution to the story telling. In Jerome Savary's production of *Le Bourgeois gentilhomme* in the mid 1980s, the male dancing master clad in an operatic tutu, and a muddy one-legged fencing master in a wheelchair, created a sensation because their surprising costume, in an extended sense of the word, added an unusual twist to Molière's comedy. But frequently costumes, or masks, or props are greeted with marveling "Ohs!" and "Ahs!" simply because they are superbly crafted, or exotic, or exceptionally intricate. In Mnouchkine's *Richard II*, staged in the Kabuki style, the colorful magic of Japanese silk gowns satisfied the audience's hunger for a cultural *performance* although no one understood what their patterns were supposed to mean.

Musicals in particular, while stressing the aesthetic appeal of their songs and dances, also rely heavily on costumes, masks, and props to achieve success with their cultural *performances*. The remarkable popularity of *Cats* on Broadway may be partly attributed to T. S. Eliot's entertaining lines, the erotic appeal of the performers, and an original staging offering the illusion of a feline perspective on the world; but the crafts of make up and costume designers, and the outsized yet realistic props also had their part of applause. The current vogue of musicals, and the trend in commercial theatres to downplay referential issues, suggest that the focus on visual and sound performances is supported by modern culture, and hence that great craftsmanship will retain for quite a while its prominent role in supplying mainstream stage productions with cultural *performances*. There are also signs, in experimental multimedia shows, that avant-garde theatre may be breaking with the tradition of "poverty" and favoring the appeal of contrived costumes and props.

Close to the seduction of arts and crafts, perhaps perverting it in some cases, is the attraction exerted by the display of wealth and other cultural manifestations of social prestige. Thus costumes, historical or modern, when their expensive material or heavy jewelry evoke great fortune or power, appeal less by their beauty, curiosity, or craftsmanship than by their concrete evidence of riches and exalted status. Exceptionally opulent furniture, rugs, crystals, and art objects also can constitute cultural *performances*. For many spectators, judging by their enthusiastic reaction, the stylized but visibly expensive furnishing of a nineteenth-century drawing room, featured in the New York production of *Dracula* (1980), was more appreciated for its remarkable display of wealth than for aesthetic or referential reasons. This taste for opulence is particularly evident in musicals, even though, starting with *A Chorus Line*, a new trend toward more sobriety appears to be growing. The same evolution is more general in traditional theatre. Whether in New York, London, or Paris, at Avignon or Edinburgh festivals, few recent *performances* have been achieved by an ostensible display of wealth and social prestige, perhaps reflecting the economic pressure to reduce staging expenses.

In contrast, the performant role of "celebrities" who are involved in a Performance, mainly but not exclusively as actors, will no doubt further grow as our culture increasingly promotes the "cult of personality" in mass media. Already in ancient Greece and Rome, then in modern times, and even more so in the commercial theatre of the nineteenth century, the draw of a star's name guaranteed the success of a production. As a rule, however, from the greatest actors, reputed playwrights, or even notoriously provocative directors, the audiences also expected properly theatrical *performances*, combining acting or directing talent with personal seduction or an intangible charisma. In some cases, private life or political activities also contributed to the total appeal of a theatre celebrity. The great Talma, Napoleon's preferred actor, owed part of his popularity to his fiery acting style, part to his bold reform of costumes, but as much to his open involvement in the French Revolution and his publicized marital adventures. Still, his triumphal *performances* always took place on the stage. They were expected, witnessed, and applauded only by spectators—a quite small group of his contemporaries. Many others could notice his name on theatre posters, read about his public and private life in the developing popular press, exchange gossip in social gatherings, but even that larger group of supporters or adversaries was relatively limited, and only few could have the occasion of really "seeing" Talma, in person or in effigy, as an actor or as public figure. The more intimate, and often sensational, aspects of a celebrity's life remained remote even for those who did hear about them.

Modern media have changed this situation in two dramatic ways. In the first place, in illustrated information media, not only are the professional, political, and sentimental activities of theatre celebrities disclosed to the public, but so too their private lives, travels, taste in clothing, dwelling, cars and restaurants, family relations, opinions on current topics, and many trivialities. Second, this information now reaches not only genuine theatre amateurs, and the circles wherein they move, but all media consumers, that is, virtually everybody. Actors can be seen not only on the stage, but in films, on television, and in photographs in the serious press as well as in specialized cheap or glossy publications, and gossip and scandal sheets. As a result, interest in theatre celebrities has increased manifold, on par with the fascination for royalty, jet-set leaders, sport figures, and criminals and victims of exceptionally sordid crimes.

Getting to know these figures satisfies indeed a double need of the public: on the one hand, gaining familiarity with celebrities, participating vicariously in their lives; on the other, experiencing indirectly many *performances* achieved by exceptional individuals in various areas valued by mass culture. No wonder, then, that some theatre spectators expect celebrities who perform outstandingly in the media to perform even better on the stage, proving to be as fascinating at close distance as they are on the screen and in the press. Such spectators are drawn to the theatre by a popular actor's presence rather than by his or her potential theatrical performance; in fact, the presence itself is the expected *performance*.

From that perspective, the appeal of a celebrity has only a marginal relation to acting or staging talents. It primarily originates in features celebrated in the media, that is in, extraordinary achievements in personal life. The range of such achievements is very wide. Watching Jane Fonda on the stage, some spectators might appreciate her as an actress, but others might be rather thrilled by a close contact with a sensational public figure: a controversial advocate of liberal causes, a most successful producer of a fitness program, an exceptionally attractive woman, a famous movie star. One would like to hope that seeing Jane Fonda acting might give such spectators a taste of great theatre, and lead to the discovery and appreciation of theatrical performances. But such conversions rarely happen. When Liv Ullmann performed at the Annenberg Center in Philadelphia, the magic of her name sold out all seats several months in advance, an unusual occurrence for that theatre, but her *performance* did not help increase the size of Annenberg's subsequent audiences, and did not win new adepts for theatre. In reality, relying on the appeal of celebrities risks having negative long-term effects on theatre, devaluing its properly theatrical function. Besides, while the presence of a star may swell the box-office take, it is costly; and many difficulties of commercial stages today derive from a general trend to increase production costs.

The variety of types of cultural *performances* in theatre—extraordinary erotic or aesthetic appeal, exceptional display of craftsmanship
or wealth, the reputation of a celebrity—makes it quite difficult to
explain how a particular cultural *performance* is found to surpass the
norm of mere competence. No such problem obtains for theatrical
*performances*. The norms to which they are compared, we have seen,
derive from a systematic observation of theatrical styles and techniques. The identification of these techniques and styles may vary
among individual spectators, but the constitution of a repertory of the
corresponding norms can be predicted for groups of spectators who
have a similar theatre education. Cultural *performances*, on the other
hand, found in any of the many achievements valued by a given
culture, cannot be related to a formal system of norms. Individual
assessment of a *performance* in any particular area always depends on an
individual's idiosyncratic interest in that area. Aesthetic and erotic
canons compete, reputations rise and fall; there is little cumulative
education in these areas. Different spectators approach them with
different bias at different times. In short, so many subjective factors are
involved in cultural judgments that, strictly speaking, no individual
acknowledgment of a cultural *performance* can be clearly explained,
reasonably discussed, and related to a shared norm. But perhaps it can
be predicted.

In most cases, indeed, considering social groups rather than individuals, it is possible to observe what cultural norms are most forcefully
promoted by the given group cultures. In that sense, in any group,
particularly when it manifests a high degree of conformity, one can
discover *probable* norms of achievement expected in any particular
field, and a *probable* inclination to value *performances* in one or several of
such fields. It is reasonable to assume, for example, that most teenagers
in the West today will turn to rock stars in order to tie a *performance* to a
celebrity. Theatre producers, interested in the box-office appeal of
cultural *performances*, make such assumptions about their expected
audience. Mnouchkine's bold choice of the Kabuki style for her *Richard
II* was very suitable, by that logic, as a cultural *performance* in exotic
aesthetics to be acknowledged as such by a Parisian public known to
appreciate exoticism in all forms. Similarly, a Broadway show deliberately produced for visiting businessmen might feature actresses whose
type of beauty or sex appeal will correspond to, and surpass, the
*probable* canons of eroticism expected from an out-of-town audience.
Conversely, a display of opulence in a play performed in a poor neigh-
borhood, or in an avant-garde theatre, will hardly meet the *probable*
interests of its audience, and hence fail as a cultural *performance*. For
any group, in short, a cultural *performance* will be all the more probable

when it more closely approaches a stereotyped achievement valued in the group's stereotyped vision of life.

A cultural *performance*, appreciated on the stage, always relates in that sense to a model located in real life. To become a cultural *performance*, a feature of the stage must be compared to that model and found to offer a clearly outstanding version. However, this quality rarely means, as in theatrical *performances*, that the stage feature is superior to a specific media illustration of the model in the particular area of targeted achievement: stronger sex appeal, better art, or more personal popularity. In fact, concrete models popularized by media usually are superior in these areas to the *performance*. They are perceived in the form of flattering images, or described by enhancing verbal signs. But they are not experienced directly. In contrast, *performances* offer the physical presence of stage features that can be directly experienced during the Performance. Even when they do not quite match their media models, they are appreciated because they are perceived to be real, that is, to exist in the same reality as the audience. In that sense, they not only contribute to theatre's performant function, they also buttress the stereotypes of cultural achievements, demonstrating that media models can have a real existence. Experiencing a cultural *performance*, spectators merge the imaginary space of their vision of life with the real space in which they are living during the Performance. Part of the appeal of cultural performances stems no doubt from this momentary but reassuring conflation of beliefs and experience.

Such moments, however, interfere with theatre's fundamental oscillation between a referential space, where spectators visualize an imaginary story, and the stage space, where they watch the real process of storytelling. Even theatrical *performances*, related to previous observations of performing styles and techniques, evoke a third space: the space of past Performances attended by the spectators. But that space is made of images of stages, and remains within the boundaries of theatrical activity; at most, it introduces a temporal dimension whereby the experience of a contingent theatre becomes an experience of all of Theatre. Cultural *performances*, in contrast, evoke a third space that is located outside of theatre: the space of the real world such as the spectators conceive it, either in the form of memories of their own life experiences or in the form of visions communicated by the media. The erotic appeal of an actor or actress shifts spectator attention from theatre to erotic figures encountered outside theatres, or to erotic fantasies. Aesthetic and craft *performances* direct the mind to comparable aesthetic or craft objects in museums, in private dwellings, in photographs: admired paintings, memorable dresses, impressive pieces of furniture. And the appearance of celebrities onstage floods the memory with all sorts of information about life in the real world. The oscillation cycle between the stage and the referential world is disrupted. Caught in the real space of the cultural *performance*, familiar and hence easy to access, the spectator forgets the story space, always somewhat unfamiliar and hard on attention. Even the stage loses its appeal as a specifically theatrical space that displays properly theatrical achievements in directing or acting.

The impact of cultural *performances* depends, of course, on expectations of individual spectators. Some spectators, particularly in social groups that are strongly influenced by media, expect to find repeated cultural *performances* in all Performances, and indeed often find them. As a result, they are rarely willing to perform the mental acrobatics between three spaces that are required in such cases for a full enjoyment of theatre. Other spectators, amateurs of pure theatre, prefer to focus on the referential world and on properly theatrical *performances*; they do not expect cultural *performances* and, when these catch them by surprise, they shrug them off as an extratheatrical experience. Most spectators move between the two extreme positions, depending on their mood and on the type of Performance they attend, accepting that theatre can be many things. Indeed, the survival of theatre as an institution owes much to their occasional enjoyment of a cultural *performance*, even though they may feel that it is always somewhat parasitically grafted on the two proper theatrical functions. When referentiality fails to interest audiences, when performing styles and techniques are not appreciated, as in decadent Roman spectacles, in carnival shows, and in many musicals today, *performances* in nontheatrical areas are taking up the slack, filling theatre seats and supporting performers. But this is a matter of historical pragmatics. Theory of theatre rarely discusses cultural *performances*, and the canon of "great" Performances does not reflect their contributions.

## Semiotics of *Performances*: Deconstructing Signs

The exact mechanism by which referentiality, theatrical *performances*, and cultural *performances* interact in a given Performance depends on many factors: conditions of production, intentions of producers, dispositions of performers, composition of audiences, evolution of culture, and social pressures. We shall return to some of these. There remains that the overall interaction, and its main variations, can only be grasped in theoretical models. Separating referentiality and the two types of *performances* in a concrete Performance, drawing precise patterns of their articulation, must be acknowledged to be artificial operations that always distort the theatrical praxis.

Indeed, most examples proposed in these pages can be controverted. Perhaps, for some spectators, Kokkos's sets did have a referential impact on *Hamlet* staged by Vitez? When I was impressed by Olivier's handsome features or his reputation, didn't I also admire his acting talent and visualize a forceful Hamlet? Weren't all these experiences mixed together in an inextricable way? Do we really analyze the various facets of a Performance while we are attending it? Can we? Consciously, perhaps not, or not very frequently. Consciously, an overwhelming majority of spectators do not distinguish between the referential and the performant function and, within the latter, between theatrical and cultural *performances*; they perceive theatre as a complex but indivisible experience. No theory can account precisely for the variety of actual theatre receptions, predict exactly how one might react to a Performance.

Yet theory is indispensable for understanding what is really taking place in theatre. The postulate of three different theatre operations, one referential and two performant, enables us, without dispelling the confusion of concrete theatre experiences, to identify what basic components make up these experiences, how they combine to promote different types of experiences, and how social factors can influence them. Besides, semiotic theory suggest that, at least unconsciously, we do respond in a different manner to the signs involved in the three operations of theatre, that we process them mentally in three distinct ways.

That referentiality involves a standard processing of signs is evident. Telling a story on the stage, and concretizing it mentally, certainly raises many questions; they will be clarified in Part II. It suffices now to repeat that, whatever its problems, referentiality requires a semiotization of the stage; that is, it requires turning all its features into signs, and that the communication of the story take place, more or less successfully, only when these signs are processed by the mechanism of semiosis. In short, when we pay attention to the referential function of theatre, visualizing in our mind an imaginary story space, we respond to signs as signs, and focus on their referents. We do not split signs between their perceptible material form, that is, their signifier, and the coded definition of their meaning, their signified; we do not deconstruct the operation of the signs; in fact, as we become involved in the referential story, we forget that it is communicated with signs. In other words, as long as we keep on semiotizing the stage, we carry out that part of the theatrical contract that requires a standard processing of signs.

But our response dramatically changes when, with our attention shuttling between the stage and the story, we operate an intermittent desemiotization of the stage, hoping to experience a concrete stage *performance*. This doesn't mean that we forget that all stage features are signs. We remember that, by the theatrical contract, everything on the stage contributes to storytelling, and hence functions as a sign. But, when we desemiotize the stage, we choose to disregard the semiotic charge of its features. In other words, although we remain aware that they are intended to be signs, we interrupt processing them as signs, closing our mind to their referentiality, their storytelling. We know that Olivier is a sign standing for Hamlet, but our attention moves away from Hamlet and focuses on Olivier as we perceive him in the real space of the stage, an actor or an individual. To that extent, any desemiotization entails a disruption in the normal operation of signs. But, depending on the nature of the *performance* we hope to witness, theatrical or cultural, this disruption involves two different ways of deconstructing signs, two different approaches to the function of signifiers.

In the case of cultural *performances*, when Olivier, for example, is admired on the stage as an exceptional incarnation of virility, referentiality is totally cut off. The character Hamlet has nothing to do with the acknowledgment of Olivier's *performance* as an individual. And, within the sign Olivier, a further split cuts off the signified, the class of all possible Hamlets, from the perceptible signifier, the striking individual Olivier. Strictly speaking, deprived of a signified, Olivier no longer can be perceived as a sign; and his virile figure, by the same token, no longer can be perceived as a signifier, that is, as a part of a sign. For the spectator who admires him as an outstanding individual, Olivier is merely perceived as a human being, removed from the theatrical frame and placed in the real world. In theory, no problem there. But, we have seen, the same spectator cannot entirely forget that Olivier serves as a sign, and hence that he is also intended to function as the signifier of a sign.

Presented with contradictory information, the spectator may block his memory of the semiotic function of Olivier, and focus on his presence as an individual. At the same time, however, no doubt unconsciously, he or she learns a lesson in semiotics, realizing the ambiguous nature of all signifiers. Shuttling between Olivier as an individual and Olivier as sign of Hamlet, the spectator learns that anything can be turned into a signifier whenever a new meaning, defined as the signified, is attached to it by an appropriate convention or code; that many signs borrow their signifiers from the existing reality; that any convention, including the theatrical contract, can thus generate new signs, and hence new referents, where no familiar signs were initially perceived; but also that conventions can be discarded, by individual decision, and that signifiers then revert to their former function as parts of reality. The experience of a cultural *performance*, in that circuitous way, better prepares the spectator to understand all semiotic operations, to manipulate signs by semiotizing, desemiotizing, and resemiotizing features of reality, to deconstruct theatrical signifiers, and perhaps thus fuller to appreciate not only the performant function of theatre but also its referential function.

Theatrical *performances* entail a different deconstructing process. When we desemiotize Olivier in order to observe him as an actor rather than as an individual, and admire him for his extraordinary acting skills, we remain acutely conscious of his primary function as a stage sign referring to Hamlet. True, we stop visualizing Hamlet in Elsinore. But our assessment of Olivier's skills still relates them to the frame of theatre, acknowledges Olivier's excellence as a specific theatre sign. By the same token, our shuttling between the stage space and the story space is regulated by our overall interest in theatre, projected on both spaces. Within that framework, Olivier's *performance* may originate in two types of perceived achievement: an extraordinary mastery of style and techniques used to convey general referential notions, such as fear or pride or intelligence or power; or an extraordinary display of style and techniques used to convey a certain image of Hamlet. In either case, it would seem, the *performance* is directly linked to an exceptionally powerful communication of an imaginary referent, simple or complex. Yet that referent, say, fear or Hamlet, has been dismissed at that time from our mind's vision. It would be then more exact to say that Olivier's *performance*, in either case, is not linked to our visualization of a specific referent, be it imaginary, because we are not aware of it at that time, but rather to our almost abstract concept of an ideal referent, a class of possible referents: the class of a special type of fear, or the class of a special image of Hamlet.

Such a class, it is important to note, corresponds more exactly to the general meaning of a sign, that is, its signified, than to a specific referent. The perceived—and admired—acting Olivier is viewed as the signifier which, in Olivier as a sign, is associated with a signified defined as a class of fear or a class of Hamlets. In other terms, when we acknowledge Olivier's acting *performance*, we actually postulate that the association between Olivier as a signifier and a certain class of Hamlets (or fear) as a signified is somehow more felicitous than the association between another actor as signifier and the same class of Hamlets (or fear). And this presents some semiotic difficulties.

It would indeed appear that all actors who act out a certain image of Hamlet, say, an Oedipal Hamlet, constitute different but "synonymous" signs: different signifiers but the same signified, different perceptible acting personalities but the same fictional character. Most semiotic codes are based on much more stable associations between signifiers and signifieds, with few true synonyms. Furthermore, since any new actor adds to the number of synonymous signs by offering a new and unpredictable personal signifier for the same signified—the class of the given character—the theatre code must be viewed to be not only open but always in the process of creation. Each theatre production, in that sense, must be expected to produce its own new signs: not only different actors playing the same role, but all sorts of other different stage features that are associated with a single and same class meaning: different ways of grouping people on the stage associated with the same class of a friendly or formal atmosphere; different concrete sets associated with the same class of interiors; different hues and plays of light associated with the same class of a mood; different costumes associated with the same class of status or professions; different chairs associated with the same functional, cultural, or social class of chairs; and so forth. Part of theatre's appeal derives from the novelty that this process brings to any new Performance of a classic. But there is more. For when we compare different performances when the same class of roles is acted out, we are reminded not only that theatre convention encourages a constant coding of new signifiers for the same signified, but also that all theatrical signs are always ephemeral and potentially unstable—a notion that generates two further observations concerning our response to the referential function.

In the first place, trained to perceive theatrical *performances*, and hence aware that a Performance always produces new signs for the given textual meaning in conformity with the overall theatre convention, a spectator is better prepared to accept that, creating its own conventions, a Performance can also produce totally original signs, associating new signifiers with new stage meanings. For such a spectator, a recurrent association of a selected stage feature—a gesture, a prop, a sound—with an arbitrarily selected class of emotions, moods, ideas, characters, even events, takes on the function of a new code, designed specifically for the given Performance. By that code, just as by the general theatre code, the repeated stage feature, the signifier, can also slightly vary from Performance to Performance although the associated class, the signified, remains the same. When, for example, a dimming light is consistently associated with a temporal dislocation, say a flashback sequence, concrete variations in the color of the light can be discounted; each time the new sign is perceived, and identified as such despite its variations, it retains the same general meaning of a "flashback." For the educated spectator, the resulting awareness that new signs can always be created, and must be watched for, opens new avenues for referential operations, expands the referential horizons, and heightens the interest in the referential story.

In the second place, a sustained concern for theatrical *performances*, when it leads to a systematic and analytic survey of all types of performances, provides spectators with a chance to deconstruct the basic nature of semiotic operations, to grasp intuitively how an individual sign, through variations in its concrete signifier, can have different referents even though its coded meaning does not change. Raised eyebrows, for example, are coded to mean a mild surprise, and most actors do indeed raise their eyebrows to convey that their referential characters are mildly surprised. Yet some do it better than others. The superiority of their performance, that is, their superior acting technique or style, cannot be attributed to the signifier as such, that is, the raising of eyebrows, since it is always identically coded. It must therefore be generated by differences in some additional features: speed and scope of the eyebrows' movement, their size or color, contraction of other muscles, individual posture, unpredictable parallel gestures, and so forth. All these features, whatever their variants, are always present when eyebrows are raised; they form an inseparable part of the total materiality of the signifier; but they are not coded. In that sense, one may say that, in terms of the code of facial expressions, they represent excess properties of the signifier, parasitic manifestations of the sign. As a rule, when we decode signs, we disregard these excess properties: we pay no attention to the exact shape, type, ink of printed letters; we rarely notice the size, texture, hue of road signs. We only see those few properties that correspond to our mental picture of an ideal signifier; the signifier specified in the code. And, inverting that relation, we tend to believe that the mental picture of the ideal signifier does indeed coincide with the total appearance of the material signifier, that the two notions are equivalent, and hence that semiotics only need to deal with concrete signifiers, dismissing their ideal models in the code. Theoretically, such a view is certainly misleading, preventing a clear understanding of semiosis. Practically, however, it can be conveniently applied to most semiotic operations, and hence appears to be shared by many semioticians.

But it doesn't work for theatre. In the field of performance, the concrete and the mental signifiers play obviously different roles. In any stage sign, we always perceive two distinct categories of properties: those that we identify as concretized features of the ideal signifier, and, grafted upon them, those that we acknowledge to be in excess. Yet the two categories are linked: ideal properties always support excess properties but are always influenced by them. When we watch the stage in order to rate theatrical performances, we identify the coded properties of the signifier in order to decode the sign, but then focus on the excess properties. We note Olivier's idiosyncratic gestures, facial expressions, or voice intonations, that is, everything he manifests, like any actor, *in excess* of those features that are coded as ideal signifiers of specific emotions or of a certain image of Hamlet. When we praise Olivier's acting *performance*, we then attribute his superiority over other actors to his unique handling of these excess properties. But this judgment is always linked to our parallel perception of the coded features of ideal signifiers. Indeed, the impact of excess properties can only be assessed in terms of their interaction with coded properties; they always reinforce or weaken or enrich the coded meaning of the sign. When we judge a performance, we thus always first split the signifier between its coded and excess properties, and then bring them back together in a more or less successful relation. By the same token, we gain an intuitive understanding of the difference between ideal and concrete signifiers, we achieve greater skills in manipulating all signifiers, we reach a better grasp of theoretical semiotics. The pursuit of theatrical *performances*, the reflection on the nature of theatre's performant function, and the resulting practice in deconstructing signs, thus train us for a fuller appreciation of theatre's semiosis, that is, its referential function.

Even better, this training enables us to explain why theatre has the ability to generate more powerful referents than most other figurative arts, more convincing characters, more interesting events, a more gripping story. As we desemiotize *and* deconstruct theatrical signs, and focus on the excess properties of signifiers, that is, on practically all stage features, we are preparing ourselves to receive, after resemiotizing the stage, a much enhanced vision of the referential world. Spectators who are mainly interested in the story and who pay little attention to finer points of theatrical performances, content to assume that they must be competent, tend to concentrate only on the coded properties of signifiers; they are aware of excess properties as well, visualizing them as elements of the referential world, but they do not grasp their special role in magnifying the hold that world has on our imagination. For these spectators, Olivier's idiosyncratic features, gestures, or intonations become Hamlet's features, gestures, or intonations, perhaps pleasing or impressive, but without any particular significance. In contrast, spectators intent on deconstructing stage signs, focusing on performance styles and techniques, can truly appreciate what excess properties bring to the referential world, how they help to concretize it, why they infuse its vision with magic. A charismatic, muscular Hamlet, evoked by a charismatic muscular Olivier, will have a special power in excess of the meaning projected by coded Olivier acting: a power that will draw a special attention to it precisely because it originates in a superior display of excess properties. Moved by a theatrical *perform-ance*, spectators thus obtain a more vivid mirror image of the referen-tial world, each feature concretized in meaningful detail.

In other terms, for such spectators, all features of concrete sig-nifiers, whether provided with a coded meaning or present in excess of that meaning, contribute simultaneously to animate the story space. In fact, the excess properties may sometimes have a greater impact than the coded properties on the concretization of referents. In that sense, theatre demonstrates the full potential that signifiers have in semiotics, leading to the distortion of normal operations of signs. When excess properties displayed by a concrete signifier transform the referent drawn from the coded meaning of the sign, that is, from its coded signified, it may even seem that decoding the sign no longer follows the normal sequence of three steps: signifier-signified-referent; in such cases, decoding seems to jump directly from signifier to referent. In reality, of course, the signified (a general meaning) has not disap-peared from the operation, but it has been modified so as to corre-spond to the total signifier, including excess properties. Thus the class of certain Hamlets, associated with selected coded properties that Olivier must display when he acts out Hamlet, is changed into the class of different Hamlets, associated with all the properties displayed by Olivier, whether intended or not to be signs. In other terms, from the perspective of a *performance*, any feature of the stage is both perceived as a signifier and processed as a signified; it functions both as a concrete manifestation of a sign and as a concretized class definition coded in the sign. Which means, in turn, that the meaning of a theatre sign tends always to be reduced to a class of one, defined as the totality of its properties; and that its referent always concretizes that class of one. The meaning of Olivier as a sign is the class of Hamlets played by Olivier; and all possible referential Hamlets will only vary as much as Olivier's acting can vary from Performance to Performance.

This near convergence of signifier and signified clearly originates in the unique iconicity of theatre signs. We shall return to iconicity in order to explain how the referential function operates in theatre. It is important to note here, however, that iconicity also both generates and exploits the manifestation of the performant function, drawing atten-tion to "excess" contributions, in technique and style, that individual performers, particularly actors, bring to the performance. By the same token, iconicity also draws attention to the dual role that any actor must play as a discrete sign and as the producer of that sign. Most other people involved in theatre do not present this duality, and other pro-ducers of signs are clearly separated from the signs. The special status of actors derives from their exemplary function as live performers. Dancers, musicians, and mimes are also perceived to be both signs and producers of these signs. This is the reason, perhaps, why each of their performances, like an actor's performance, is expected to be slightly different. Any live performer, like the actor, always adds some idiosyncratic and unstable excess properties to the sign he or she is supposed to produce. The unpredictability of the resulting total sign reflects the responsibility, freedom, and hazards of a performer's function as producer of signs. In that sense, acting performances always involve a creative process present in all production of signs, as well as an expenditure of physical or mental resources. This process is not limited to performers, but they show it ostensibly to their public. As such, it doesn't create a semiotic problem; it rather raises issues related to the performant function. We do not question an actor's dual role as a sign and the producer of that sign; but we applaud his *performance* when he performs that dual task better than merely competent actors.

## Notes

1. I am making a distinction here between the word "performance," in its usual theatrical meaning of a staged production, and the word *performance*, understood as an exceptional achievement. This italicized *performance* corresponds to the meaning that word has in French but also in such English expressions as "This production was marked by a performance by the leading actor."

2. But these points happen to deal with the relation between the referential and performant functions, which changes with the translation. See Tadeusz Kowzan, "Aristote, théoricien de l'art du spectacle," *Théâtre de toujours d'Aristote à Kalisky* (Bruxelles: Editions de l'Université de Bruxelles, 1983).

3. Aristotle, *Poetics*, p. 9.

4. Jean Duvignaud, *L'Acteur. Esquisse d'une sociologie du comédien* (Paris: Gallimard, 1965).

5. See Keir Elam, "Much Ado About Doing Things With Words (and Other Means): Some Problems in the Pragmatics of Theatre and Drama," in *Performing Texts*, ed. Michael Issacharoff and Robin F. Jones (Philadelphia: University of Pennsylvania Press, 1988). See also Marco De Marinis, *Semiotica del teatro* (Milano: Bompiani, 1982). One notes that Elam is mainly interested in the text and its readers, while De Marinis deals with performances and spectators.

6. Marco De Marinis, "Vers une pragmatique de la communication théâtrale," *Versus 30* (Sep.–Dec. 1981), p. 75. My translation.

7. See Ernest Theodore Kirby, *Ur-Drama: The Origins of Theatre* (New York: New York University Press, 1972).

8. David Cole, *The Theatrical Event. A Mythos, a Vocabulary, a Perspective*. Middletown, Conn.: Wesleyan University Press, 1975), pp. 3–4, 8.

9. Obviously, any activity, however playful, has some effect on the player's

life, be it only through the satisfaction of a need or desire. Also, the pleasure derived from playing a game has some beneficial results. And many serious activities, not considered to be games, follow arbitrary rules. The key notion in the definition above is not the gratuitousness of the ludic activity, which is illusory, but the gratuitousness of the specific outcome of that activity. Any game is profitable while it lasts, and to that extent may be said to improve the player's situation, though usually in a nonquantifiable way; but the concrete results of the game are postulated not to change the milieu of the player, nor to modify the player's endeavor to master the milieu. Ideally, a game of chess or tennis, a crossword puzzle, a painting, a film, or a novel, while providing pleasure and perhaps increasing physical and mental skills, is not expected, after its completion, to affect the situation and the behavior of players, spectators, and readers. Practically, of course, many games are treated as integral parts of life, just as integral parts of life can be treated as games. But such cases testify to a dysfunction of the game principle, just as an amateur sportsman who is paid for his performance testifies to a dysfunction of amateurism rather than to its failure as a concept.

10. Johan Huizinga, *Homo Ludens* (Boston: Beacon Press, 1955).

11. Roger Caillois, *Les jeux et les hommes* (Paris: Gallimard, 1967).

12. See Jean Piaget, *Biologie et connaissance* (Paris: Gallimard [Idées], 1967).

13. Morse Peckham, *Man's Rage for Chaos: Biology, Behavior and the Arts* (New York, Schocken Books, 1967).

14. Henri Laborit, "Le geste et la parole," *Degrés* no. 29 (Winter 1982), pp. b–b24.

15. See, for a very specific application of that approach, Charles Mauron, *Phèdre* (Paris: Corti, 1968).

16. Anne Ubersfeld, *L'Ecole du spectateur*, p. 165. My translation.

17. See Jerzy Grotowski, *Toward a Poor Theatre* (New York: Simon & Schuster, 1968). See also Zbigniew Osinski, *Grotowski and His Laboratory* (New York: PAJ Publications, 1986), especially Robert Findlay's "1976–1986: A Necessary Afterword," pp. 166–80.

18. See Erving Goffman, *Frame Analysis* (New York: Harper and Row, 1974).

19. In extreme cases, the title may simply indicate the artistic character of the work, identifying it as, say, "sonata" or "painting." Such identifications, serving as a frame within which the work appears, refer not only to its nature but also to its aesthetic dimension. In a painting titled "painting" we are supposed to note both the content of the painting and its beauty. The term "painting" operates as a double sign: linguistically, to refer to the object, and culturally, to refer to an artistic form. But what about the painting itself, or an untitled painting? Even when its content seems not to represent anything, the frame in which it appears, usually a wall, indicates a similar representational function: at the very least, it represents a general concept of painting as art, manifested in an unique form.

20. One may object that some "artistic" manifestations, offering an aes-

thetic experience, have no permanence, either because no material form has recorded them, or by design. For example, to illustrate the first hypothesis, a poem or the text of a play may be totally lost, though some note may recall that the poem was at one time recited or the play performed. In theory, they did qualify at that time as potential art forms, but pragmatically, because they cannot be experienced today, their artistic status is only a matter for idle speculation. As for the second category, exemplified by "happenings" or the Canadian public contests of improvised acting, it is doubtful whether the notion of art applies at all. For many observers, happenings are rather a form of play, or soul-expanding exercises. At any rate, they appear to be dying out, confirming that forms without permanence cannot be successfully integrated in the mainstream development of art.

21. For theory and application, see Eugenio Barba, *The Dilated Body*, followed by *The Gospel According to Oxyrhincus* (Rome: Zeami Libri, 1985). See also a similar trend in Jean Caune, *La dramatisation*, (Louvain: Cahiers théâtre Louvain, 1981).

22. Part of the difficulty resides in the ambiguity of the term "beautiful" when it is applied to mental concepts. Obviously, we experience an aesthetic pleasure when we follow a well-constructed story. And we are pleased by a generous or heroic action, a surprising idea, a happy ending. But such pleasures are not clearly aesthetic, and, when we use in such cases the term "beautiful," we understand it in the derived meaning of "pleasant." As to the beauty of an imagined character, it no doubt is dictated by a prior decision, or command, or desire, to attribute beauty to that character, and the mental aesthetic experience probably lacks the pleasure attending real discovery of beauty. There are many other problems with aesthetics, even in the case of sensual perceptions, related to the influence of conventions, diversity of beauty, and so forth. But the nature of aesthetic judgments is not at issue here, only the acknowledgment of their role.

23. Jerzy Faryno, "From Everyday Life to the Theatre." Unpublished paper read at the International Symposium on the Theory of Drama and Theatre, Ruhr-University at Bochum, 28 April 1984.

24. See Paul Bouissac, *Circus and Culture. A Semiotic Approach* (Bloomington: Indiana University Press, 1976); an outstanding semiotic analysis of circus, still unmatched despite the more recent Hugues Hotier, *Signes du cirque: approche semiologique* (Bruxelles: AISS-IASPA, 1984. Coll. Treteaux), which examines various circus acts one by one, providing anecdotal information but few theoretical insights. Most of my examples of referentiality in circus are borrowed from Bouissac, and my reservations concern what he doesn't say rather than what he says.

25. See Anne Ubersfeld, "Notes sur la dénégation théâtrale," in *La relation théâtrale*, ed. Régis Durand (Lille: Presses Universitaires de Lille, 1980) pp. 11–25. Ubersfeld notes correctly that "illusion" in theatre is not really an illusion because nobody believes in it. She claims that spectators are aware of the reality of the stage, which is also correct, but then states that for them "the actress present there is Cleopatra and is not Cleopatra" (p. 12, my translation): a

simultaneous affirmation and negation of reality. This process, which Ubersfeld calls "denegation" (Freud's *Verneinung*), expresses a conscious judgment whereby a perceived reality is denied the property of reality. But this notion, just as the notion of "illusion," posits that spectators see Cleopatra on the stage, whereas a properly semiotic approach indicates that they only see a sign referring to a Cleopatra who must be concretized in a mental story space.

26. Apuleius, *The Golden Ass* (cited in A. M. Nagler, *A Source Book in Theatrical History* [New York: Dover, 1959], pp. 34–35).

# II: A Grammar of Theatre Referentiality

## 1. A Story Told with Signs

A theatre performance always tells a story. It has other functions as well, and storytelling may serve them in various ways. But there is always a story. The role of that story in the overall economy of theatre may also vary, but such variations do not affect the nature of storytelling and need not be examined at this juncture. Nor would there be a point discussing in detail what constitutes a story. Too many definitions have been proposed, with various degrees of rigor. One can simply state that, traditionally, the story told on the stage always deals with an action, usually carried out by human beings but sometimes by humanized gods, animals, elemental powers, plants, objects, or abstract notions. Traditionally, that action involves a number of events perceived distinctly as being separate but somehow connected by causality or theme. Even traditional avant-garde follows that pattern. A totally disembodied voice delivering, on a dark stage, a totally meaningless monologue, would still tell an action with at least three events: the strange story of a voice that first started babbling, then babbled for a time, then stopped babbling.[1]

The theatre story, whether minimal or complex, realistic or absurd, also always involves two distinct spaces and times. The telling of the story takes place on the stage, in a continuous present time, that is, within the spatial and temporal continuum of the audience. But the story itself takes place in some space offstage, at some different time. The imaginary story space and time will vary depending on the story. Some stories occur in a historical or mythical past, others are timeless, still others are set in future or fictional worlds; and some concern events that could be roughly contemporary to the time of their telling, but not really simultaneous, taking place in a close proximity of the theatrical space, but not in it. Even the story of the babbling voice must be located, by virtue of the theatrical convention, in a space and time that are quite obscure but different from the space and time of the action perceived on the stage. Indeed, in contrast with storytelling, which is experienced directly by performers and spectators as part of their reality, a story cannot be experienced as part of that reality. In that sense, stories are always fictions, even when their events are acknowledged to be true in history books. A play about Danton and Robespierre, for example, may tell about historical events, but the story it tells is not occurring in their historical continuum; told on the stage, it can be only fictional.

To that extent, theatre stories do not differ from stories told in verbal narratives, in pictures, in films, in dances. In each of these media, the story tellers communicate an "absent" story: a story that cannot be experienced directly, and hence must be communicated with *signs* that stand for, or refer to, some selected features of the story. The need to use signs is common to all media, but they use different signs. In verbal narratives, signs are primarily words drawn from a particular system of natural language. Ballets, paintings, pantomimes favor different systems of signs, relying on different codes. Even music is assumed to be able to convey, with coded musical sounds, at least such minimal elements of story as emotions or sensations. For some people, however, music does not refer to any story and, as a direct experience, is appreciated in the same way as food, drink, sex, or pleasant sensorial stimuli.

Theatre no doubt can also be enjoyed as a direct experience. The desemiotized stage, as we have seen, always offers potential *performances*, to be perceived directly. More generally, an audience can be stimulated by all sorts of sensorial pleasures, by the magic of a ritual communion, or by emotional responses to intangible charismatic pulsions. These forms of enjoyment of theatre experience can be very powerful. In various ways, they influence our enjoyment of theatre stories, even substitute for it. But whatever their impact, they do not eliminate the basic theatre function of storytelling. They do not refer to stories, they do not use signs, they do not participate in theatre's referential process. One need not take them into account to explain how theatre tells stories with signs.

That theatre tells stories with stage signs—those features of the stage that refer to what they are not—was first proposed, as a systematic theory, by theatre semioticians of the Prague Circle before World War II: Otokar Zich, Jan Mukařovský, Jiří Veltruský, Petr Bogatyrev, Karel Brušák, Jindřich Honzl; their names and contributions are now theatrical history. Their central idea, that everything on the stage is semiotized during the referential process, becoming a sign for something else, still underlies all theatre semiotics. Their early taxonomies of theatre signs provided the model for more recent classifications by Tadeusz Kowzan, Keir Elam, and Erika Fischer-Lichte, to name a few. To a large extent, they were also responsible for the still popular notion that theatre is a polysemic medium. Noting the great diversity of signs on the stage, they concluded that theatre does not rely on a single system of signs, like the system of natural language for verbal narratives, but offers a polyphony of competing and overlapping signs that belong to many systems: verbal, paralinguistic, gestural, clothing, proxemic, color, and sound, and so forth. They tried to establish priorities among these systems, find the laws of their interaction and group them in larger categories such as signs carried by actors, sets, or props. They also noted that theatre tradition has generated its own system of properly theatrical signs that refer to features of past theatre practice rather than to culturally coded meanings. Thus wigs worn on the stage today can stand for a classical staging style rather than for a fashionable seventeenth-century coiffure, and T-shirts for avant-garde performance styles rather than for outfits of teenagers.

Most of these categories provide useful tools for a precise identification of referential processes. Sensitized to the diversity of theatre signs, spectators can better understand how each discrete feature on the stage generates a discrete feature in the imaginary story space; and their vision of the referential world gains in details. However, as these classifications proliferate and grow more complex, it becomes increasingly more difficult to grasp the process by which various signs actually combine, to find an organizing mechanism that makes sense of their totality. At one time, the verbal system used in the dialogue was believed to be the prime source of semiotic order, directing the display of all other signs. But now we have learned that meanings of words are always transformed on the stage by intonations, mimicry, and gestures; we know that staging strategies can distort verbal intentions. Is there then no order among stage signs? Is theatre a mere aggregate of autonomous signs, miraculously put together to yield concerted meanings? Doesn't theatre have its own specific sign system, defining its specificity as a medium?

Most semioticians today, persuaded by the same arguments as the Prague Circle, still deny such a semiotic specificity to theatre; or rather believe that this specificity lies precisely in the absence of a specific theatrical sign system. Thus, in a most influential interview first published in 1963, Roland Barthes defined theatricality as "genuine informational polyphony," exciting but unruly, whereby spectators are always solicited at the same time by many stage signs belonging to different systems.[2] In his 1987 *Dictionnaire du théâtre*, Patrice Pavis notes that this view still represents the current thinking about theatre semiotics.[3] And no wonder, since it does correspond to the experience of most theatre spectators and, among scholars, it benefits from the popularity of trendy notions of "polyphonic dialogism," "open-ended work," and "deconstruction."

Yet polyphony helps little to understand the referential process in theatre. It precludes any systematic analysis of strategies by which theatre produces concerted meanings. It reduces theatre to a smorgasbord of signs offered for our consumption; they may not be equally appealing but their display is supposed to account for all semiotized features on the stage. By that logic, no space is left for features that seem to have no meaning, for signs that do seem to carry meaningful references to the story: neutral gestures, intonations, colors. To that extent, the polyphonic theory of stage signs contradicts rather than reflects our experience of theatre: it fails to explain why most spectators attribute meaning only to a few features of the story world. It does not clarify why many stage signs can be processed as signs that tell a story and yet be denied any further function as signs operating within that story's world. Besides, why would theatre be the only major art medium deprived of a proper semiotic system? The popularity of the polyphonic theory manifests, one suspects, a reluctance to think over semiotic theory in order to solve problems raised by theatre semiotics.

Let us then start with some basic notions. In the first place, polyphony of signs is not a specific feature of theatre. In "real" life, we also use several signs belonging to different systems in order to convey a single meaning, coherent or contradictory. To indicate strong disapproval, for example, we say "no!" shake our head and finger, shudder, and make an appropriate face. In other terms, we superpose, within the same time span, converging signs belonging to natural language, body language, and the semiotic system of facial expressions. Each sign, however, remains autonomous, operating within its own system, independently from the other signs. We could substitute "yes" for "no," while keeping the other signs intact: the resulting—and presumably intended—meaning would be contradictory, ambiguous and/or ironic, but each sign would still have its own impact. But *superposition* is not the only polyphonic strategy. We can also have recourse to *insertion*. By that second strategy, a sign in one system will refer to another sign in another system, inserting the secondary semiotic operation within the frame of the primary operation. When we want to reinforce a meaning, or undermine it through irony, we thus use one system of signs, usually our natural language, in order to refer to various cultural signs that have the same or antithetic meaning within their proper systems.

For example, by stating that a widow "claims to be sad, wears a black dress, dabs at her eyes with a handkerchief, but has a red rose pinned in her hair," I am using English as my primary sign system, but only the word "sad" directly refers to the widow's bereavement in that system. The other words only refer to a color of dress, a gesture, and a flower, that is, they have no other direct meaning. However, once these verbal signs are decoded, their referents—black dress, dabbing at eyes, red rose—operate in turn as cultural signs in systems of color, gestures, and flowers, communicating inserted meanings that both reinforce the notion of bereavement and undermine it with an ironic suggestion of amorous inclination. Within this insertion structure, verbal signs are autonomous; they do not depend on the operation of the cultural signs; one can miss the suggestion of amorous inclination communicated by the red rose but one will not miss the vision of the rose. The inserted cultural signs, in contrast, always depend on an initial correct decoding of the verbal signs. We may know the flower code, but shall miss the meaning of the red rose if we do not know English and fail to visualize the rose.

The shortcomings of the polyphonic/polysemic theory stem from its tacit assumption that *all* signs produced at the same time on the stage are organized by the *superposition* scheme, that is, that they operate independently one from another, creating a polyphony. But such an assumption has no theoretical justification. On the contrary, comparison with other representational arts, literature or painting or cinema, suggests that semiotic operations in theatre are rather based on the *insertion* scheme. Each of these arts, indeed, relies on a dominant primary system of signs that must be decoded in order to provide access to signs coded in secondary cultural systems.[4] By a general logic of representation, theatre may then be expected also to rely on a dominant primary system which uses its proper signs in order to insert signs of other systems. Such a dominant system will constitute the primary theatre system, both overseeing and organizing the polyphonic operations of other signs. But what is that system?

## 2. Primary Signs: Iconicity

The clearest model of the primary theatrical system can be found in the semiosis of narrative literature. Literary theory has long accepted that narratives, in order to tell a story, always first rely on a primary system derived from natural language, that is, the subsystem of "literary language" using a special set of verbal signs.[5] In theory, all literary verbal signs that are present in a narrative must be decoded to yield the basic lines of the story: who did what, where, when, why, and how. Whether we actually read all the signs, or how we concretize the story in our imagination, does not affect the absolute priority of this initial decoding process: we must start with understanding the words in order to visualize the referential world. Then, but only then, can we perceive, within that world, the *occasional* presence of further signs belonging to various cultural systems. Most of these, such as body language, clothing, or colors, usually are as familiar to us as to the writer, and we decode their signs without problems. Some texts, however, may refer to systems that we do not know well, either because they originate in a different culture or have become obsolete; and we miss or misunderstand their signs. And sometimes a given text creates its own new system, requiring us to learn its code in order to identify and understand its signs. Whichever the case, our decoding of cultural signs always depends on a previous decoding of verbal signs, but only processes a small proportion of verbal references to give more cultural meaning to the story.

When we read *Madame Bovary*, for example, we first decode its primary verbal signs in order to concretize in our mind all objective information concerning Emma and her provincial milieu. But now and then, in Emma's world, we notice a feature that we identify as a cultural sign referring, more or less obviously, to psychological or ideological notions that the verbal signs do not convey directly. An early description of Emma, arching her neck backward while sipping a sweet liquor and licking her lips, provides us, through primary verbal decoding, with an objective vision of her action; but, through cultural decoding, it also suggests Emma's basic sensuality that foreshadows and explains much of her later behavior. *Madame Bovary* contains many such inserted cultural signs, directing our interpretation of its meaning, but they are dispersed among many more features of Emma's world that are not coded in any cultural system and suggest no hidden meaning. Attentive to these features, different readers notice different cultural signs, and often draw different conclusions from their combination. Hence the unresolved arguments about the "real" meaning of Emma's story and/or Flaubert's novel. In contrast, even when we contest interpretations of the text, we agree by convention that we have read the same text and understood in the same way all its verbal signs. In other words, we assume that all readers equally competent in literary language, that is, in the primary system of written narratives, are equally competent in decoding the basic story of a narrative even though some of its meanings may elude them. But we also acknowledge, with or without regret, that many readers do not reach beyond the surface story: they are not interested in finding cultural meanings. For them, mere competence in the primary verbal system is a necessary but sufficient condition for the reception of storytelling.

What then about theatre? What is the primary system that enables its competent practitioners to tell and decode stories on the stage? Competence in literary language fulfills that function for theatre read as literature; but one does not read a theatre performance. Verbal competence is also needed to understand what is said on the stage, especially when dialogue plays an important role. But such understanding is not absolutely necessary. Many spectators have been known to enjoy plays performed in a foreign language; in fact, several festivals now feature foreign companies, and the Théâtre de l'Europe in Paris has institutionalized that practice. Nor is it necessary to have a formal knowledge of all nonverbal systems of stage signs: Western audiences have been flocking to performances of No and Kabuki plays without understanding their coded costumes, body language, mimicry, paralinguistic signs. All stage systems, including natural language, are useful but neither necessary nor sufficient for communicating a story in theatre. And for a good reason: for their signs are always inserted in a primary theatre system which, operating continuously during the performance, regulates and orders the alleged polyphony of all cultural signs.

\*    \*    \*

So again: What is that system? What semiotic competence is really necessary in theatre? It would seem that there is only one such a sine qua non requirement: a competence in the use of an *iconic code* whereby *all signs on the stage refer to their mirror image in the imaginary story space outside stage*. This code suffices to define the properly theatrical primary system. It underlies the basic "theatrical pact"—or convention—by which spectators, as well as performers, agree that what takes place on the stage is always referring to what takes place in the story world, and that the corresponding real and mental spaces must not be confused one with the other even though they look very much alike.

Theatre is not the only figurative medium that relies on iconicity. Codes of painting, sculpture, photography, and cinema also postulate a strong resemblance between what is perceived and what is represented. However, even when we rely on resemblance to identify the model in legal documents, as in the case of passport pictures, we remain aware that the materiality of the sign differs from the materiality of the referent: dots, lines, and pigmentation on photographic paper have no material relation to flesh or hair. In theatre alone iconicity reaches its full material potential, especially in the two categories of signs that draw most attention on the stage: live actors and verbal statements. In the case of actors, human beings stand for other human beings, lending them all their physical attributes. In the case of verbal statements, words stand for other words, lending them all their paralinguistic features at the time of enunciation. This shared materiality of signs and referents legitimates the role of iconicity as the primary theatre code, and facilitates mental shifting from the stage to the story space. It also accounts to a large extent for the universal appeal of theatre.

Yet iconicity does not mean real identity. By its definition, a sign cannot stand for itself nor refer to itself. The most iconic theatre signs are never totally identical to their referents in the story. Statements made by actors on the stage are not intended, nor should be taken, to be the exact statements made by characters in the referential world; by the theatre convention, they are always assumed to be somehow different in vocabulary, rhythm, syntax. Similarly, characters are not expected to look and act exactly like the actors who portray them; a certain stylization always interferes. Besides, there is always a gap between referents of the producer of the sign and referents concretized by individual spectators. However, these differences tend to be minimized or even disregarded when the "magic" of theatre operates its "illusion." Despite some apparent exceptions (about which more later), the metaphor that best evokes this special relation between features on the stage and features in the story space is that of a *mirror image*. Even the best mirrors distort a little, but even the worst mirrors retain exceptionally high iconicity. The fact that theatre, in contrast to real mirrors, also involves a close *material* identity between signs and referents further magnifies the iconic power of the mirror image. The stage operates like Lewis Carroll's magic looking glass: seeing through it, we perceive reflections embodied in flesh.

In other terms, iconicity as code of the primary theatre system demands that, as a necessary and sufficient condition of theatrical experience, we shift from stage features to their mirror images appearing, as through a looking glass, in an imaginary story space. By this specular code, Laurence Olivier as a sign of Hamlet evokes a Hamlet who looks like Laurence Olivier but is not Laurence Olivier; Olivier's gestures evoke mirror image gestures of Hamlet but are not Hamlet's gestures; and Hamlet speaks like Olivier, but his statements are not Olivier's. Seen through such a looking-glass distortion, the referential story always lacks some precision, and individual spectators must draw on their own experience or imagination to round up its concretization in their minds. They are also expected to decode, within the imaginary world, various inserted cultural signs that might help them to clarify what the primary signs neither show nor say about that world. Finally, at any time, spectators can turn away from the looking glass, return to a desemiotized stage and enjoy theatre's performant function. But, as long as the referential function prevails, iconicity rules the basic theatre decoding.

At least two major objections can be made to this theory. In the first place, many signs on the stage visibly are *not* iconic. In the second place, some referential strategies seem to bypass the primary iconic system, suggesting that the story somewhat takes place on the stage and not, behind the looking glass, in an imaginary world. The first objection derives from the acknowledged frequent use of stage *symbols*: signs that do not look like their referents and only stand for them by dint of convention. Sometimes a certain iconicity may be detected in the symbols, as in the New York production of Peter Shaffer's *Equus* (1974), where wire headgear did bear some resemblance to horse heads; but even then only by convention could the actors with the headgear be taken to stand for real horses. More often there is but a minimal resemblance, if any at all. Thus a plastic slab has some similarity to a table, a bed, a chair, or an altar, but will stand for any one of them, or for all in succession, only by an arbitrary agreement. Such nuances are irrelevant to the objection. Whether partly iconic, slightly metaphoric or metonymic, or totally conventional, theatre symbols clearly subvert a strict iconic code. If iconicity indeed provides the key to the primary theatre system, this subversion must be explained as a natural function of that system.

The pragmatic reasons for the use of stage symbols is not at issue. Obviously, only symbols can represent gods, monsters, or magic powers in any theatre space, and horses must be symbolic on small modern stages; but most symbols have no such justification. A plastic slab standing for a table can be easily replaced by an iconic table. Nor are economic constraints a persuasive factor. Most symbols substitute for iconic props that are readily available at small cost. In fact, because they are minor signs, such symbols benefit from the deictic power of actors who project on them their own high iconicity, turning them with gestures and words into recognizable features of the story world. But deictic contamination is also a matter of convention and choice; it helps clarify symbols, it moderates their subversion of iconicity, but does not explain why they are chosen in the first place. Clearly the recourse to symbols has other than pragmatic reasons. It can be shown that the real reasons are inherent in the nature of theatre as artistic communication.

Literature again provides a model. Its own primary system, we have seen, is literary language, with its clearly coded use of words and syntax. Yet most literary texts contain verbal forms that deviate from coded meanings or grammatical structures. Whether we call them "poetic," "rhetorical," or "artistic," many such stylistic figures, notably metaphor and metonymy, usually retain some relation between the coded and the noncoded references, between the sail and the ship for which it stands, between a lion and a man of courage. Others, however, appear to be more arbitrary, like Paul Valéry's image of doves standing for sails. In either case, the subversion of the literary code is not justified by an improvement in referential communication; it is motivated by the desire to produce a more effective artistic impact, playing on aesthetic or emotional responses. The underlying assumption appears to be that literature, to the extent that it is *art*, has the special mission of conveying something that normal verbal communication cannot transmit, and that it accomplishes that task precisely through a subversion of its own primary code of meanings and usage of words.

By the same logic, the presence of symbolic signs on the stage may be explained as a poetic subversion of the primary iconic code that occurs when theatre seeks to stress its function as art—a debatable function, as we have seen, but one that has been claimed for theatre since its early development and now is widely accepted by producers and consumers alike. In that sense, subversion through symbols does not undermine the validity of a proper theatrical system based on iconicity; it rather testifies to its flexibility. Because it can accommodate symbols at the price of an acceptable subversion, it demonstrates that it can not only communicate that which is intended to be clearly conceptualized, but also convey, through an "artistic" manipulation of its code, that which cannot be coded with precision and must only be suggested. To that extent, one could say that symbolic signs are the poetry of the stage.

The second objection is more serious. It stems from the observation that some theatrical performances, by an overt design, seem to locate on the stage at least a part of the referential story, and thus need no operation of any primary system, iconic or not, that shifts mental vision to an imaginary space. I am not referring to planned collapses of referentiality when the imaginary story is interrupted and the spectators are lured back to the stage by dancing or singing *performances*—a procedure commonly followed in musicals. I am referring to two *referential* strategies whereby an action on the stage, perceived without transition through the looking glass, appears to relate directly to events or meanings of the story. The first strategy uses the stage as the forum from which *performers* make comments on the story that is taking place in a mental space outside the stage. The second strategy has *characters* interact with performers or spectators, and thus seeks to break down the separation between the reality of the entire theatrical space and the imaginary referential space. In both cases, one may claim, the primary iconic system is breached. But what does really happen?

The first strategy is now associated with Bertolt Brecht's *Verfrem-dungseffekt*, or "alienation," but can be traced back to the commedia dell'arte and beyond. It requires the actors to inform the spectators, by the means of common cultural signs—intonations, gestures, facial expressions—how one should interpret the actions of the imaginary characters portrayed by these actors. Inspired by Brecht, an actress playing the role of Mother Courage, a war profiteer, will visibly exaggerate repulsive traits of behavior, say, gloating over profits, in order to show her disapproval of Mother Courage's activity. In theory, such cultural signs produced by the performers as performers cannot be perceived as taking place in the specular story space. Spectators are expected to locate them on the stage, as a direct commentary that actors provide about the meaning of the story. Yet, because this commentary affects the understanding and concretization of characters, it also contributes to storytelling and shapes the story world in the mind of spectators. But no strict iconicity is involved: performers are viewed as performers, not as signs. The point of the strategy is simply to tell parts of the story with a commentary made on the stage rather than with signs referring to the story world.

In many cases, at least, it may so seem. But at the price of a quasi-desemiotization of the stage. For, when they focus on the performers' commentary, spectators briefly lose track of the characters. Not completely, since the commentary always evokes the characters to whom it refers, but sufficiently to cause a fluttering of attention. A similar fluttering also occurs when, as often in Brecht's plays, characters rather than performers offer, in discrete satirical songs, various social or political comments on topics related to the story's meaning. In either situation, the referential function is displaced, from the central area of the story, toward its boundaries: an ambiguous region where imagination interfaces with reality. A step farther, and the boundaries are crossed: comments about the story are offered by a theatre official before the curtain is raised, or by a printed text distributed to the spectators—two forms of communication clearly situated outside the theater performance even though they take place within the theatrical space. Actors' commentary or characters' songs do not go so far. But they bring to the stage a similar nontheatrical function: neither properly referential, that is, involved in telling a story, nor properly performant, or focused on the stage. It is rather a critical function, normally fulfilled outside theatre by all sorts of written or oral observations about the world, the meaning of life, or, in some cases, the meaning of a play. Of course, the story told on the stage can include such statements, or suggest them in various ways, but it does so through characters evoked by the primary iconic system. Critical commentary offered by Brechtian actors, when it is noticed at all, takes place outside that system, but does not disturb its monopoly as the basic referential medium of theatre. It rather undermines the traditional division of theatre between the referential and performant functions, suggesting that it can also have a critical function that uses a hybrid technique. At any rate, these moments of alienation are rare and rapidly dissipate in a return to the norm.

In fact, in many cases, the primary iconicity reasserts itself at the very moment it is denied. The stage commentary about the behavior of characters engineers an instant move back to the referential world. Commentary signs displayed by the actors are carried through the looking glass, repositioned in the story space, and concretized as signs offered by the characters themselves in order to comment on their own behavior. At that point, in a manner not anticipated by Brecht, iconicity produces the desired estrangement not on the stage but within the specular space. The primary code yields the vision of a world where people have split personalities: they make critical observations about their own actions and yet are unable to change these actions in light of their own judgments. It is a deterministic world that lucidly exposes its lack of freedom, encouraging the spectators to react to it with a greater determination to preserve freedom in their real world. The audience might find such a world to be quite improbable, and very theatrical, but no more so than other highly improbable worlds portrayed commonly in theatre, for didactic or artistic reasons, from Aristophanes to Beckett. True, the blurred boundary between stage and story spaces exposes this strategy to many perils, as Brechtian performances have amply demonstrated. It is important to note, however, that most of these perils originate in fact in an awkward tampering with the primary code of theatre, thus confirming rather than denying the dominant function of iconicity.

The second strategy that undermines iconicity seeks to break a different barrier—the barrier between, on the one hand, the mental plane of imagination and, on the other, the reality of the entire theatre space, both stage *and* audience. Under normal circumstances, spectators share with the actors the awareness that they collaborate in a common experience that requires a moderate interaction, limited to communication: actors adjust their performances to the responses of spectators, and spectators communicate their reactions to actors. But the story space, while viewed as a mirror image of the stage, is situated in an imaginary realm that excludes both actors and spectators. A mild transgression of that barrier occurs when the story involves both fictional actors and fictional characters, as in Pirandello's plays; or a fictional theatre stage and spectators as in *Hamlet*; or even, outside a fictional theatre, a fictional urban space that is connected to the real urban space outside the real theatre, as in Jean Genet's *The Blacks*.[6] As a result, it is claimed, spectators forget the difference between the theatre space and the story space, situate imaginary actors on the same plane as real actors, believe that the events taking place on an imaginary stage actually take place on the real stage; in short, they gain the impression that they see directly the imaginary action, without going through the looking glass of iconic signs. But it is only an impression. Spectators educated in theatre conventions know well that the imaginary stage is not the stage they see but only its mirror image. And they apply the iconic code to concretize the mental image of a play within a play.

A more radical version of that strategy has characters directly address the audience during the performance. To what extent they do so while retaining their fictional personality, or assume a special new role, is not always easy to determine nor is it very important; the three assassins explaining their actions in T. S. Eliot's *Murder in the Cathedral* offer a case in point. In either case such addresses, as well as more aggressive forms of physical interaction with the spectators practiced in the 1960s, notably in the *Dionysius in 69* production, are perceived to take place outside the imaginary story and yet, as integral features of the story world, to be related to that story. For the spectators, forcibly involved in a direct communication with story characters, the space of the imaginary world overlaps for a moment with the reality of their own theatre space. By the same token, the same characters who were seen through the looking glass of iconicity are now experienced as real people.

Fleetingly, the traditional function of actors as primary theatre signs seems to be superseded by a direct access to the roles they portray; hence an impression of disorientation, highly prized by advocates of defamiliarizing art. But this effect does not imply an overall negation of the iconic code. It rather relies on an unexpected shattering of the basic theatre convention, including the operation of the primary theatre system—a breach of contract that actually reinforces, by its scandalous character, the normative power of iconicity as proper code of theatrical referentiality.

It can further be argued that some spectators, well trained in theatre semiotics, remain involved in the operation of iconic signs even when these signs intrude on the plane of reality. When we attend *Murder in the Cathedral*, for example, and are addressed by the assassins, we are aware that their speeches, though seemingly directed at us in our individual reality, in fact are intended for all spectators, present, past, and future, not as real people but in their role as spectators of the play. In that sense, while we remain individuals who are watching a performance, we also participate in an ideal series of performances that includes us as temporary characters. We fulfill the function of signs that refer, by the iconic code, to all possible spectators of these performances. By the same token, the entire theatre space becomes the stage for the serial performances which, through the looking glass, present the story of an imaginary performance where we play the role of imaginary spectators as close to us as mirror images but not totally identical. Experienced in that spirit, theatre offers both the appeal and the drawbacks of many rituals where participants are at the same time actors, characters, and spectators. That these multiple roles involve paradoxes is evident. But such paradoxes, and the resulting mental acrobatics, account for the sophistication of highly theatrical theatre, with plays about plays, performances about performances, and other self-reflecting referential games that could not be played, nor fully appreciated, without the assumed trust in a primary iconic code.

## 3. Cultural Stage Signs

### Modes of Insertion: Primary and Cultural Signs

Decoded as icons, primary stage signs provide all the information that spectators need to concretize an imaginary world, where characters looking like actors are engaged in a series of actions. But the story of these characters would remain quite opaque if it only contained information supplied by the primary signs. It would appear as a succession of events, without explanation, value judgment, or interpretation; in short, it would lack "meaning." To be sure, as will be discussed later, individual spectators always project their own meanings on the story when they concretize it or when they reflect upon it. But they normally also expect that performances themselves suggest at least some meaning beyond the objective facts. This enlightening commentary, which concerns the story and not the stage, is properly offered directly by the story world itself. It is communicated to us by signs that we perceive as features of that world, but that we also recognize as signs coded in any of the semiotic cultural systems operating in our society. To distinguish them from the primary theatre signs, they shall be henceforth called *cultural* signs. It is to be expected that some of these cultural signs will be exchanged as such between the characters in the story world, if its culture is similar to ours; but others will be exclusively directed at us. We shall return to this difference. At this point, it is more important to note how all cultural signs, regardless of their intended receivers, are connected to corresponding primary signs, and how they interact with them.

Because they are features of the story world, all cultural signs must be communicated, like any feature of that world, by appropriate primary signs placed on the stage. And because primary signs are iconic, the cultural signs that we concretize in the story world must look like their primary mirror images. Yet, strictly speaking, the related primary and cultural signs are not identical, and operate by different codes. When, playing Hamlet, Olivier frowns fiercely, his frown as a primary sign only refers to a nearly identical frown produced by Hamlet; it doesn't say anything about Olivier's nor Hamlet's mood despite the fact that, in our cultural system of facial expressions, a frown clearly stands for irritation or perplexity. But when it is concretized by us as Hamlet's frown, it functions as a cultural sign informing us about Hamlet's anger or worry. Similarly, a provocatively décolleté red dress tells us nothing about the actress who wears it on the stage; but, seen through the looking glass, it first yields a mirror image décolleté dress worn by the corresponding character: primary operation; and then serves as a commentary on her erotic inclination, motivation, psychology: cultural operation.

This dual semiotic process is simple but involves some complex problems. The choice of cultural signs appropriate for commentary is not always easy. In theory, any cultural system familiar to the audience could be used for that purpose. In practice, however, some systems have more effective signs than others because their codes are more reliable. In contrast, many inevitable features of the referential world, such as clothing, colors, light, and postures, function as cultural signs in notoriously unreliable systems, with fragmentary or unstable codes. A beige dress on the stage and an average electric light, while fulfilling their primary missions by yielding a mirror-image dress and light in the specular world, do not have any precisely coded meaning as cultural signs. They supply no intentional commentary, and are not received as intentional signs by the audience. They function as nonsignifying features of the story, that is, as semiotically neutral features.

Most features of the imaginary world, and hence most mirror-image features of the stage, may be expected to share that neutral condition. Some are not noticed at all. Some do not belong to any cultural system, are not coded in and by the performance, and hence cannot operate as signs. In many cases, the code is trivialized and its signs do not elicit any strong response. Recreating a relatively complex referential world, and intent on following the story, spectators can hardly pay attention to all of its potential signs. Besides, even when they recognize familiar signs, they rarely focus on their semiotic messages; they are rather drawn to features that play an important role in the development of the story, or satisfy the needs of the performant function that leads to desemiotization: a pretty face, an inventive costume, a pleasing light which do not mean anything. In that sense, most primary signs present on the stage have a low probability to generate meaningful cultural signs. And many productions, handling iconicity with care and inventiveness but without much concern for cultural codes, fail to communicate precise meanings.

In semiotic terms, the reciprocal relation between primary and cultural signs implies a near identity of their signifiers. The material manifestation of the primary sign on the stage yields a mirror-image manifestation of the cultural sign in the imaginary world. The meaningful Hamlet's frown is concretized as the mirror image of Olivier's meaningless frown. Restated somewhat loosely, substituting "identity" for "near identity," this means that cultural signs share their signifiers with primary signs. Or, in even looser terms, that any *cultural sign always already also operates as a primary sign*. But the opposite is far from true. As was noted, *only a few primary signs also operate as cultural signs*. Which means in turn that, in a performance that comments on its own story with a careful selection of cultural signs, a corresponding number of "identical" primary signs must be chosen and displayed in order to allow for this commentary. To that extent, the intended interpretation of the story, or its "meaning," directly influences the choice of appropriate primary features of that story. In contrast, primary signs that are not intended to serve as supports for cultural signs have no such constraints, and their choice only reflects a particular vision of the referential world, neither necessarily meaningful nor coherent.

Let us assume, for instance, that we want to suggest a tragic interpretation of Hamlet as a character doomed to seek a fatal destiny. In order to indicate that he follows a death wish, which is *not* told in the story, we shall clothe him in a totally black outfit, coded in our culture as a sign of death. This requires that the actor playing Hamlet also be clad in black. It further means that, in order to focus tragedy on Hamlet, other actors must wear outfits that sharply contrast with a black costume: bright-colored rather than gray or dark-blue costumes. As a result, our free use of primary signs will be curtailed, and hence our freedom to shape the vision of Hamlet's world. But let us assume that we limit our commentary to the cultural meaning of the black outfit, an unlikely but possible strategy. We shall be free to choose other primary signs, say, other costumes, in conformity with our vision of fashion in medieval Denmark. The specular story world could be quite coherent. But will the suggestion of a tragic Hamlet be powerful enough to communicate its meaning to the spectators? Or will such a minimal recourse to cultural signs result in a flat performance that, however successful its storytelling or its performant function, will yield a very ambiguous Hamlet?

The selection of cultural signs demands that a subtle balance be maintained between meaningless and meaningful features of a story. But there are various ways of achieving it. A large number of cultural suggestions, notably when they reinforce each other, normally produces a strong commentary. Yet a commentary limited to a single meaning risks being overly reductive; it forces a potentially complex story into the straitjacket of a single interpretation. Conversely, too many comments risk to creating confusion. A spectator solicited by too many cultural signs may give up trying to reconcile them: overabundance of suggestions can have the same effect as their total absence. Furthermore, as noted before, not all cultural codes are equally normative, nor are all signs in the same system equally effective. Sometimes a single sign, when it is striking and appears alone in a world deprived of other commentary, will convey a more powerful meaning than a network of coordinated but trite signs: a hunchback Hamlet will suffice, with his hump coded as a sign of monstrosity, humiliation, and inferiority, to generate a powerful interpretation of Hamlet as a warped character even if no other cultural signs support that interpretation. But then, is it always advisable to feed definitive meanings to spectators? In some cases, for various reasons, it may be preferable to hint at several possible meanings, inviting the audience to participate in an active interpretation.

Under ideal conditions, the selection of cultural signs thus requires many thoughtful and concerted decisions by the producers of the performance: authors, directors, actors, technical staff. In reality, contingent conditions of theatrical production limit their choices. Various pragmatic factors dictate the presence of primary signs that cannot serve as supports of desirable cultural signs. In a theatre company getting ready to stage *Hamlet*, for example, all the leading male actors may be small and/or corpulent, and have relatively common faces—features that do not hamper great acting but could hardly suggest, as cultural signs displayed by Hamlet, that he is an ascetic and yet domineering redeemer. Such a company must then select a different image for Hamlet, or indicate his redeeming role with other, more subtle cultural signs. Or let us suppose that, intending to stage *Hamlet* on Broadway, the producers have located an ideal actor; they may not be able to afford him and, for a Broadway production, costs are a determining factor. In still another situation, the choice of actors is arbitrarily imposed by "angels." Besides, even a physically ideal actor may have his own idiosyncratic likes or dislikes of given interpretations.

Then, one must also take into account various demands of the performant function: many producers will sacrifice concerns for cultural signs for the sake of a star's aesthetic, erotic, or celebrity appeal, promising fat box-office returns. And further complications derive from contract stipulations, relationships between actors, directors and producers, political conditions. Though these and other similar factors are not always present, their influence exerts a constant pressure on the manipulation of cultural signs, precludes the implementation of the simplest strategies and, in many cases, leads to contrived performances where special directorial signs, to be discussed later, are brought on the stage for the sole purpose of sharpening a diluted commentary.

## Simple and Complex Signs

In the section above, the suitability of actors to suggest an interpretation of their characters was related to their display of discrete physical signs belonging to discrete cultural systems: facial expressions, body figures, clothes, colors. One could object that this perspective on actors as signs is artificial; that actors are not mere aggregates of discrete semiotic features; that they project on the stage their entire personality; that, even within the limited area of their referential function, they produce and communicate all their signs in a continuous process of total acting. In short, that an actor is an indivisible complex sign, and that any simple sign that he or she might display always operates as an integrated part of a combined complex sign manifested by the actor's personality.

In terms of strict theory, such an argument leads to a tautological fallacy. There is no semiotic code wherein the totality of an actor's features, the complex signifier of the actor as a complex sign, is conventionally associated with the total personality of that actor, that is, a complex signified; besides, if such a code existed, then actors could refer to themselves, which is semiotic heresy. Yet one must not dismiss the objection simply because it is theoretically invalid. For it draws attention to the difference between simple and complex signs—a question that has much wider implications for theatre than the specific problem of the actor's semiosis. In fact, differences between simple and complex signs explain a basic difference between primary and cultural signs, and by the same token permit to clarify the problem of the actor's semiosis, both total and partial.

Let us first consider theatre's primary system and its iconic signs. The theoretical distinction between simple and complex signs has very little pertinence for that system which only involves various degrees of complexity. Since all its signs operate as icons, all features perceived on the stage constitute a global iconic sign that is always complex and refers to an equally complex mirror-image world. As spectators, we tend to isolate certain stage features in order to focus on selected parts of the global icon, or to structure its complexity. In particular, we center our attention on actors because they are the main supports of the story action. To that extent, we process them as single signs. However, even as we isolate them, we nevertheless perceive them to be very complex signs, distinctly identified with a number of individual properties: stature, voice, facial expression, clothes.

Furthermore, this focused perception requires that we keep our focus on the actors and prevent our eyes from being drawn to other features of the stage: a most improbable achievement. As a rule, for various reasons, we rapidly expand the scope of our attention and connect actors with their direct surroundings, objects they handle, furniture they use, places where they move, till we reach the limits of the global icon, that is, the limits of the illuminated stage. At any stage of that process, we perceive a different complex sign. Conversely, we sometimes try to restrict our attention to an actor's particular feature, for example, a facial expression, treating it in turn as if it were a distinct complex sign involving several features of the face. A further narrowing of the focus brings up a close vision of the mouth, or forehead, or eyes, each of these single signs still presenting some complexity since each one involves distinct movements of muscles and distinct texture and color of skin. In theory, no doubt, beyond the limit of what we can practically see, one could posit the presence of a simple and indivisible feature, but we cannot perceive it nor process it as a primary sign. Besides, even when we try to focus on a minimal complex sign, say an actor's lips, noticing their curve, color, movement, we remain aware of their relation to other features of the face, and we progressively expand our attention to the entire body and its surroundings, encountering an increasing complexity in each larger sign. Whatever the individual focus, then, for a performance's audience *all iconic signs are always complex*, and differences in focus only generate differences in the degree of complexity, impossible to quantify.

Similar differences in degree of complexity also mark differences between distinct global icons, that is, between total stage features, perceived in different performances. The actual number of stage features obviously depends on individual staging styles. A bare stage, where three actors encased in jars deliver sparse monologues under a uniform light, as in a performance of Beckett's *Play*, may seem in that sense to offer a less complex global sign than an opulent staging of a historical drama, with many costumed actors and a profusion of evocative props. Yet even these extreme examples only differ by a degree of complexity that eludes quantification. Besides, it is difficult to assess the impact of such vague differences. A greater complexity of iconic signs surely facilitates multiplying cultural signs that are attached to them, but there are many other factors that influence that strategy in a more decisive way. Furthermore, the referential function of primary signs is never affected by their degree of complexity; fictional story worlds are more or less believable and/or interesting regardless of their complexity.

In contrast, *cultural signs always operate in theatre in the form of simple signs*. Since they belong to various cultural systems, with distinct codes, each one must be perceived clearly as a discrete sign operating within its particular system. Furthermore, many of these systems rely on a "one-on-one" code, where each distinct signifier is associated with a distinct signified, with as much precision as possible even in the case of multiple associations. A smile may stand for happiness or amusement, sympathy or complicity, and the context indicates its specific reference; but, within that context, it operates only if its coded meanings are clearly identified regardless of the context. This does not mean that all cultural signs always respect their codes. Various strategies aim at creating ambiguous references, or at figurative (or poetic) uses of signs that subvert the code. Such subversions, we have seen, in special circumstances can affect even the primary system of iconic signs; they also affect the operation of cultural signs in similar circumstances. But they do not undermine the general perception of cultural signs as simple signs. Only one contextual situation leads to an apparent violation of that rule: when simple signs aggregate to form a gestalt.

Such an aggregation is inevitable because, it bears repeating, cultural signs always coexist with corresponding primary signs. When primary signs aggregate to form their complex gestalts, cultural signs remain attached to the same gestalts. Of course, complex primary signs convey no commentary at all in the story world they help to visualize. Furthermore, in larger iconic gestalts, only a few features also serve as cultural signs. Still, when two or more cultural signs are perceived as a part of the same primary gestalt, say, the gestalt of an actor, one could be tempted to believe that they form together a complex sign. But it would be a mistake.

Let us suppose, for instance, that an actress with heavy make up, a come-on smile, and swinging hips, enters the stage wearing a red, tight, low-cut dress. Most Western spectators will surely perceive these features as a single gestalt, operating as a complex sign of sexual invitation. In reality, however, this general cultural gestalt proposes its commentary by aggregating six quite distinct simple signs, each one conveying independently, in its own cultural system, the same meaning of sexual invitation: heavy make up in the make-up system, come-on smile in the facial expressions system, swinging hips in the body language, red in the color system, and tightness and low décolleté in the contemporary system of clothes. Their aggregation into a gestalt reinforces, by concerted superposition, the intended suggestion of sexuality, but the gestalt as such does not modify the autonomous nature of each simple sign, nor turn them together into a complex sign. In fact, aggregation does not have necessarily to offer a convergence of signs. Some gestalts, seeking irony or ambiguity, display signs with contradictory messages. Whatever the strategy, however, analysis always shows, in the most complex gestalts, only a finite number of simple cultural signs.

There is no exception to that rule, not even for the special category of coded theatrical signs. Within the theatrical system, primary signs refer to mirror images of traditional theatre forms that have acquired the status of clichés, and some of these clichés are visibly more complex than others. But the attached cultural signs remain simple signs. A stylized gesture coded as melodramatic acting, or a certain intonation coded, in French theatre, as classical delivery, are obviously simple signs that create no theoretical problems. But some theatrical signs involve much more: physical appearance of actors, ritualized gestures, costumes, colors, intonations, combining into a complex gestalt. In order to evoke the complex cliché of a Scaramouche, or of a black-hatted villain, a complex mirror-image figure must appear on the stage. Such theatrical signs are complex in their primary iconic function. But they also operate as cultural signs, suggesting through their commentary that "the world is a stage" and the meaning of a theatre story is theatrical. Can they be considered as complex cultural signs? Not really. For their cultural gestalts are not really complex, cannot be broken down into autonomous, discrete cultural signs; prescribed costume, gestures, and colors would mean nothing, taken separately. Some primary features of such gestalts have no cultural meaning, but a minimum core must be preserved in its integrity lest the signs become meaningless. And that indivisible core is always coded in the theatrical system in the form of a simple sign, however complex its material properties. Scaramouche forms an integrated theatrical figure, not an assembly of features that are independently Scaramouche-like. Theatre clichés function in that sense like all other cultural signs.

The paradox of the actor who is viewed both as a total person and as an aggregate of some discrete features can now be clarified. When we process the actor as a primary iconic sign, referring to a mirror image in the story world, we respond to the totality of his or her personality, to everything that can be perceived on the stage. We see indeed a complex primary gestalt; and though we may focus on those features that seem to us particularly important or striking, we integrate them with all other features in order to concretize the corresponding character. In that process, we also carry through the looking glass any special charisma that, in addition to all discrete features, is somehow projected by the unique configuration of the gestalt, that is, by the actor as an individual personality. However, when we look at the actor in order to detect cultural signs, displayed by the character as a commentary on the specular world, we focus only on those few discrete features, if any, that are coded in any of our cultural systems. We note a raised fist as an aggregated gestalt of aggressiveness; we identify clenched fingers and the upward movement of the arm as simple signs conveying that message; but we dismiss the shape or size of the fist, the color of the skin, the texture of the sleeve—in short, all other features displayed by the actor. We keep seeing them, but we do not attribute to them any power to suggest the meaning of the story. Simply stated, as a cultural sign, an actor can be deconstructed as a combination of simple signs, without input of a total personality.

## Story Signs: Intentionality and Causality[7]

While they always operate in the story world, cultural signs are nevertheless clearly understood to serve two different types of communication, originating in two different sources of commentary. A vast number of signs, notably almost all verbal signs, are produced by the story characters in order to communicate between themselves. As spectators, we perceive them from the outside. We can respond to them like voyeurs, and/or draw from them conclusions about the story world; we know that they are intended to elicit some reaction on our part; but we remain aware that their meaning must first be related to the intentions of characters. Other signs, in contrast, are directly addressed to us as the intended receivers of a performance-to-audience communication. The comments made by the two categories of signs serve different purposes and must be examined separately.

The first category, that of *story signs*, enables characters to communicate to each other information, desires, feelings, and ideas, aimed at achieving some specific goals. In most cases, these signs are coded in the same cultural systems that we use to communicate in our real world. We could then be expected to identify and decode them without trouble when we perceive them in the story world. Yet problems occur, contributing ambiguity to our understanding of characters and the meaning of their actions.

The main question is: How can we be sure whether cultural signs displayed by story characters are truly intentional, that is, that they are used for the purpose of conscious communication? We have no difficulty with verbal exchanges. Words, especially dialogues, are normally taken to be both intentional and conscious; and even monologues operate in the manner of purposeful speech acts addressed by characters to themselves. Unconscious verbal utterances constitute exceptions, but they are rare and need not bother us now.[8] We have also few problems with paralinguistic signs, such as intonations: as a rule, we assume that they are intentionally produced to sharpen the meaning of words. However, there are many other signs, notably in the systems of body language and facial expressions, that have been coded on the model of involuntary "reflex" reactions to direct stimuli—reactions that produce unconscious smiles or instinctive aggressive/defensive gestures. Perception of such signs creates as many doubts about their intentionality in theatre's story world as it does in real life.

When, in our mental story world, Hamlet smiles at Ophelia, we know by theatre convention that we are intended to notice that smile. But is it an intentional sign produced by Hamlet in order to let Ophelia believe that he is content or amused? Perhaps. But perhaps not. Hamlet could be also smiling unconsciously, because he is amused for some secret reason, and because amusement, by a biological law, causes an instinctive contraction of facial muscles that we call a smile. Such a smile is not a sign intended to communicate a feeling to another character; it is only the visible result of an emotion that cannot be perceived. Yet it is not devoid of information. If we believe that Hamlet is merely amused, and not trying to inform Ophelia about his true or pretended feelings, we may attempt to deduce the cause of his amusement, and hence learn something new about Hamlet. But such a deduction would not rely on our knowledge of coded signs of facial expressions; it would rest on our belief in *causality* underlying an appropriate psychological law. This is an essential notion that needs further elaboration.

As a general rule, when we perceive a visible result and deduce the existence of an invisible cause, we testify to our belief that the causal relationship between that cause and its result has the validity of a law. Applying such a law, we deduce the occurrence of fire from the perception of smoke, and sleepiness from a yawn. We accept that causality governs such sequences, and that no other explanations are needed, no communication takes place, no signs are at work. But, perhaps because most causal sequences were initially discovered to operate in nature, and formulated as "natural" laws, many semioticians use the term "natural signs" to refer to all those perceptible results that enable us to deduce hidden causes. Others prefer to call them "symptoms," or

"indexes," or "indices" in French: an unnecessary complication of terminology. Although the term "natural signs" can be quite misleading,
because it conceals the causality that underlies it and implies communication when there is none, it nevertheless remains within the area of
the basic semiotic vocabulary. Furthermore, it is easy to use. I shall then
refer to "natural" signs whenever it is convenient, but always with the
understanding that these are not truly conventional and "intentional"
signs, coded to stand for what they are not, but only results of causes
that have no part in communication. With this caveat in mind, the
question about Hamlet's smile can be restated as: Is his smile to be
interpreted as an intentional sign or as a "natural" sign? As a conscious
act of communication or an unconscious product of causality? In other
terms, is it a properly cultural sign?

Most performances provide indications that dispel the audience's
confusion: specific observations, coherence of the story, logic of a
character's behavior. In some instances, a careful manipulation of such
clues helps to generate dramatic irony. An appropriate staging can
make it clear that Ophelia trusts in Hamlet's smile, believing that it
unconsciously manifests his good mood; but the spectators may be
informed, by other staging strategies, that Hamlet wants to deceive
Ophelia about his real feelings. Irony in this case, and in many others,
derives from contrasted readings of the smile: for the naive character,
it is a "natural" sign guaranteed by causality, hence not an intentional
sign; for the educated audience, it is a true conventional sign intended
to achieve a deceitful communication. A similar irony will obtain when
the two interpretations are reversed or distributed among two characters. Yet much more than irony rests on a correct identification of story
signs. Indeed, "natural" and intentional signs offer two different ways
of apprehending the meaning of the story, two different ways of access-
ing the different dimensions of its world.

The processing of "natural" signs, let us repeat, always relies on a
causality postulated by a general law. To deduce absent causes, we must
believe in the basic validity of the law. We know that some laws are not
very reliable, especially in the field of psychology. Yet, even when in
doubt, we rely on them to make sense of what happens in both real and
story worlds. When a character staggers in, flops down on a chair, and
sighs in relief, we deduce from this visible action that, by a general law,
tiredness must be its absent cause; however, when asked to think it
over, we could find other general laws that could account for the same
behavior, though with less probability. In that sense, many general laws
are probable rather than reliable, especially when they derive from our
personal experience raised to the level of generalization. Through this
lawmaking process, we formulate ad-hoc causalities even for individ-

uals; as Sartre observed, we decree that a boy who has stolen several times must be expected to steal again because he *is* a thief. That we thus may negate human freedom is not at issue here. Right or wrong, our attitude betrays our trust in subjectively postulated laws even when no objective laws support them. More generally, we tend to believe that human actions result from built-in causes—causes that are already identified in an appropriate law.

In theatre's story world, as in life, this recourse to built-in causality provides us with instant explanation of human behavior. Most actions carried out by characters are, in that sense, self-explanatory, pointing to their probable causes. When we visualize these actions, our instinctive acknowledgment of their causes thus enriches our knowledge of the story world; it opens up a causal dimension that our observation of mere actions, mirror images of primary signs, cannot disclose. Processing each action as a "natural" sign, we double the surface events with an underlying layer of their sources, and sources of sources, knit together in a network of causalities.

This detection of causes beneath the surface of actions takes place continuously, effortlessly, automatically. Most frequently, we are not even aware that we rely on causalities. Now and then, however, when it is processed in terms of a familiar law, a particular action leads us to a built-in cause that seems to make no sense in the context of other actions. When we visualize a smile on Hamlet's face, clearly *not* addressed to another character, we normally attribute its source, by a natural causal law, to an amusing event that he is witnessing, say, a scene or a remark that he can be expected to find humorous; and we give it no second thought. But if Hamlet smiles during a tragic scene, we are puzzled. By the theatrical pact, we know that all story actions are purposeful, that Hamlet's amusement must have a reason. But which one? The built-in cause does not fit the context. The smile becomes a provocation, a signal for further investigation. "Why is Hamlet smiling?" leads to "Why is Hamlet amused?"—a question that, in the absence of a satisfactory answer, rips our complacent reliance on "natural" signs. Under the layer of causalities, granted a general validity, we perceive the operation of an individual psyche that cannot be accessed without additional information. And, to find that information, we begin to look for a commentary conveyed in the story world by truly intentional signs, including signs that characters use to communicate to each other their personal feelings, desires, and ideas.

Now, communication between characters, like all intentional signs, is not totally reliable. Characters, like people, can lie, and their accounts of their emotional or mental states, including reasons they give for their actions, can be deceitful. Yet, by a tacit convention of theatre, we must assume that, unless we are otherwise informed, characters in the story are telling the truth. When Hamlet tells his mother that he feels anger and disgust, we believe that he really does feel anger and disgust. The exceptions are rare, in fact, scandalous and specifically signaled as such. When they lead to tragedy, like Iago's lies in *Othello*, we respond with outrage; in comedies, we may enjoy a feeling of mischievous complicity with dissimulating lovers; whatever the strategy, however, liars are marked as liars. No doubt it is also possible that characters waver in their opinions, fool themselves about their real emotions, or are not aware of hidden reasons for their actions. But such problematic states are also clearly marked, either by signs exchanged between characters or, as will be shown later, by signs directed toward the audience. In the absence of such marks, we take statements made by characters about reasons for their action, that is, cultural signs in the story world, to be as reliable as information provided by primary signs about actions in the story world.

There follows that communication within the story world fulfills a double cognitive function. It lets us know what the characters say or do, what their actions are. But, in an overwhelming majority of cases, it also tells us what they feel, want, or think, and why they act the way they do. Reaching beneath a behavioristic vision of story events, then beneath the second layer of "built-in" general causalities, signs exchanged between characters open a third dimension of personal psychology. They transform typical characters into complex individuals, and help to explain otherwise enigmatic actions. With their commentary on secret personalities and hidden motivations, they enable us to distinguish between natural signs and intentional signs, between truth and lies, between Hamlet's genuine and deceitful smiles. But they do more. Through their referential function, they also expand the story world beyond the temporal and spatial limits dictated by the constraints of the primary signs: they incite our imagination to recreate past events that cannot be perceived through the looking glass, to visualize events that cannot be shown on the stage. In short, with the magic of verbal signs, they supply theatre with the resources of literature.

No wonder, then, that traditional theatre has always so much relied on dialogue to tell its stories, and that dialogue remains a favored form of communication even among many avant-garde characters. But one can also appreciate why, eager to disassociate theatre from literature, many modern directors and actors rebel against the priority of words in communicating hidden meanings. Verbal tradition, from their perspective, hampers a truly creative exploration of other cultural systems that better serve theatrical practice: body language, clothes, pictorial representations, theatre clichés. Modernity on the stage involves today an intensive work with all such nonverbal signs, not only in order to supply a commentary to the audience, but also to vie with natural language when characters exchange information about events, emotions, or ideas that cannot be perceived directly.

For example, nonverbal signs would provide both commentary and information, though at the price of an anachronism, if Hamlet, when he first encounters his father's ghost, were to put on a black armband: to other characters, this sign would be showing his will to display a proper family mourning; to the audience, it would suggest Hamlet's basically conformist personality, perhaps a bourgeois mentality. By the same double function, in Daniel Mesguich's *Hamlet* (1986), when a silent Ophelia erotically assaults Laertes, she not only informs her brother about her sexual desire for him, but also directs the audience to perceive the incestuous climate of Elsinore. Whether bold or mild, such performance signs, added to the verbal text, justify the current acknowledgment of directors as prime supplies of stage commentary, that is, as authorized interpreters of the story's meaning.

## Signs for the Audience: Commentary

Like commentary supplied by characters when they exchange information between themselves, commentary addressed from the stage to the audience has an important cognitive function: it expands our knowledge of the story world as it reveals unconscious motivations, evokes an atmosphere, suggests social conflicts or cultural backgrounds. Most of this cognitive enrichment, however, does not represent as such the primary goal of commentary for the audience. It is rather a by-product of commentary's main function: to clarify those features of the story world that neither general causalities nor statements made by characters suffice to explain. In other terms, the basic purpose of commentary is not to add features to the story world but to supply answers for the questions "why?" that existing features keep on raising. By theatrical convention, we understand that Hamlet berates his mother *because* he really feels anger and disgust, but neither standard built-in causes of anger and disgust, nor Hamlet's words to Gertrude, offer precise reasons for his emotions. We do not know exactly why he is angry and disgusted, and this lack of explanation disturbs us.

Or at least some of us. My rhetorical *we*, here and elsewhere, obviously does not refer to all possible spectators. More modestly, *we* stands only for those spectators who want to understand the meanings of the story. But even these spectators have varying expectations. Some are curious by temperament, others are passive and satisfied with ready-made explanations. All believe in some general laws ruling human behavior, but their grasp of these laws varies considerably in nature and sophistication. Many performances, trying to please passive audiences and minimize occasions to wonder "why?", thus offer stories with an abundance of built-in causalities corresponding to most widely acknowledged laws. Broadway productions, among others, favor characters who, however contrived the plot, behave predictably in terms of psychological clichés. Wives lie because they are unfaithful, husbands throw tantrums because they are jealous, lovers separate because of family responsibilities; the rich are eccentric because they are bored, or nasty because they are greedy, or unhappy because money doesn't bring happiness; sacrifice evidences generosity, success rewards hard work, and so forth. Melodramas and light comedies feed on such stuff. But even a performance of *Hamlet* need not be problematic. For many spectators, anger and disgust are natural feelings like love, ambition, envy, or greed; as such they need no explanations; and they fully account for Hamlet's action, leaving no opening for further "why?" questions. Such spectators are content to be entertained, or moved, by a story that takes them to an imaginary world where people behave in the same way as they think people behave in their real world.

For other spectators, however, the tritest performances tend to become problematic. A long practice of theatre surely contributes to this loss of innocence. But personality also plays a role. Individual history, profession, cultural interests, perhaps a perverse bend of the mind, sensitize such spectators to contradictions, ambiguities, disguises. Beneath supposedly natural actions, and overtly stated motivations, they learn to suspect unconscious drives or complexes, covert social prejudices, deeply buried causes that successive "why's" must try to identify. *They* want to know why Hamlet feels anger and disgust. Or why he could be amused by a tragic scene. Or why he hesitates to kill Claudius. And so, dismissing easy causalities and explicitly stated reasons, they scrutinize the performance in order to find signs which, in the form of a commentary on Hamlet's story, could assist them to answer all their "why's." True, not all of us who form the rhetorical *we* always react like these fanatics of the "why?" Sometimes we share the passivity or indifference of Broadway audiences. When we go to theatre, we expect to follow a good story, but we also want to see *performances*; we look for emotional purges, or aesthetic satisfaction, or ritual communion; we like to discharge social or family obligations. As a rule, however, when a story does interest us, we do ask "why's" when our curiosity is not fully satisfied, and watch for commentary signs that could help us to answer our questions.

Such commentary signs clearly must belong to cultural systems commonly used for communication. But they are addressed specifically to the audience, not to the characters. They trigger an intermittent communication between the performance and those spectators who notice the presence of cultural signs that are deliberately produced for them and that they proceed to decode. The notion of such a communication presents no real difficulty. However, it raises two theoretical questions: Who is really responsible for the production of signs that we attribute to the performance? And are these signs communicated consciously?

The first question has no simple answer. One may claim that final responsibility rests with the director who interprets the story and decides what commentary is needed to sharpen its meaning; or with actors or technicians who actually produce commentary signs; or with a social ideology that commands the director's interpretation. In reality, various spectators locate the source of production in various combinations of these agents, depending on individual perception of specific signs. For purposes of brevity and clarity, however, it is convenient to subsume all the possible producers under the concept of the directorial function, whoever may be carrying it out; or, more succinctly, to agree that all commentary for the audience is communicated by the "director," a single person or a collective. It is the formula we shall adopt here, while keeping in mind that the term "director" refers to the actual source of staging decisions rather than to a professional title.

The second question, whether commentary signs are produced consciously as such, echoes the question about the intentionality of primary stage signs, and can be answered in the same spirit. We noted that, when an actor stumbles and there are no reasons to believe that it is an accident, spectators must assume that he stumbles on purpose so that the mirror-image character will be visualized in the act of stumbling. In the same way, when we identify a commentary sign, and there are no obvious reasons to explain it by accident or chance, we must attribute it to the director's design to help us interpret the story. And, indeed, in actual theatre practice, with few exceptions, all signs addressed to the audience are received, when they are recognized as such, as if they were consciously intentional.

A different problem, more pragmatic in nature, results from the fact that all cultural signs, including commentary signs addressed to the audience, must always also serve on the stage as primary signs yielding the mirror-image vision of the referential world. Any directorial comment on the story must therefore be integrated into that story as one of its features and justified by the fictional logic. In most cases, this dual function of a feature of the imaginary world, visualized as a part of that world but also decoded as a commentary on the meaning of that world, creates no special difficulty. We deal easily with a similar situation when, visualizing verbal or nonverbal information exchanged between characters, we process these exchanges on two separate levels, considering them as communication that takes place between characters in the story, but also as a source of additional knowledge about these characters and their story. Most directorial commentary can be similarly processed as a feature of the imaginary world *and* a source of additional knowledge about that world. Mother Courage's exaggerated manifestations of greed, inspired by Brechtian "alienation," serve to convey a vision of the protagonist that fits within the logic of the story, but also inform us that war profiteering is bad. In some cases, however, signs designed by the director to offer commentary may strain, as features of the story world, the internal coherence of that world. Such instances occur particularly in avant-garde performances, reflecting the growing role of the directorial function; and since they could multiply in the future, they deserve a closer observation.

Let us imagine that we are attending an avant-garde Freudian performance of *Hamlet*. In our mental Elsinore, while Hamlet berates Gertrude with anger and disgust, we notice his display of cultural signs of lust and guilt: hands straining to caress his mother's body, face contorted by desire and horror. At the same time, shadowy shapes of a phallus and scissors appear on the wall over the bed. A simplistic example, no doubt, but it will serve as a telling caricature of more sophisticated versions of similar staging strategies. If we know well the codes of body language and facial expressions, and are familiar with the Freudian symbolic system, we shall acknowledge we are offered a directorial reference to Hamlet's incestuous passion for Gertrude. We shall deduce that he is suffering from the Oedipus complex, or at least that the director's commentary suggests that we reach that conclusion. One of our "why's" might be thus answered: Hamlet's anger and disgust are caused by an acute case of a complex that, since Freud, has been made into a law of psychological disorders.

Of course, we may disbelieve that law and hence, while understanding it, we could reject the director's Oedipal explanation of Hamlet's behavior. We would then have to look for other answers to the "why?" Or we may suspect the director of playing games, offering the Freudian commentary in a parodist spirit to amuse or to deceive us, perhaps to conceal a different interpretation, accessible to initiated spectators, say, the vision of Hamlet as a homosexual. It is also possible that some spectators would not know Freud at all, or at least not the Oedipus complex theory, and thus miss the director's signs. But these are the perils of all communication. They can undermine the efficiency of commentary, not its function. A more basic problem is that the Oedipus complex, while providing an answer to one "why," does not offer a final cause. An inquisitive spectator might want to know why Hamlet is afflicted with the complex, and then the why of the proposed cause, and so forth. The ensuing succession of "why's" will keep postponing a fully satisfactory understanding of *Hamlet*, though not infinitely, as shall be seen.

So much for our commentary signs decoded as such. But what happens to them when they are processed as primary signs? Hands, face and shapes on the wall, visualized as factual features of the story world, add to our knowledge of Hamlet and Elsinore. But what? Surely they are not perceived as intentional communication signs exchanged in the story. Hamlet cannot have conscious intentions to use hands and face to tell Gertrude about his lust for her; an Oedipus complex must be unconscious. And walls normally do not communicate messages, unless inspired by God or supernatural powers; but in *Hamlet* the ghost speaks with his own voice, not with shapes on a wall. Hamlet's hands and face, and shapes on the wall, must be then perceived not as signs but as *natural* features of the story world, and hence as results of some built-in causes ruled by natural laws. For Hamlet, this perception creates no logical problems. Educated in Freudian laws, we accept that the Oedipus complex, by an established causality, produces unconscious gestures and expressions that manifest incestuous lust and guilt. But the shapes on the wall? How do they fit? How can they be inserted in a coherent imaginary world?

No agency can be assumed to have produced them. No acceptable built-in causes can account for their presence. No shapes on the wall appear in the real world, hence no natural causalities can be applied to their presence in the imaginary world. True, *Hamlet* also has a ghost, and we do not much believe in ghosts; but, by a long tradition, the appearance of ghosts in legends and fiction has been attributed an acceptable a built-in cause: an irregular death that must be avenged or redeemed. But shapes on a wall? And any other bizarre occurrence that, placed in the story world by a daring director, cannot be explained in terms of general laws in which we believe, that is, which has no recognizable built-in cause? Must we renounce rational answers to the question "why," and posit that the story world is ruled by magic? There would be some logic in that solution, since the story world is always fictional, and many fictions involve magic. In some cases, then, magic will provide a satisfactory cause for otherwise inexplicable events. But in others, including *Hamlet*, recourse to magic would destroy the coherence of the fictional world because nothing in it suggests the presence of magic.

There is another and much simpler answer. As noted above, and as most seasoned spectators learn from experience, the iconicity of primary signs is often subverted by "poetic" symbols. We have no problem identifying a plastic slab as the sign for a table, an altar, a throne, or a rampart, and concretizing it with appropriate added features in the imaginary world. Within the same frame of theatrical poetry, a phallus and scissors would be perceived, at least by some spectators, as primary symbols for lust and guilt. By poetic subversion of iconicity, the shapes on the wall on the stage would thus be concretized, by the operation of the primary system, not as their mirror images but as manifestations of the presence of lust and guilt in Gertrude's bedroom. As such, they would not say anything directly about Hamlet's feelings; but they would evoke an Oedipal atmosphere in the room: a very coherent feature in *Hamlet*'s fictional world. Indeed, in fictional worlds, by a well-established law, characters project their emotions on their surroundings; and, by that law, the appearance of an Oedipal atmosphere in Gertrude's bedroom has an acceptable built-in cause: a surge in Oedipal feelings of Hamlet. At this point, the function of our cultural signs as features of the imaginary world coincides with their function as commentary about the meaning of the story.

This example illustrates how all commentary signs operate and how they can be grafted on the primary signs without undermining the coherence of the story world. No wonder then that modern directors, determined to control the reception of their performances, indulge in many forms of commentary to coach spectators in the search of meanings. Addressing cultural signs to the audience, they tell it directly how the story should be interpreted for the same reason that novelists insert their own commentary in their fictional texts: to influence the fate of their work after it is surrendered to the public. In the last analysis, however, each spectator, like each reader, decides alone whether the story has indeed a meaning, and what it could be.

## 4. The "Absent" Cause: Point and Meaning of Story

Let us recapitulate. No story told with signs supplies its full meaning. However skillful the storyteller, the story world always needs to be concretized in the mind of the receiver of signs, and completed in that process. In theatre, multiplying primary signs increases information about the surface features of the story world: outside appearance of characters and their surroundings, physical and verbal action. Through built-in causalities, these features generate a layer of "natural" causes, not visible but deduced from those story events that can be explained by general laws: an automatic cognitive gain. But some causes are problematic or elusive, concealed in individual psyches or reaching the realm of speculation. Grafted on primary signs, cultural signs serve to suggest what these causes might be. Many absent causes are thus identified by verbal and nonverbal signs with which characters communicate in the story, revealing emotional or ideological reasons for their action. But some actions are unconscious, caused by forces that control characters without their knowledge. Thus new questions "why" arise. To answer them, directors and actors have recourse to a special category of cultural signs that they address directly to the audience. These signs, in the form of a commentary on the story, suggest where to look for more built-in causalities in order to answer an ever-receding succession of "why's." But, as we now shall see returning to our staging of *Hamlet*, at some point the performance runs out of answers.

The bedroom scene, as interpreted above, has generated several links in the causal chain: Hamlet berates his mother because he feels anger and disgust; he experiences these feelings because of his lust and guilt; and his lust and guilt result from a classical case of Oedipus complex. But this answer is not final. It begs the next question: *why* is Hamlet afflicted with the Oedipus complex? No doubt, by Freudian causality, because he is shocked back and locked into the Oedipal stage. But why this shock? A directorial commentary, using crude signs, could suggest as an answer that the carnal relationship between Claudius and Gertrude reenacts for him the primitive Scene. But why does he experience that relationship in the form of the Primitive Scene? Because an uncle is a substitute father, and, as appropriate commentary signs can indicate, Hamlet sees his uncle acting like a father in the mother's bed. But why should Claudius be Hamlet's uncle rather than an unrelated prince? Because it says so in the story. But why does the story say so?

At this point, the causal chain reaches the boundaries of the story world. Why a story is the way it is can only be explained, outside that story, by the fiat of the storyteller. We know that Shakespeare did not totally invent Hamlet's story; he reworked the legend of a historical figure that had inspired other texts before his. Why did he chose to write a version that stresses that Claudius is Hamlet's uncle? To look for an answer, we must interrogate Shakespeare and his time, and search for reasons in personal, social, or cultural circumstances. A similar move from fictional to real world is needed to answer questions raised by a specific performance. To account for a director's choice of a Freudian commentary, and the staging of phallus and scissors as poetic icons of incest, we shall have to cross the boundaries of performance as a text. Why should a director single out the Oedipus complex among all possible causes of Hamlet's behavior? Because he or she believes it to be the most suitable explanation. But why this belief? Nothing in the performance can explain it. The director's reasons, like Shakespeare's, can only lie in his or her own real world.

Another staging of the bedroom scene could yield other causal sequences but no better answers to the final "why?" A different director could choose, for example, to arrange primary and cultural signs in a way to stress the impact of historical tensions. In this version, Hamlet feels anger and disgust because Gertrude has married a "vice of kings," a "murderer," and a "villain." And why is Claudius thus branded? Because he "stole" the crown by killing the old king. But why is this killing wrong when killing other kings raises no problems? Because it did not take place in a fair fight. Why is that wrong? Because it violates the feudal code of honor. And why is that wrong? Because it manifests a new spirit oriented by individual values. But why hate Gertrude as much as Claudius? Because her marriage, as a legitimate queen, sanctions the replacement of feudalism by the new spirit. And why would Hamlet find that spirit wrong? Because it is morally, socially, and politically rotten, promoting slyness, decadence, and bourgeois values. How do we know it? Because Shakespeare and the director tell us it is so. And what are their reasons to feel that way? Neither text nor performance offer an answer. The pursuit of causalities in the historical version opens again on motivations that are located outside the story.

One could object that a single scene never accounts for a full meaning of a play. My argument certainly can be faulted for anchoring the chain of causes in only one scene. A coherent performance of *Hamlet*, one could argue, involves many related causes which, through their interaction within the story, must converge on one precise final cause that will account for all of them. But will that cause be really final? What will happen when our imaginary staging of the bedroom scene is integrated into a coherent interpretation of all main characters and actions in *Hamlet*? Shall we obtain a final meaning? André Green's *Hamlet et **Hamlet*** is exemplary in that sense because it expands the Freudian reading to the entire structure of the text, including its theatrical references.[9] Yet, to find the ultimate reason for Shakespeare's intentions, he reaches beyond the story into the playwright's personal history and problems. And what obtains for the text obtains also for a performance. Let us develop our imaginary historical interpretation, adding directorial commentary to verbal indications in the dialogue.

With standard primary and cultural signs, such a staging will strongly contrast two generations: parents and children. Among the older generation, three male "power" characters instruct the young:

Hamlet's father, Claudius, and Polonius. But they offer three different social models. Old Denmark embodies the figure of feudal warrior king; he stands for strength, prowess with the sword, trust in loyalty, concern for his kingdom. In contrast, Polonius manifests the familiar signs of bourgeois mentality: a comfortable body, a sense for the pragmatics, faith in reason and cleverness, and interest in family matters. Posited in between, Claudius: proudly bearing the insignia of his new royalty, he betrays by posture, gestures, facial expression, and voice his affinity with Polonius; he is sly and acutely aware of his self-interest; he prefers poison, a decadent weapon, to the noble sword. An appropriate staging further suggests that the entire feudal age has passed away with old Denmark; only its ghosts still haunt the young generation, deploring the criminal act by which new bourgeois rulers overthrew the old order. Under Claudius, the Machiavellian principles prevail: sophisticated amorality, recognition of individual ambition, practice of political intrigue, a touch of hedonism, promotion of arts, and respect for bourgeois policies of profitable peace. The commentary suggests that this performance of the Renaissance drama reenacts the drama of the Renaissance.

To this rotten state of affairs, three young men are brought from outside in order to set things right, to restore the golden (feudal) past: a typical strategy of heroic tales. Two fail in their mission: Laertes and Hamlet. Laertes, made up to resemble his father Polonius, replaces him as a middle-class figure: strong family ties, respect for education, popularity among commoners, a bent for conspiracy. He has learned swordplay but smears his blade with poison. A gentrified bourgeois, a second-generation nobleman, he reverts to his bourgeois nature under stress, and achieves nothing. Hamlet, whom Claudius calls his son, has the same appearance as Claudius, and a similar duality.

As a blood prince, he is as problematic as Claudius is as a king. From feudal paternal origins, he draws pride, loyalty, and prowess with the sword. He dispatches the crafty Polonius, setting some things right, then kills the upstart Laertes and the "villain" Claudius. But he takes his time. For, tainted champion of the old order, he lacks its single-mindedness. Already partly bourgeois, he shares with Laertes new manners and education, and with Claudius dissimulation and private passions. He thinks and talks too much, knows theatre too well for a feudal lord. Worse: he disregards caste barriers and, like his mentor/father Yorick, a "fool" who moves across classes, he measures all men by their wits. All sorts of cultural signs show that Hamlet's madness stands for the folly of the Renaissance, the rot that he was to clean out. So, despite his service to feudalism, Hamlet is out—and tragedy is in. Like many tragic heroes, he cannot be fully trusted.

This leaves the third young man: Fortinbras. And Fortinbras fulfills the mission. He is the son that Old Denmark should have had. Appearing clad in the ghost's bloody armor, he replaces the unreliable Hamlet. A ruler by birth, a rough warrior, dedicated to the aggrandizement of his kingdom, he will restore a feudal Denmark, bring back the old order to society, straighten out its problems. Under him, one feels, each man will do what he is expected to do, without asking foolish questions.

The surprisingly harsh fates of Gertrude and Ophelia then become justified. The queen is guilty because, married to Claudius, she both inspires and legitimates the criminal transition from feudal to bourgeois age. She renounces honor and, enjoying the royal bed and courtly pleasures, she endorses the sensual Renaissance spirit. Her example disorients and corrupts young women around her. No wonder that Hamlet is shocked by her changed behavior, especially a blatant sexuality. His real target, however, is general hedonism that replaces the sense of duty. As for Ophelia, she is shown as a silly imitation of Gertrude: same fashionable dresses, same hairdo, similar gestures and voice inflections. She adopts Gertrude's Renaissance license, forsakes virtue, invites seduction. But there is a darker side to Ophelia, a troubled split personality. As Polonius's daughter and Laertes's sister, she participates in her family's assault on the old feudal principles, and seeks to transgress social boundaries. Her wild dream of a marriage with the crown prince manifests the ambition of rich bourgeois girls who fancy marrying into nobility. Gertrude is a traitor, Ophelia must be mad. The reborn old-style society has no place for either of them.

There is little point continuing this expansion in more detail. Let us simply note that, strengthening coherence, Guildenstern and Rosencrantz act like amoral Renaissance figures rather than like obedient courtiers manipulated by political power; that the grave digger philosophizes like a humanist; that the play within the play, with the metacommentary on theatre, serves further to denounce a deceitful Renaissance culture wherein art and masklike appearances substitute for truth. Altogether, blanking out ambiguities, these features yield a tightly knit network of causalities, converging on a single total cause: *Hamlet*'s story is the way it is because it dramatizes an important historical moment—the time when the last phase of the feudal society shifted into the early phase of the bourgeois society. But that total cause is not the final cause.

Why indeed was Shakespeare interested in the transition from feudalism to bourgeoisie, why did he censure it in his story, canceling its results by the magic of fiction? And why did our imaginary director support that interpretation through stage commentary? No doubt they had their own reasons, not necessarily the same. But what were they? What could they be? What are my own reasons for choosing that particular interpretation for my hypothetical staging? Like questions about the single bedroom scene, the "why's" generated by an answer that is drawn from the entire performance, taking into account all features of the story, still open on an "absent" cause, a cause located outside the performance. We may study thoroughly a performance, understand its articulations and potential interpretations, but its final explanation eludes us as long as we remain within its boundaries, leaving us without "cause" or "meaning." Indeed, in our minds, the frustrating question "Why is the story (or the performance) the way it is?" merges with the question "What does it really mean?" In our final answer, we merge the final "absent" cause with the final "meaning," equating "why" with "what."

In fact, of course, few final meanings of a performance are ever proposed. Most spectators and critics, aware of the failure of internal causalities to lead to the "absent" cause, are reluctant to turn to their own guesses in order to find a valid meaning for stories produced by others, or to turn to the producers' intentions, always hidden and perhaps irrelevant. Some readily concede that they cannot get any meaning, that they find the performance to be meaningless, that it "makes no sense." Others, more sophisticated, appeal to relativity to justify giving up their search for definite meanings since there are always many meanings. In the chaotic reality outside the performance, they claim, lies a multitude of possible "absent" causes, all equally valid. Any choice of one over the others must then be always reductive. These spectators and critics favor "neutral" stagings where, in the same spirit of relativity, ambiguities are retained and potential meanings are multiplied at the expense of coherence. Still others reach the same conclusion but from more radical theoretical premises. In their opinion, looking for final causes is always futile and hence wrong methodology. For them, the only "meaning" of a performance is the ephemeral totality of that performance, autonomous, unique, and experienced as such by the spectators. Irreducible to any explanation, it is justified by its own existence.

Yet many of us, addicted to explanations, keep on searching for causes and formulating meanings. To satisfy that yearning, we have the choice between three basic strategies. By the first, and most trivial, we interrupt the sequential "why's" at a point where the answers can still be deduced from the performance signs. For example, without looking farther, we explain the meaning of *Hamlet* by the Oedipus complex, or by stresses resulting from the ascendancy of the bourgeois spirit in England. Many such meanings are proposed in scholarly works and media, often answering only a couple of "why's." That strategy is not devoid of pragmatic value; it enables us to suggest a variety of intermediate meanings without needing to formulate a final justification; it aborts the frustrating quests for the "absent" cause. But it has little theoretical interest.

The second strategy deliberately situates the "absent" cause in the world of the producers of performances: playwrights, directors, actors. Treating the performance as their combined "speech act," we can process it as a "natural" sign of conditions that produced it, that is, as the result of built-in causalities that add up to a final cause. Reading *Hamlet* as Shakespeare's work, we would apply our knowledge of laws that rule the production of dramatic texts; and, depending on what law we uphold, we would explain that Shakespeare—unconsciously— wrote *Hamlet* to relieve his own Oedipal troubles, as Green tries to demonstrate, or that he needed to solve some social problems of his times by projecting them on a fictional medieval Denmark.

The latter approach, properly sociocritical, would point to the emergence of conflicts in Elizabethan England. It would note that its dynastic changes in fact manifested a more profound transformation brought about by the rising middle class. The resulting unconscious tensions between the old and the new, would claim an adept of so- ciocriticism, were both disguised and resolved unconsciously by Shake- speare in the form of a fictional rehabilitation of past values, a mythical restoration of feudalism. The sociocritic would grant that Claudius and Hamlet were certainly closer to Shakespeare than Fortinbras, but he would argue that the logic of unconscious fictional projection requires the playwright to glorify the past and censure the present regardless of his personal feelings. In fact, by the same logic, most ambiguities in *Hamlet* would be explained by the need to defend feudal values in which Shakespeare himself no longer believed. The "absent" cause, social tensions in Elizabethan England, would thus yield a general meaning that can account both for converging and contradictory struc- tures of the drama. Of course, sociocriticism may be questioned as a law of dramatic production, different tensions can be singled out as the "absent" cause, one can even translate social problems into political lessons consciously offered by Shakespeare. The world of any play- wright is always very complex and hence always forms a very fertile source of meanings.

By the same strategy, substituting performances for texts but posit- ing similar laws of their production, we would explain a modern staging of *Hamlet* by the director's response to his or her own psychic obsessions or to unconscious tensions in his or her society. My hypothetical version of a sociocritical performance of *Hamlet*, concretized on a real stage, could surely be traced to an "absent" cause in my own unconscious or in the unconscious of my social group, yielding two different meanings. But there is no need to speculate. I shall attempt, in the next section, to apply this approach to a real production of another Shakespeare drama, *Richard II*, showing that its transformation of textual references, generating a new meaning, can be attributed to a contemporary tension in the French cultural milieu.

But a meaning related to conditions of production is not always found to be totally satisfactory. It does tell us why texts and performances are produced, and what meaning they could have for their producers, but not what meaning they may have for us. Genetic strategy works for genetic studies, expanding our knowledge of creative processes in theatre. It also works for those among us who give priority to intended meanings, whether conscious or not, and thus satisfy both a nostalgic desire for fixed meanings and a sense of loyalty toward original creators. But seekers of genetic meanings do not fully respond to theatre as a speech act communication: content to understand the sender's message, they do not relate it to their own reality, that is, they do not react as intended receivers. They seem to assume that theatre merely serves to solve tensions in a playwright's or director's unconscious problems, and, more generally, that theatre production always originates in the need to solve problems, that it is always oriented by a practical goal. The meaning they attribute to texts or performances is grounded in the fictional solution of such problems at the time they occur, without regard for other meanings that could be formulated by readers or spectators.

The pragmatic orientation of this strategy has terminological implications. The question "why?" that leads to the determination of genetic "causes" could indeed be more appropriately rephrased, from that perspective, as the question "what for?" that leads to the determination of "goals" rather than "causes." The fictional solution of a problem, disclosed by genetic strategy as the goal of production, corresponds better to the notion of the "point" of a text or performance than to its "meaning." By that logic, the term "meaning" as such should be rather reserved for those final answers that, by a third strategy, spectators derive from their own world, in full response to the communication of the fictional world. But there is no point suggesting a reform of the language.

The third strategy, because it better meets the speech-act goals of communication, is somewhat solipsist. It locates the "absent" cause of a theatre work in our personal vision of our own world. By that strategy, as we reach the end of answers supplied by performance signs, and concretize a vision of the story world that only lacks a final meaning, we turn that story world into an special global sign intended for us as receivers. For example, after decoding *Hamlet*'s primary and cultural signs, and concretizing in our mind a relatively complex world of Hamlet, we attribute to that fictional world the status of a sign that we are invited to decode to obtain its meaning. By this strategy, as I conceive it, we assume that, as a global sign, Hamlet's world refers to still another world—a potential world that must have a meaning for us, a world that we can identify as a potential version of our world. Obviously, then, in order to decode Hamlet's world as a sign, and obtain as referent a potential vision of our world, we must also assume that a special code provides for this type of operation. And obviously that special code necessarily determines a special semiotic system: a system that enables fictional worlds to operate as signs of potential real worlds. I shall call it "the system of world visions."

In semiotic terms, the signs of that system can be defined as all fictional visions of a world, that is, all visions of worlds communicated in fiction. Among them, many are story worlds offered by theatre performances, including Hamlet's world. Each of these worlds, within this system, is perceived as such only as a signifier; by itself, it merely *is*, without referring to anything; in order to operate as a sign, it must be associated with a signified, in this case defined, as we shall see, as a certain class of possible worlds. The association between signifier and signified is provided by the special code of the system of world visions. It is a cipher code, establishing, for all its signs, a single principle of association that can be formulated as follows: *Each vision of a fictional world*, that is, the signifier, is associated by convention with *all possible visions of the real world that need only a minimal transformation to achieve compatibility with the fictional world.*[10] This minimally transformed vision of the real world is only the signified of the sign. But, when the code is observed, the fictional world functions as a full sign; it then refers to a *specific* vision of the real world that requires a minimal transformation to be compatible with the fictional world. The referent of Hamlet's world, by this operation, is that vision of our own world that seems to us to be most compatible with Hamlet's world.

After we obtain a vision of Hamlet's world, we scan our mental vision of our world till we identify the version that best corresponds to Hamlet's world. This identification depends on many factors. It is relatively easy when the given performance of *Hamlet* yields for us a world similar to ours. A very different world might require, in order to achieve compatibility with ours, many radical transformations that could impede the entire process. Or: a world with incoherent or anachronistic features will demand more scanning than a world that is historically coherent. But the greatest influence is exerted by the nature of our individual vision of what our real world is, was, or should be. We may believe that our world is ruled by psychic complexes, or by social conflicts, or by random events; and, depending on our convictions, we shall be inclined to perceive good reasons why the corresponding vision of our world would indeed be closest to the fictional world.

Individual spectators might then give different meanings to Hamlet's story, drawing different "absent" causes from their own vision of reality. Indeed, by the logic of this strategy, the same causalities will operate in Hamlet's world as in a minimally transformed vision of our own world. Looking for causes, and reaching the boundaries of what the performance can tell us, we can move into the territory of our own general laws, and apply them safely to answer final questions about *Hamlet*. If, within our vision of our world, the Oedipal complex explains our behavior, then we shall accept that it also explains Hamlet's behavior. And why? Because we know that such is human nature. If we believe that our world is ruled by social conflicts, then social conflicts must also account for tensions in Hamlet's story. Why? Because we know that such is the nature of society. If our vision of the world were mainly made of random events, then we would interpret Hamlet's story as mainly a series of random events. Why? Because such is the nature of life. In each case, the meaning we give to our condition as human beings or social beings, and final causes that we attribute to our behavior, are projected as meaning or causes in Hamlet's world. But not as meaning or causes that the creators of that world might have had in mind, consciously or unconsciously. Resigned to the failure of a theatre performance to communicate final causes and meanings with its coded primary and cultural signs, we shift as it were to a different level of communication with a different code: we minimize the sender's intentions, focus on the receiver's processing of the message, and transform the fictional work into a true *opera aperta*.

By the same token, as we explain the world of fiction with general laws operating in our world, we generalize individual behaviors, motivations, and concepts. The mediating mental vision of a minimally transformed world stands for a class of possible visions of the real world; Hamlet stands for a class of human beings who generally behave like he does; social conflicts in *Hamlet* are assimilated to a class of basic social conflicts. As we keep on asking "why," our answers reach lofty levels of general statements about human nature, society, and the meaning of life. For practical reasons, we rarely move that far, preferring to stop at the level of causes that seem to suit our specific inquiry: a fleeting curiosity, a discussion, a newspaper review. But in most cases, books and dissertations excluded, our formulation of general meanings tends to take the form of stereotyped statements about human nature or society, worn out clichés of the *doxa*. At our most original, we produce paradoxical meanings which, in fact, either merely modify old clichés or propose new ones in the imitation of old models. The third strategy may best fulfill our need for a total understanding of theatre fiction, but it rarely yields most interesting explanations.

## 5. A Case Study: Mnouchkine's *Richard II*

There is no need to state in detail why a verbal account never faithfully conveys the experience of a live performance. Words, even supported with photographs, cannot communicate the visual dynamics of action on the stage, nor fully indicate how the referential story is visualized in the mind's eye. Besides, all sorts of subjective bias always distort the account, drawing attention to some features of the performance while downgrading others. In that sense, any description of a theatre production is already an interpretation, one among several transformations that attend theatre reception.

Yet, as a reception text, a verbal account forms an integral part of the entire theatrical process and, despite distortions, can contribute to a fuller understanding of a performance. This is particularly true when a classical text, expected to be known by the reader, and hence needing no explanation, receives an innovative staging that the reader might not have seen, or has partly forgotten, or found to be puzzling if not outrageous. In such cases, a verbal account can focus on those staging features that, at least in the writer's vision, best explain the originality of the performance, that is, its unique and unexpected character. By the same occasion, as some of these accounts have shown,[11] the overall semiotic strategy can be clarified, and related to ideological concerns of both producers and receivers. For the last purpose, involving the central notion of meaning, it is particularly interesting to examine a performance that, despite or because of its innovations, manages to capture public enthusiasm: an avant-garde play that is acknowledged as one of the small number of legendary *testi spettacolari*, points of reference that theatre amateurs recall with smug satisfaction or are embarrassed to have missed.[12]

For all these reasons I have chosen, in order to test my grammar of referentiality, to recreate from memory Arianne Mnouchkine's staging of Shakespeare's *Richard II*. It opened in 1982, at the Cartoucherie theatre in Vincennes, as the long awaited new show of the Théâtre du Soleil, a company reputed for its avant-garde style, a moderate leftist ideology, and the excellence of its performers. It was an instant hit, by all accounts *the* performance of the year in France. It moved to Avignon as the centerpiece of its festival, then back for another run in Paris. It was then succeeded by other Mnouchkine stagings of Shakespeare: *Twelfth Night* and *Henry V*, which used devices derived from *Richard II* but less successfully.

The key to *Richard II*'s success was, by consensus, Mnouchkine's bold decision to do what seemed unthinkable at the time: to stage a Shakespeare text in the style of the Kabuki performances.[13] Some Parisian spectators had already seen Japanese companies and could recognize the Kabuki style, even though they could not understand it; others were told by the media what they would see. The majority simply expected to be introduced to an exotic staging tradition, boldly grafted on a Shakespeare text also quite new to them.

And, as they were uncomfortably packed on wooden benches, but prepared to be amazed, this is what they perceived on a bright and nearly bare stage with a faintly oriental backdrop cloth. First, a noise: a clash of cymbals and a loud beating of drums, summoning the performers. In a single file, about ten of them ran in from the back, costumed like stereotyped images of samurai in ample gold, black, and red silk robes, curved swords at their sides; running in step, they twice circled the open space to the tune of the drums; then, facing the public, they formed a semicircle, alternately lowering and raising their (presumably) bowed legs under their concealing skirts, bobbing up and down in the rhythm of respiration, while their leader, identified later as Richard II, jumped onto a platform in the middle and froze in the hieratic stance of a Japanese warlord. Tableau vivant, silence, applause. Then the king, his chalk-white face slashed with red, shook his sword and, in well-articulated French, launched his opening speech. Shakespeare's words, in a modern and clear translation, began to weave their spell. Significantly, at no time was their delivery sacrificed to visual or sound effects. As the actors went into their strange movements, ritual shaking of arms or clever evocation of prancing horsemen, their voices declaimed each line with a neutral poise and precision worthy of the staid Comédie Française. Contrasting with the opaque signs of the Kabuki body language, natural language kept the communication channel open: the only stable, effective, and impressive support of the story, barely assisted by distinct fixed masks of alien faces. With one exception, about which more later, this is how the performance proceeded and ended.

By the primary iconic code, conventionally adjusted to translation paradoxes, verbal signs thus clearly referred, through names, titles, places, and events, to a story space located in medieval England, during the unfortunate reign of Richard II. But, by the same primary iconicity, all the other signs, especially costumes, gestures, postures, backstage sounds, and the rare props, pointed as systematically to another distinct space and time, the world of samurai, situated in some medieval Japan. Both spaces were unfamiliar to the Parisian spectators; they lacked exact temporal and geographical features; they had to be visualized as legendary rather than historical lands; but nonetheless they were sharply contrasted, as opposed one to the other as their insular locations, west of the European continent and east of Asia.

The potential disorientation created by this dual reference escaped neither Mnouchkine nor most theatre critics. They tried to dispel it by pointing to resemblances beyond the differences. Elaborating on Mnouchkine's suggestions, identifying specifically the two worlds as Plantagenet England and Ashikaga Japan, Claude Roy made a learned and persuasive case, in the illustrated *Double Page* program sold during the intermission, that both countries experienced, if at different times, the same dynastic power struggles and feudal family bloodbath.[14] From that perspective, Mnouchkine's placement of the story of Richard II in a different middle age was to enlighten rather than to confuse the audience; the Kabuki style was offering a proper visual *metaphor* for medieval England, and samurai were serving as fitting *symbolic* signs for the English lords. By that argument, while Shakespeare's text still played the dominant semiotic role, the massive subversion of strict iconicity with Kabuki stage symbols was justified by a thematic identity between two feudal societies.

But did the two spaces actually coalesce in one symbolic world of feudal decadence? In order to generate such a synthesis, the referential space of the Elizabethan drama would have to be metaphorically transformed by the audience into a half-English and half-Japanese hybrid space: a most difficult feat for most spectators. Besides, such an outcome could not claim to refresh Shakespeare's text; rather, it would modify thoroughly its meaning. If, on the other hand, no convergence of the two spaces occurred in the spectators' imagination, then no metaphor could operate successfully nor could the Kabuki forms be perceived as symbols of an English story; they would remain standard iconic signs of a Japanese society. The two worlds could still be compared and associated before or after the performance, but during the performance the feeling of schizophrenic disorientation would prevail. That neither hypothesis seemed to be confirmed by the audience's reaction indicates that the entire argument leaves much to be desired, that the spectators concretized neither two separate worlds nor a single hybrid world.

It is then understandable why, not content with the thematic justification of the dual referentiality, Mnouchkine and the critics offered yet another explanation. The recourse to the Kabuki style has been inspired, according to this version, by a general need to regenerate the worn-out staging conventions of the West. Adapting the formalist device of "ostranienie," that is, the creation of new forms that enable the artist to defamiliarize reality and endow it with a new look, Mnouchkine claimed to seek a new theatrical style in order to rejuvenate classical texts, that is, the reality with which the director deals in his or her artistic work. As such, this approach would not have been particularly original nor surprising. Many modern directors, at least since Brecht, have been searching for a new look in oriental, African, and folkloric theatrical practices. Yet the forced marriage between a wholesale import of Kabuki forms and a canonical Shakespearean text, without mediation or adaptation, would have been indeed quite a revolutionary concept. But did Mnouchkine really do what she proclaimed? Did she really rejuvenate *Richard II* with the Kabuki style?

There is no reason to suspect the sincerity of Mnouchkine's explanation. In fact, measuring the challenge inherent in such a radical project, she might have been genuinely tempted to demonstrate a great directorial *performance*, to offer an exceptional staging achievement. But why did she seek rejuvenation in borrowed forms rather than, as in her earlier productions, in her own formal innovations? Up until *Richard II*, her impatience with conventional styles had generated performances that struck blows at all traditions, attempting each time to be truly original. Flouting expectations was a distinct Mnouchkine quality, but there was no Mnouchkine style; and audiences were only prepared to be surprised. While *Richard II* managed very well to create that surprise effect, it did so however by giving up the iconoclastic treatment of forms. Instead of subverting theatre conventions qua conventions, it paid homage to the well-established Kabuki convention, however stilted it might have become in its own tradition. No doubt it was foreign to the Western audiences, but that very exoticism made the form of the "defamiliarizing device" more interesting than the world it was supposed to defamiliarize. The display of Kabuki style concealed rather than revealed a new vision of Shakespeare's drama. Paradoxically, the avowed strategy of putting "old wine in new bottles" drew attention to the bottles and away from the wine. Whatever Mnouchkine's intentions, her praxis downgraded the story and focused on the telling.

The "equal but separate" treatment of Shakespeare's verbal world and the world of Kabuki staging involved a similar paradox. On the one hand, it testified to great respect for the integrity of each set of signs, to the will to let each one tell its distinct story in its own mirror-image space. On the other hand, however, it deprived each world of an essential dimension. The Shakespeare story, communicated with words in the dialogue, lacked visible human support: actors, and hence characters, looked Japanese and not English. Conversely, actors or characters, while quite convincing in their Japanese appearance, were estranged from their statements that referred to English psyches and circumstances. True, the two worlds were admirably superposed, yielding a harmonious if dual total gestalt; but neither complemented the missing dimension of the other. To that extent, Mnouchkine created a two-headed monster, whose heads spoke at the same time but in different languages; and while their duet was certainly pleasing, it could not communicate a story as effectively as a single voice.

Both paradoxes reveal Mnouchkine's basic ambivalence about the role of the referential function. The strategy of "old wine in new bottles" and the "equal but separate" treatment shared a dichotomy between a declared desire to strengthen the communication of the story and an actual sabotage of that communication. A similar ambiguity seems to have motivated Mnouchkine's radical polarization of all primary signs, verbal and nonverbal, between minimal and maximal complexity. Actors, but only actors, were loaded with primary signs: extensive dialogues, powerful enunciation, expressive body language, stylized facial expressions, impressive costumes—all of them heightened by an exceptional level of achievement meeting the expectations of the performant function. In contrast, the simplicity of sets and props, at first reminiscent of Grotowski's practice of "poor theatre" but moving away from its total bareness, drew practically no attention, offered no information. The two stationary side walls had no marked reference, and changes in the backdrop cloth, alternating meaningless color patterns, merely indicated switches in location. Stylized seats, bed, and table had a vaguely Japanese look but appeared very briefly, as did a playful replica of a Loire valley type castle, a neutral cage, and equally neutral all-purpose blocks. In short, sets and props were neither rich nor coherent enough to point to any specific space: not medieval England, nor old Japan, nor even an avant-garde theatre stage.

As signs of ambient world, the minimal sets and props were thus suitable for any imaginary action, clearly a referential gain, but, by the same token, they offered no help in localizing that action in any precise imaginary world, a referential loss in this case. Indeed, appearing in such neutral surroundings, *Richard II*'s characters fully preserved their competing images as English lords and Japanese samurai, both powerfully conveyed by complex signs carried by actors, but neither profiting from reinforcement through other stage signs. Solicited to concretize two parallel but different worlds, or rather their two bare outlines, the majority of spectators faced the difficult task of following the action of two superimposed sets of characters, neither of which could be viewed as more real than the other, or inversely as a metaphor. In that sense, the performance visibly impeded a clear reception of any story, whether communicated by Shakespeare's words or by Kabuki signs or by their impossible combination. But then, the real point of the performance was quite different, involving a more subtle manipulation of both primary and cultural theatre systems.

In fact, indeed, contrarily to what Mnouchkine and critics have asserted, actors performing in the Kabuki style did not refer at all to Japanese samurai, could not be concretized as such by most audiences. Parisian spectators knew very well that Mnouchkine's actors, mainly French, were *not* genuine Kabuki actors. Their costumes, facial masks, gestures, and postures, perceived as primary signs, could only refer to the appearance and style of imaginary Kabuki actors who, in their function as characters, would be performing on an imaginary stage. By the strict operation of iconicity, despite the special nature of the verbal text, Mnouchkine's company merely *stood for* a Kabuki company. Whether Kabuki actors look in fact like samurai or not, whether they can stand for imaginary samurai, is a different matter that concerns cultural rather than primary signs of the performance; it applies to the interpretation but not the concretization of the referential Kabuki space; we shall return to it later. The troubling Shakespeare text, on the other hand, posed no iconic problem: most spectators, not versed in the formal constraints of real Kabuki performances, could readily accept that the imaginary Kabuki characters were acting out, in an imaginary Kabuki performance, *Richard II* translated into French. Such an event might be unlikely but is conceivable, whereas a vision of imaginary samurai bearing English names and speaking in French obviously would make no sense. In short, the Cartoucherie space essentially referred to a mirror-image space identified as a Kabuki stage.

By its overall primary code, Mnouchkine's *Richard II* thus offered a daring illustration of the respectable tradition of theatre within theatre, with a total coincidence of the frame play and the inserted play. The troubling dichotomy between referents of verbal and nonverbal signs, medieval England and feudal Japan, was dissolved in the logic of the inserted fictional play, that is, a Kabuki performance of *Richard II*. But this imaginary performance, in turn, generated its own mirror-image space, an imaginary Kabuki vision of an imaginary England; and in that third space, it told the story of Richard II. The French actor playing the role of a Kabuki actor was made to look like a Kabuki actor, and Richard II, played by the fictional Kabuki actor, looked like the

French actor with a Kabuki make up. Parisian spectators were simultaneously watching three activities: real events on the Cartoucherie stage, imaginary events taking place during an imaginary Kabuki performance, and imaginary events that this imaginary performance staged in an imaginary medieval England.

In the absence of clearly delineated frames, these three spaces had to coalesce in the spectators' vision. Much confusion would have been prevented had Mnouchkine drawn attention, as Brecht had done in *The Caucasian Chalk Circle*, to the play within play structure, placing some oriental-looking actors/spectators on the stage. But she did not. Maybe she was not aware of the basic nature of her strategy, maybe she did not care to clarify its aims, to explain why her imaginary Kabuki actors would indeed want to stage *Richard II* in French. At any rate, her performance deviated from the tradition of theatre within theatre, where the inserted play always clearly contributes to the understanding of the frame play, either as a feature of the main story (*Hamlet*), or as a figurative illustration (*The Caucasian Chalk Circle*), or as a commentary on meaning, say, theatricality (Corneille's *L'Illusion comique*). Mnouchkine's articulation of the two referential spaces had no referential justification: it was an arbitrary decision, adding nothing to the story, though quite fertile in *performance* potential. The frame play, the story of a Kabuki performance, might have used a Western text for the inserted play in order to create a strong effect of contrast, but any well-known French or English text would have done as well if not better than *Richard II*.

The choice of a Kabuki performance as topic of the frame play also evidences little regard for the referential function. For Western spectators, the main attraction of a Kabuki performance qua performance cannot lie in the decoding of its signs, nor in guessing at the story of its staging. Promoted as an exotic theatre convention, the Kabuki style appeals precisely by its exoticism, by its extraordinary and incomprehensible nature. Somewhat like a circus act, it is guaranteed to be an exceptional achievement by sole authority of its producers; the Western public, like the "good" circus public, gives up its own function as qualified judge. Besides, Kabuki forms, while recognized as cultural signs, cannot operate semiotically for an audience that knows none of their special codes. In Paris, these forms/signs could not be assessed as means of communication, nor could they help to interpret the story of their own production. It is even questionable whether, for most spectators, they evoked any cultural features of samurai, as critics claimed, and hence the mentality and rituals of feudal Japan. Perceived as opaque signifiers, they could only seduce, playing on nonreferential sources of appeal: demonstration of outstanding physical skills, striking aesthetic displays, masklike faces, stylized gestures and postures, unusual music. All of these features constitute, of course, common stimuli of the performant function. And all of them were manifested by the imaginary Kabuki performers, and admired by the public. Insofar as the frame play is concerned, it mattered little not only what Western play was performed by the Kabuki characters, but also in what exact style they performed it, as long as their performance offered *performances*.

The choice of *Richard II* as the play within the play, and the way in which it was performed by the imaginary characters, did not serve better the referential function. The story of Richard II, as told by Shakespeare, can be staged powerfully, generating great interest in the audience. But, for a French public, *Richard II* is not the most accessible of Shakespeare's plays. In the first place, it largely refers to totally unfamiliar matters. Many Parisian spectators, at one time or another, have read, or seen, or heard about *Hamlet*, or *Macbeth*, or *Romeo and Juliet*; but few have any knowledge of English kings, with the possible exception of Henry V and Richard III. The always problematic concretization of a referential story, drawing on information stored in memory, had thus to take place in a vacuum, without any solid support in History: at best, a frustrating process. In the second place, in contrast with other unfamiliar plays, such as *Twelfth Night*, *The Tempest*, or *The Taming of the Shrew*, *Richard II* does not build its referential world as it were from scratch, supplying itself all the needed information: it largely relies on the public knowledge of historical events, dynastic problems, laws of succession to the throne, Irish wars, and so forth. To reconstitute, from fragmentary cross-indications, all such needed and yet missing background, would have again demanded considerable attention and effort on the part of a French audience, even if that audience had not been distracted by a dazzling display of Kabuki forms. It would also have required a strong motivation. But while the Cartoucherie public had been very eager in the past to see fresh images of the French Revolution, however distorted, or scenes from the life of immigrant workers, however biased, it was not much interested in the story of a long-dead English king.

One may assume that Mnouchkine was aware of that problem, as well as of the trap created by performant achievements of the Kabuki frame play. True, as such, the use of foreign stage signs does not always impede the communication of a story; they can be "domesticated" or distorted in a way to become comprehensible to the public, as an American *Kabuki Othello* demonstrated with some success. But Mnouchkine wanted to preserve all the exotic power of the Kabuki style. To protect the play within the play, she chose instead to magnify the role of Shakespeare's verbal signs, having them delivered as clearly as possible, without contamination by the confusing but overwhelming Kabuki signs. Each word enunciated by the imaginary performers was made to stand out distinctly, each figure of speech unfolded carefully its fragile or violent poetry. As a result, both the beauty of the text, and the drama of its story, could have been expected to come across strongly, competing effectively with the performant appeal of the Kabuki style. But these expectations failed to materialize; the text failed to generate a sustained interest in the fate of Richard II. In fact, the outstanding delivery of the text turned it into a poetry recital rather than into a theatrical dialogue. The audience was given a choice between two *performances*: beauty of Kabuki forms, and beauty of Shakespeare's text. To salvage referentiality, Mnouchkine was forced to break the constraints of her dual iconic system; and she did, at the expense of coherence.

For suddenly, in the last act, the primary signs dissolved, and the frame story of a Kabuki performance of *Richard II* was suspended. A naked man in a cage, under cruel spotlights, appeared in the center of the stage. During one unforgettable scene, waiting for his assassins to come, he delivered alone in an empty space unfortunate Richard's final soliloquy about life, death, and the vanity of human plans. For a short time, before the Kabuki convention resumed, words, gestures, body language, and props converged on an exemplary figure with a powerful referentiality. In the audience's vision, not an actor but a man embodying all mankind denounced and accepted his fate. There was nothing kingly in his appearance, nothing English in his surroundings. Estranged from any historic context, and the story of Richard II, the naked man in the cage stood for all men stripped to their bare condition, constrained, and about to die. As a universal sign, he was sure to move deeply any but the most blasé audience. He did not fail to impress Parisian spectators, eager to wallow in humanist universals, away from uncomfortable History. Sweating their purge, emotional needs satisfied, they felt they had participated in a great theatre experience. With a good conscience, they could return to the dazzling *performance* of Mnouchkine's actors, and the exotic appeal of Kabuki forms. The *Richard II* they saw, and remembered, was both moving and beautiful, even though it did not mean much.

With the exception of the death scene, there were indeed very few cultural signs that could have given meaning to Richard's story. Various signs in the dialogues, even in French translation, could have suggested an interpretation of the story, accounted for the king's or Bolingbroke's mystifying behavior. But most such references inevitably escaped a Parisian public which, as already mentioned, is not familiar with most semiotic systems operating in Shakespeare's society. Verbal signs, as often the case, needed support or clarification by nonverbal signs, and obviously the Kabuki signs could not provide it. A few could be decoded, such as the shaking of arms as a sign of furor, but they did not go far in answering questions "why?" The overwhelming mass of gestures, postures, facial expressions, costumes, colors, and sounds formed a bright but totally opaque pattern of features, without indication as to which ones, if any, served as cultural signs.

Still, a couple of systems emerged from the opacity of the Kabuki style: intonations and lights. But, with the exception of her use of glaring light to suggest the total truth of the naked man in the cage, Mnouchkine systematically minimized potential contributions of light. Her generally bright light, required by the logic of iconicity, displayed no meaningful contrasts, evoked no coded variations of emotions. Nor was any special meaning projected by the modulation of voices, no special intonation communicated nuances of surprise, negation, irony, stress, embarrassment, sexual interest, or social manners. Neither Shakespearean nor directorial commentary could be heard in the pitch of voices and the rhythm of enunciation. The few spectators who were searching for a meaning received only primary signs that referred to two equally gratuitous sets of surface events: gestures and moves of an imaginary company of Kabuki actors, and actions in an imaginary English society. On one level, they were thus reduced to appreciating the outward forms of a pseudo-Kabuki performance, on the other, to appreciating the formal quality of a dialogue exploding with poetry. Frustrated in their quest for meaningful references, they had to join the captivated majority of the audience by switching attention to the achievements of the performant function. The Cartoucherie's public loved the show but, I suspect, with the exception of one pathetic scene, experienced it as a beautiful tale full of sound and fury, and signifying nothing.

This overall favoring of *performances* at the expense of the story, while not accidental, cannot be attributed to a deliberate decision of the director. One must trust Mnouchkine's stated intention to revive *Richard II* through a new staging style, to extract new meanings from its text. It is likely, however, that Mnouchkine, like many traditional and avant-garde directors today, yielded to a general pressure in contemporary society to stress performances over references. Instinctively, by osmosis with the ambient culture, she probably sensed that it is better to show than to tell, that showing needs not to tell anything significant, that telling is superfluous and largely unreliable. The current primacy of visual media no doubt contributes to that feeling, but it is doubtful that it creates it. For images can also tell stories, and film or mime has as much telling power as literature or theatre. It is important to note, however, that images, even when they operate as signs, have a much greater potential than words to serve as vehicles for the performant function. Because they elicit direct responses to aesthetic, erotic, or violent features, images encourage producers of shows to appeal directly to such responses without a semiotic mediation, to entertain without communicating meanings. What happened on Mnouchkine's stage, and has been happening for some time in Broadway musicals, can in that sense be best related to increasingly popular forms of sheer showing in comic strips, or French BDs, where flat, incoherent, and often banal stories serve to support truly impressive graphics; there is a similar lack of interest for meaning, a similar indifference to semiotic processes.

To check that hypothesis, and explore it further, let us return to Mnouchkine's *Richard II* and retrieve, from the rubble of its referentiality, the few references that should have survived the competition offered by *performances*. By the logic of our theatre grammar, four sets of signs, overcoming cultural communication problems, had the potential to generate distinct, clear, and easy concretizations in the audience's mind: the man in the cage, Mnouchkine's actors impersonating Kabuki actors, opaque forms of Kabuki style, and the text of the dialogue. In theory, even the Parisian audience could have perceived each of these sets of signs and decoded it without ambiguity. But what did actually happen at the Cartoucherie?

The first set posed no problems. The cage scene, through its primary and cultural signs, ensured an effective understanding of its moving but trite message about the vanity of human life. Much more problematic, however, was the reception of the second set: French enactment of a Kabuki performance. Most spectators, in their oral and written reactions, failed to evidence any understanding that the Cartoucherie's stage and actors could only refer, as primary signs, to mirror-image Kabuki stage and actors, *not* to characters in medieval England. These spectators, by the same token, missed the implications of the structure of a play within a play. On the other hand, however illogically, they did appreciate the performance achievements that this structure generated, praising Mnouchkine's actors for their admirable mastery of the Kabuki style as well as for their interpretation of Shakespeare's characters.

In contrast, the third reference was no doubt correctly received on the level of primary iconicity: the intended vision of Kabuki forms was apparently successfully concretized by all spectators, except for a small number of Kabuki experts. But, with the same exception, the audience was unable to decode most cultural signs supported by these forms, hence to access the layer of psychological or philosophical meaning. As a result, the successful reference to the Kabuki style generated an admiration for its exotic beauty, viewed as a *performance*, rather than an appreciation of its exotic semiotic operations.

Finally, on the basis of personal observation, it appeared that very few spectators paid any sustained attention to the poetic or dramatic virtuosity of Shakespeare's text. They may have been distracted by the competing visual and sound effects, or else, unable to track the intricacies of the textual story, they might have given up paying attention to all verbal signs. Now and then, no doubt, they perceived and appreciated disconnected images, or moving arguments, but these referential segments, severed from their ties to the story, could not stand up as forms of a consistent verbal *performance*.

This overall setback of the referential function of signs, misunderstood or desemiotized, suggests that the gap between production and reception of meaning reached quite serious proportions at the Cartoucherie. The ideal scheme of theatre communication was not followed, theatre codes were not observed, and basic semiotic theatre conventions were ignored. It is irrelevant that *Richard II*, as a spectacular production, profited rather than suffered from this referential dysfunction. It is also secondary whether the collapse of signs was caused by the directorial mishandling of primary and cultural systems, or by a flawed reception by a public lacking semiotic skills. It is important to know, however, whether the Cartoucherie experience could have been symptomatic of a general semiotic crisis: the malaise of a changing society that has trouble dealing with its own signs, or fears using its signs to deal with reality.

A firm diagnosis of such a cultural malaise, conceived as a source of multiple semiotic problems, including the preference for showing over telling, would be clearly relevant to a general sociosemiotic analysis of our society. But let us stay a while with theatre. My hypothesis about a semiotic malaise at the Cartoucherie was drawn from a single experience, involving an experimental staging of an unfamiliar text and a rather small group of snobbish bourgeois. The first question must be: Can this hypothesis be expanded to apply to other types of theatre performances, mainly traditional, where no special communication problems occur? And only second: What else can it reveal about our culture?

We need to go back to *Richard II*. A happy few, we can assume, must have had no problems with a correct decoding of Mnouchkine's performance. Bypassing communication gaps, they no doubt reached an exact understanding of the basic system of references to real and imaginary spaces: the Cartoucherie stage, a Kabuki stage, and medieval

England. It is important to note, however, that their successful semiosis would *not* yield natural visions of reality, nor potentially "normal" stories. All three spaces indeed refer primarily to an artifice, with little relation to real individual or social concerns. First, then, the frame story: what happens when a Kabuki company performs Shakespeare in French. As a story, it is certainly peculiar, telling about a hypothetical event much more unlikely than events in most imaginary tales. But it is particularly arresting because, contrary to most stories, it deals with two contrived art forms rather than with a direct experience of life: Shakespeare's artistic vision of Richard II, and a Kabuki artistic vision of Shakespeare's text. The combination of the two visions only heightens connotation of artificiality: they merge into an art work three times removed from its historical model.

Second referent: Kabuki style. By definition, it concerns theatrical practices qua theatrical practices, that is, art forms. Kabuki costumes, gestures, postures, and music are manifested concretely, but always on a stage, in an enclosed theatre space, and within the frame of an artistic vision of reality. In that sense, the reference to the Kabuki style pointedly deals with artificial conventions that arbitrarily distort lived reality. The imaginary Kabuki actors play a game directed by the rules of a discrete art, exotic and incomprehensible in its forms: a gratuitous activity, indeed, an artifice that lacks connections even to artificial but familiar forms of Western theatre.

Third: Shakespeare's literary text, again many times removed from its inspiration in reality. Richard II had a real life, but in Shakespeare's time his story was already mediated by all sorts of conventional documents. Shakespeare distorted it further by the magic forms of his art as a playwright; and the French version of his text was further transformed by the formal constraints of a different language and different poetic conventions. The verbal poetry heard on the stage thus mainly refers to its own existence as literature, an eminently artistic artifice.

In each instance, in short, reference is made not to real human life and/or society, but to art, and not to a form of traditional art, interfacing with reality, but to art about art. The first conclusion to be drawn from this focus on artifice is rather obvious: for the happy few who understood its signs, the global reference of Mnouchkine's *Richard II* was a possible artificial world, a world where reality is art. For them, for us, the question becomes: What meaning can we attribute to the vision of that world? In other terms: What "absent" cause, what answer to the last "why?" can we find in a vision of our own society? By the code of world visions, as proposed above, the vision of Mnouchkine's world, processed as a complex sign, must refer to a minimally transformed vision of our own world. In this case, visibly, this minimal transformation yields a vision of our world wherein interest in reality is replaced by interest in art, labeled and packaged as such; a world where our drive to structure reality is satisfied when we structure signs representing reality; a world of artificial conventions. In that sense, Mnouchkine's _Richard II_, viewed as the closest mirror image of our world, manifests indeed its semiotic malaise: a discomfort with a culture wherein signs proliferate, get out of control, conceal the very reality they are supposed to designate. Which brings us back to general sociosemiotics.

For surely, when signs increasingly refer to other signs, and reality eludes their grasp, it is tempting to give up trying to deal with real History, social issues, ideologies, even everyday problems. Creative artists in particular, such as Mnouchkine, may be expected to respond to the world covered by signs by focusing on artifacts build with signs, artificial visions of reality, fixed artistic achievements of the past. Shakespeare's text, Kabuki style, a Kabuki imaginary performance, all conventional sign structures, offer stable and safe media to restructure with signs. In the same spirit, Rosencrantz and Guildenstern, imaginary characters in _Hamlet_, engender Stoppard's fictional reworking of their own fictional story; a Borges character rewrites _Don Quixote_; new novels deal with old novels, and films with films. Mnouchkine's _Richard II_ exemplifies but one of the many ways in which modern art tends to feed on itself in a growing trend toward self-referentiality.

But there are also other ways of adapting to the semiotic malaise. Frustration with signs that fail to communicate a clear understanding of reality can lead one to suspect and reject all forms of sign communications. Some avant-garde artists thus turn to different channels of expression: mystical communion, aesthetic appreciation, emotions. Discounting references, they stress the performant function, give priority to showing over telling, promote images that please, or excite, or frighten even when their message is opaque. In that sense, many experimental shows are as symptomatic of the semiotic malaise as the artificial referentiality of Mnouchkine's performance. In fact, as we have seen, _Richard II_ heavily borrows from this fashion, stressing its own aesthetic and exotic _performances_. And no doubt the Parisian audience was more interested in emotions created by forms than in meanings proposed by signs, even though these meanings referred to art rather than to reality. Hence the communication gap. Paris spectators, one suspects, were not sophisticated enough to understand Mnouchkine's commentary on the semiotic malaise of their own culture, but they played their part in it by focusing on the "show."

But what about Broadway productions, best-selling novels, successful films that generate few communication problems? How do they fit with the hypothesis of a semiotic malaise? No doubt, more often than not, they do deal with reality, and their signs are well understood. But at a price. Indeed, as a rule, they do not convey much truly new information about that reality. As a rule, they communicate conventional meanings that are carried by conventional signs, familiar to many. For most media and arts, whatever their formal achievement, rarely try to reach beyond such fixed images of the real world. Through their expected use of expected signs, they eschew structuring new fictional worlds, and offer worn-out schemes that consumers follow mechanically, without effort nor danger to their view of their world. They promote adaptation to the semiotic malaise when they avoid acknowledging it, and do not question its perils. Their response is as symptomatic of the malaise of large numbers as Mnouchkine's *Richard II* was exemplary of the malaise of the small Parisian theatre world.

## Notes

1. This hypothetical example is clearly inspired by Samuel Beckett's *Not I*, where, on a dark stage, only a luminous mouth is perceived while it delivers a disorganized monologue. But this monologue is not really meaningless, the mouth is attributed some degree of identity, and the puzzling story of a specific disembodied mouth delivering a specific scrambled monologue must be concretized, by theatrical convention, as taking place in an imaginary space and time continuum that is different from the space and time of action on the stage. No doubt this referential story, and its referential world, are very strange, but that strangeness is only experienced in a mental mirror image of the stage and not on it.

2. Roland Barthes, *Essais critiques* (Paris: Seuil, 1964), p. 258. The essay titled "Littérature et signification" reprints an interview that Barthes gave to *Tel Quel* in 1963.

3. Patrice Pavis, *Dictionnaire du théâtre* (Paris: Editions Sociales, 1987), p. 396.

4. This is quite evident for literature that relies primarily on natural language, as will be discussed below. But it is also true for the pictorial system which, by its proper code, associates shapes, lines, and colors with what they are supposed to represent, and then allows for decoding, in the represented object, all sorts of cultural signs referring to psychological, social, or religious meanings. Similarly, in a ballet, various dance figures are primarily decoded as various types of behavior of fictional characters, and then some of these types of behavior are culturally decoded to yield psychological, social, or religious meanings.

5. Obviously there are many literary languages, corresponding to various natural languages, social groups, historical periods, conventions of various genres and styles, and so forth. Language used in classical French tragedies, for

example, differs in many ways from language used in modern guerilla theatre or in Proust's novels. But all such languages are clearly recognized, by vocabulary as well as by syntax or formal constraints, as properly literary, i.e., always somewhat artificial. They all use a special set of verbal signs, drawn from the larger set of verbal signs coded in natural language. In turn, the so-called "poetic" language is a subset of the "literary language."

6. One recalls that black characters stage a play about white official figures in order to expose colonialism but also to distract a fictional audience from the signs of a revolution planned outside the fictional performance space. Then a shot is heard from outside, and a man runs in to announce that the revolution has began. But he runs through the real audience, implying that the revolution has taken place in the real space outside the real theatre. The fictional black performance tends to merge with the real black performance.

7. Parts of this section, as well as of the following, draw on ideas in my paper, "Meaning and Theatre: Reassigning Performance Signs," published in *Semiotica 85*, ed. John Deely (Lanham, Md: University Press of America, 1986), pp. 85–96.

8. An unconscious utterance, or any other action, cannot be a real sign because it is not intentionally produced within the process of communication. On the other hand, as we observe it from the outside, we often are able to apply our knowledge of psychological laws in order to explain its production as the result of an unconscious cause. We shall return to this problem when dealing with "natural" signs.

9. See André Green, *Hamlet et **Hamlet**. Une interprétation psychanalytique de la représentation* (Paris: Balland, 1982).

10. The notion of a minimal gap between the vision of the real world and the vision of a fictional world, or a possible world, is by no means new. Too often, however, it takes the vision of the real world as a given, as a stable reality by itself, and not as a referent of a complex set of internalized signs, as variable as the referent yielded by the complex set of signs in a fiction. For a further consideration of that problem, see Marie-Laure Ryan, "Fiction, Non-Factuals, and the Principle of Minimal Departure," in *Poetics 8* (1980), pp. 403–22.

11. Particularly impressive, and enriching in that sense, are Michel Corvin's studies of iconoclastic versions of Molière's comedies by Benoin, Planchon, and Vitez, models of a semiotic analysis that explains a performance as an interaction between potential meanings of a text and concerns of its modern interpreters. See, in bibliography, Corvin, *Molière et ses metteurs en scène* (1985) and "Sémiologie et spectacle" (1985).

12. The actual composition of that legendary corpus obviously depends on individual experience, taste, geographical location, age, memory, perception of what "has to be seen," and so forth. Over the last few decades, I have noticed that, when I scan my memory of great theatre performances, a couple of dozen keep on coming to mind: Peter Brook's *Les Iks* and *Mahabharata*, Planchon's *Tartuffe*, Chéreau's *La Dispute*, Vitez's *Dom Juan*, Mnouchkine's *L'Age d'or* and *Richard II*, Luca Ronconi's *Orlando Furioso*, Schechner's *Dionysius in 69*, Mesguich's *Hamlet*, Grotowski's *Apocalypsis cum figuris*, Wilson's *Einstein on the*

*Beach*, Ludlam's *Camille*, etc., but also *A Chorus Line*, *Rex*, and *Cats*.

13. A notion that made its way to the United States, with a much different "adaptation" of Shakespeare in *Kabuki Othello*: a hodgepodge of old and modern borrowing from various styles, without much interest.

14. "Le Théâtre du Soleil: Shakespeare," *Double Page* (Paris: SNEP, 1982), pp. 3–4.

# III: Transformational Processes: Production/Reception

## 1. Theatricality: Theatre as a Series of Transformations

A public performance clearly constitutes the central manifestation of theatre, associating actors and spectators in a single event. Yet, for most types of theatre, it forms only one stage in a complex process that involves a series of production and reception sequences. A semiotic theory that views theatre as a total process must no doubt first focus on the performance, as I have done here, establishing its nature, its referential and performant functions, and its use of signs. But it must also account for the other stages in that process, especially those which most directly interact with the performance, either preceding or following it. Particular attention must be paid in that sense to the reception of the verbal text, including its own transformations, then to the transformations whereby that text is turned into a performance, and finally to the reception of that performance that results in further transformations carried out by the spectators. Within these three sequences, the second one, the transition from text to stage, has assumed an increasingly important role in the traditional practice of theatre. By the same occasion, it has drawn much recent theoretical attention. Indeed, it would appear that the distinct nature of theatre as a transformational process can be best grasped in the text-to-stage transition: its unique tension between its two poles, but also its unique potential for free creation. That tension and creative freedom define in that sense theatre's basic *theatricality*.

No doubt, as a total process, theatre also involves many other phases. One might even claim that it is determined by a circular series of production and reception operations, starting with the playwright

who receives all sorts of existential and theatrical stimuli when producing a dramatic text; then moving to the director who reads that text
and, through an exchange of views with the actors, stages it as a
performance; then to the spectators who attend the performance and
produce reception texts; then to the readers of those texts who produce further texts about texts; and finally back to another playwright,
who in turn receives the stimuli of performances, dramatic texts, reception texts or texts about reception texts, and responds to them with
a new textual production. A similar circle can be traced for theatre
based on oral tradition or ritual forms. A complete account of theatrical activity would have to reconstitute the entire circular movement: a
Herculean project that could be impossible to achieve. Practically, a
certain selection must be made among the many interactions.

Most theatre studies single out one link in the total chain, or one set
of interactions between two links. For a long time, priority was given to
the production of the text, then to techniques of performances, and
most recently to problems of reception, arbitrarily set as the final stage
in the theatrical process. All three stages are parts of theatrical activity,
but they must be connected one to another in order to yield a clear understanding of theatre. And such connections introduce, within the
triad text-performance-reception, various additional stages, with competing pragmatic and theoretical interests. The reduction of the total
theatrical process to only a few phases thus requires reassessing the importance of each step, weighing its theatricality content, and deciding
whether the transformations it carries out justify an extensive examination.

Viewed from that transformational perspective, the production of
the verbal text does not deserve much special attention. No doubt, as a
general rule, the dramatic text constitutes the first coherent manifestation of the theatrical process, that is, the first concrete step that initiates
all the others. To that extent, texts have a capital function, and we shall
see in Part IV how they can be analyzed in the spirit of sociocritical
inquiry. It is also important to acknowledge that dramatic texts form a
distinct genre. They differ from other literary narratives because only
in them is a story told with the expectation of being staged, and hence
transformed on the stage. The awareness of the demands of the expected performance—the various constraints of theatrical forms—
thus plays a special role in the production of the dramatic text, channeling in a special way the more general social (and individual) concerns. All these sources contribute to the constitution of the text and,
by the same token, to the diversification of meanings that this text will
be given in its reception. In that sense, formal, social, and individual
influences must all be taken into account to explain the full potentiality

of a text. But such explanations concern only the nature of the text as it already exists at the beginning of theatrical transformations. Strictly speaking, they deal with a given text, and not with its contribution to theatre as a total process.

To be sure, even approached from that angle, a given text can be made to yield hypotheses about its own transformational processes. Analyzing the text, one can attribute its various features to various transformations that must have taken place during its production: transformations of social reality into a fictional world, and transformations of textual dramatic forms. Yet, however convincing such hypotheses might be, however fertile their overall implications, they can hardly generate a close understanding of actual processes of transformation. Indeed, as a rule, it is impossible to get a firm grasp on the reality of any textual production. For various reasons, its very notion is quite difficult to define in exact terms.

In the first place, in many cases, there are several texts rather than a single text, and their production spans an uncertain period of time. Plays attributed to Shakespeare, and modified by him and others over the years, have many versions, each one transforming the previous ones. When, then, was a given version produced? At the time of creation of an Ur-text, perhaps lost? At the time of its most recent modification? And which one of its successive producers should be considered as its author? No such problem of authorship exists for Racine's tragedies, but he changed himself several texts just before his death; what was the production time for the last version? Or, when Molière created his *Dom Juan* with material taken from Tirso de Molina's play, with whom and when did *that* production actually begin?

Nor is it clear when textual production stops. Even the most stable dramatic texts, performed in their canonical form, inspire many different stagings that, now and then, stimulate the production of reception texts, often documented with illustrations. The commentary thus produced, and popularized through education and media, always somewhat modifies the perception of the initial dramatic text, without changing its verbal signs. Can one say truthfully that the production of *Hamlet* has ever reached a final point? Or is it going on, adding the contributions of Marx or Freud, Brecht or Olivier? More generally, does the production of a dramatic text always precede the performance? In many cases the performance comes first, and the text simply records what has been staged; in other cases, performances produce changes in the text, more or less stable.

But let us consider the ideal situation of a (relatively) original dramatic text produced by a single author within a known period of time. Let us also assume that the playwright had nothing to do with the staging of that play, and that its text has not been contaminated by any performance. The notion of such a production presents none of the problems discussed above. But how can we grasp its concrete processes? Even when we have written traces of early drafts or changes made by the author, a rather rare opportunity that might totally disappear with the use of word processors, we can only speculate about the intentions, or unconscious pulsions, that directed the creative activity. And the mental or psychological production of oral texts is even more secret. At best, we can perceive what objective factors are present at the time of production, and how they are transformed into a dramatic text at the end; but the author's creation takes place in a black box, like all artistic production. We are thus reduced to hypotheses, which may be illuminating but yield no reliable knowledge of theatrical transformations.

A dependable transformational grammar of theatre must thus posit, as its given basis, the existence of an already produced text. And not any possible version of that text, whether first offered by the author or revised at one time or another, but the specific version that is used as the starting point for the successive transformations carried out during a particular theatrical process. The first phase that will be closely examined concerns, then, the reception of that text, after it has been selected to be staged but before the actual staging takes place. Actually, as shall be seen in the following sections, this first reception already involves a series of textual transformations. The given text, encountered initially in its literary form, or in an oral presentation, is always somewhat transformed when it is read or heard as a dramatic text, that is, as a text to be staged. Some modifications affect its formal features, accounting for properly textual transformations; others concern the story it tells, and its intended meanings. During that last process, the fictional world suggested by a literary reading is transformed into a different world to be suggested on the stage: these are specifically referential changes.

At this point, the first phase merges into the crucial second phase: transition from text to stage. During that transition, the text transformed by its initial reception generates the production of a concrete performance. And any such production inevitably results in further transformations, some developing and concretizing changes already made during the reception of the text, others bringing new changes. This central phase is quite complex and needs to be examined in some detail. It will be necessary to account for both its basic rules and its methodological strategies. Yet again some choices must be made among all successive and/or overlapping steps in that phase. Thus, quite paradoxically, the sequence of *rehearsals*, no doubt most intensely marked by all sorts of constant transformations, does not require a particular attention.

Rehearsing, to be sure, takes a long time and demands many activities from all the producers of the performance: director, actors, set, costume, and lighting designers, technical staff. It involves various approaches and specialized techniques: blocking, scripts, video-recording, and so forth. Like any performing art, theatre uses rehearsals to perfect the execution of a given task; but, probably more than in other arts, this task is largely formulated in theatre during the actual rehearsing process. In other terms, rehearsals rarely serve only to implement a previously determined staging plan; as they proceed, they transform that plan, they create the staging. In that sense, they can be compared to the creative phase in textual production: the mysterious black box where an author's secret intentions are cast and recast in the form of verbal signs. At the input end, rehearsing artists are fed a set of general or precise instructions about the intended performance; at the output end, the performance comes into existence. However, since we do not know the instructions, we cannot match them with the finished product; and hence an exact knowledge of transformations within the black box eludes us. In most cases, we even lack information about the importance assigned to initial instructions, the part played by the director and actors in formulating and modifying them, the impact of change. We can only assume that the performance includes, among its manifold transformations, those which were initiated during the rehearsals. In short, though rehearsals have an important role in the concrete theatrical process, their contribution to theatrical transformations yields few useful insights.

The last phase that must be discussed concerns the reception of performances. Here again some problems are evident. In its most general sense, this reception means the way in which spectators respond to a performance: a rather clear notion. But there are several types of responses that, to be sure, correspond to different functions of theatre but are usually interconnected. On the one hand, spectators are invited to follow the story that takes place in the referential world. Their response takes the form of a mental activity whereby stage signs are decoded and concretized in an imaginary story space. In that restricted sense, reception involves comprehension of events and meanings of that story. On the other hand, spectators are also expected to experience emotional states such as amusement, sympathy, pity, outrage, anxiety, fear, and so forth. These emotions mainly express reactions to the story, but can vary a lot with the personal ideas or

sensitivity of individual spectators. Besides, the intensity of such feelings partly also depends on the operation of the performant function:
an exceptional display of love or hatred will generate a stronger reaction than a merely competent enactment of the same passions. One
must also account for a different type of reception, strictly commanded
by the performant function operating on its own. Sustained by the
hope for a *performance*, it generates an evaluation, appreciation, or
censure of both theatrical and cultural achievements, without direct
relation to the story. In short, total reception is a complex process,
difficult to unravel.

It is even more difficult to grasp in a concrete form at the time it
takes place. A few emotions have direct manifestations: laughter, tears,
ahs! and ohs! produced by awe or admiration. But most emotional
responses cannot be directly perceived. Nor can an observer ascertain
how a story is concretized in a spectator's mind, hence what meanings it
receives. Actual reception, like textual production and performance
rehearsals, occurs in a black box. Worse: unlike the other two activities,
it is not intended to be communicated, and does not result in a finished
product. The only way to approach reception is through reception
texts, that is, texts that have been produced about reception some time
after it took place. Which raises other problems. First, the validity of
such texts as a reliable testimony of actual reception is very questionable. For obvious reasons, fragility of memory and space limitation,
they are always reductive. At best, they can only convey an incomplete
and delayed reception, a few remembered fragments of performance
reshaped by personal structuring constraints. At worst, they offer de-
ceptive information, oriented by pragmatic concerns. Also, even the
most reliable texts, composed with notes and an open mind, are never
very representative: they may suggest the reception of a single individual, or several amateurs of theatre, but they cannot claim to account for
the responses of most spectators. Nor do various surveys of entire
audiences provide more reliable data. Besides, they are rare and, in
that sense, also unrepresentative of general public responses. In fact,
all serious reception texts always risk being exceptional because they
refer to a limited number of performances: selected productions in
large cities that support sophisticated media. The overwhelming majority of performances leave no useful reception traces.

This doesn't mean that reception presents no interest. The most
unreliable reception texts contribute some knowledge about the total
cycle of theatre, notably about its insertion in the cultural and social
environment. To that extent, reception deserves to be examined in
some detail, if with a critical eye. But no interest in reception can match
the fascination exerted by the text-to-stage transition. In the last anal-

ysis, relations between text and stage always play the central role in the traditional theatrical process.

\*   \*   \*

The text-to-stage transition is not only an exemplary locus of transformational theatricality. It also draws attention to a traditional competition between two different meanings of the word "theatre": literature and performances. Indeed, while the dramatic text serves, within the transitional phase, as a matrix for performances, it also often assumes, outside that phase, a second role as an autonomous literary form. An overall understanding of theatre requires at least some clarification of that curious duplication of functions, that surprising spin-off of the theatrical text into the medium of literature.

The properly theatrical mission of the text cannot explain this split between two functions. No doubt, even as a part of a total theatrical process, a text has a function that greatly exceeds its transitory role as a pre-text for performances. While it supplies contingent verbal material to be transformed, it also traditionally provides, or at least is intended to provide, a (relatively) permanent formal document that, without changing itself, can inspire a great number of ephemeral and always different performances. The dramatic text, in that sense, operates as a single fixed notation of complex activities that are performed many times and with many variations. It plays therefore a fundamental role in the constitution of theatre history. Its transformations generate not only a single performance, nor only a sequence of repeated performances, but, in the case of the best-known texts, open series of past, present, and future performances. It is essential for that function of the text that it be preserved and made widely available in an unchanged form: in writing rather than orally, and in print (or on computer disks) rather than by long hand. As a permanent notation, in short, a dramatic text always must have an autonomous and continuous material existence. But that is not sufficient to account for its transformation into literature.

For not only theatre but all performing arts need to have some form of notation, some permanent matrix of activities to be performed. Music relies on scores, ballet on choreographic notations. Whether these notations require the performers to provide little or much new material is not relevant here, nor is the degree of technical virtuosity that they must display. Whatever their differences, all performing arts, including theatre, expect and encourage variations in performances but on the condition that these variations be inspired by a fixed notation. As a result, all performing arts support the availability of their notations, preserving them in an autonomous material form.

Yet, with the exception of scholars, connoisseurs and performers themselves, whether professional or amateur, very few people consult, read, or buy music or ballet notations. Nor are these notations acknowledged as a form of a different art medium. The function of dramatic texts as basic notations in theatre cannot then explain why they alone have obtained a distinct status as literature, or why only in theatre a tension occurs between the appeal of performances and the appeal of notations as literature—a tension that leads many readers of dramatic texts to show no interest at all in dramatic performances.

The popularity of dramatic texts, read as literature and not as theatrical notations, must rather be related, in various ways, to a special operation of their semiotic system, that is, their verbal signs. In the first place, among all performing arts, theatre alone transfers its signs, essentially words, from the notation to the performance, without much alteration in their formal integrity. The written dialogue, which forms the permanent basis of the dramatic text, is expected by theatre convention to reappear integrally on the stage as an oral dialogue. As we shall see, the transition between written and oral forms certainly encourages, in fact always dictates, various transformations in textual references, but not in the coded meaning of verbal signs. The reader and the spectator rely on the same linguistic competence to decode the text and the performance, and that linguistic competence is taken to be equally shared by amateurs of literature and theatre. In contrast, reading musical scores, or deciphering ballet notations, demands a specialized competence; and, in the process of concretization, even specialists experience a basic difference of nature between the notational signs and imaginary or real performances. No wonder, then, that only in theatre does semiotic identity between written and oral dialogue lead to a conflation of verbal signs in the text and verbal signs on the stage, as if they had the same function and the same meaning; and no wonder that, for many people, reading drama replaces seeing it performed, literature substituting for theatre.

This literary fallacy, still evidenced by many serious "theatre" scholars, benefits from the additional circumstance that, among performing arts, theatre alone has been traditionally granting a special status to its verbal signs, somewhat set apart from other signs on the stage. To be sure, various other arts also combine verbal and nonverbal signs in their performances: many musical works have words, operas and operettas have dialogues and arias, films make extensive use of written and oral language. In each case, however, when it is present at all, the verbal text is clearly subordinated to other semiotic systems. Opera mainly stresses music and voice performances. Some films are very verbose, especially when they record or imitate plays, but others have no words at all or only a few: the proper art of cinema lies rather in the production of visual (and now sound) effects. Only in musical comedies, as in theatre, the verbal signs of lyrics compete on an equal footing with the musical score and/or the performant appeal of costumes and sets; but then musicals have always formed a hybrid genre par excellence, drawing from its theatrical component the special function of words.

In contrast, already in ancient Greece, the verbal text played a major role in theatre, especially in its serious forms. Aristotle, while acknowledging that other signs were produced by actors and musicians, singled out the plot, carried out by the dialogue, as the main feature of tragedy. Plato was more alert to body language, censuring its mimetic influence on the audience, and disregarding words. The question is not who was right, nor whether verbal signs are *more* important than other stage signs—an issue that frustrated Prague semioticians. The point is that verbal and nonverbal signs have always been consistently contrasted, whatever the position taken. Even zealots of a modern theatre centered on the body also perpetuate the notion, in their very protest against it, that dialogue plays a special role in a theatrical performance, that words operate unlike other signs.

This split between verbal and nonverbal signs, assigned different functions on the stage, contributes certainly to the more radical notion that the verbal text, in the form of dialogue, forms a distinct literary body within the theatrical performance. It is also plausible, however, that acknowledgment of a special power of words onstage reflects a more fundamental difference between two general types of signs—the difference between the "show" signs and the "tell" signs, affecting theatre but also other communication media.

On the one hand, in its most general meaning, "showing" is essentially done with iconic signs: sculptures, sounds, images, actors. With various distortions, technical or artistic, these iconic signs provide information about outward manifestations of reality (or its imaginary vision); they communicate what can be grasped with senses: what is, was, or could be. However, iconic signs, unless they are symbolically coded, poorly convey operations of mind, psychological states, abstract notions—in short, everything that takes place under a perceptible surface. And special symbolic systems that use iconic signs are rare, fragmentary, and often unreliable, depending on culturally unstable codes. "Telling," on the other hand, is principally done with precise verbal signs, oral or written words, coded symbolically in the natural language. The natural language, as a result, is an extremely versatile system on which is based most of our knowledge of our past and present world. Up till recent semiotic (and deconstructing) reservations, it enjoyed the unquestionable prestige as the model system of communication. Yet, because of their abstract meaning, verbal signs cannot convey very detailed information about material appearances, cannot "show" like iconic signs. They are particularly suitable, in contrast, for communicating ideas, emotions, and desires that can be conceptualized; for ordering and summarizing sequences of events; for carrying out arguments; and for offering ambiguous statements. In short, they can tell, discuss, and explain that which cannot be shown with iconic signs.

In practice, this fundamental difference tends to be masked by artistic and semiotic strategies whereby, at some risk of misunderstanding, words are made to evoke images and images to evoke ideas. A more efficient way toward well-rounded information combines both telling and showing in a single medium; thus illustrated books, films, and comics owe much of their popularity to their ability both to tell and to show. This combined approach is somewhat more complex in theatre since, as we have seen, two different semiotic operations take place during a performance. First, let us recall, everything on the stage serves as an iconic sign, referring spectators to a mirror-image imaginary world. Second, within that world, in addition to situations and action, spectators also perceive dialogue words that tell explicitly that which cannot be shown, and thus communicate meanings. While there are many reasons why theatre has always held a special fascination for naive audiences, drawing on its ritual power, the magic of live performers, and various seductions of the performant function, part of its appeal as a storytelling medium surely results from this complementary use of verbal and nonverbal signs.[1]

Yet, although verbal and nonverbal signs are clearly complementary, the different types of information they provide are rarely given an equal weight. Knowing *what* is happening is as essential, no doubt, as understanding *why* it is happening. But, for most educated spectators, events shown on the stage with iconic signs are always somewhat tainted by the knowledge that they lack stability, that they are apt to change from performance to performance, from one director's capricious staging to another's, evoking contingent worlds. In contrast, the fundamental reasons for these events, and hence their meaning, conveyed with verbal signs, are assumed to deal with general human, social, or philosophical truths, offering permanent visions of the world. They are attributed to fixed intentions of the author/creator, who once and for all has given them a final form in the dramatic text—as happens in literature. This essentialist attitude also prevails among many theatre directors who, whatever their own talent, claim they must respect the literary legacy of the authors of dramatic texts. But even directors with more existential leanings, dedicated to the right to create visions on equal basis with the playwright, show more consideration for the verbal signs of the dialogue than for nonverbal signs displayed in past performances of the text. They too rely on the fixed dramatic text to inspire or trigger their own new meanings.

All these reasons account for the special status attributed to words as stage signs. The same reasons explain also why so many people, including practitioners of theatre, trust in the power of dramatic texts. Directors want to stage a play, and actors to have a part in it, "because it is such a great text," regardless of its intended future transformations. Critics censure a production for failing to do justice to "an outstanding text." And some spectators have claimed to perceive, in concrete performances, a tension between the meaning structured by the underlying verbal text and meanings conveyed by the staging. Yet, granted an autonomous existence, the dramatic text still is viewed in each case as a theatre text: as a text to be staged. None of the reasons discussed above explain satisfactorily why that text is also read and viewed as literature, without ties to theatre. Another factor is at work, extrinsic but decisive: a similarity of form between printed dramatic texts and printed literary texts.

The similarity of written form does not necessarily entail a similar reading process. Theatrical and literary readings are quite different, involving different mental operations. They will be further discussed in the next section. Nor does similarity of form entail a total identity. A number of formal marks enable most readers to distinguish a dramatic text from the text of a prose narrative or essay or poetry. Printed plays are identified by subtitles (tragedy, comedy, drama), and, more generally, draw attention to their distinct nature by a list of characters, repeated identification of speakers before each set of lines, an overwhelming presence of dialogue, different graphics and brevity of stage directions. These conventions are not always totally reliable. Some novels (such as Roger Martin du Gard's *Jean Barois*) use only dialogues with brief commentary that looks like stage directions. Some dialogues (such as Plato's) have never been intended as dramatic texts to be staged. Some plays (such as Bernard Shaw's) have very extensive stage directions and commentaries. But these sources of confusion concern marginal cases. As a rule, we know the text of a play when we see it. Yet we still can read it as literature.

One can speculate, without much profit, on the reading practice of dramatic texts in ancient Greece or during the Middle Ages. Even after Gutenberg, say, in seventeenth-century France, few people were buying printed plays; and discussions of plays were first triggered by (successful) performances. By the nineteenth century, however, dramatic texts became widely available and purchased as *books* and, together with all their special formal marks, entered the stream of literary production following economic and cultural goals. Since then, plays have been printed to be sold, and sold to be read by the largest possible public; and, as means of production improved, and prices went down, many people undertook to read plays without seeing them performed. Their reading practice, not informed by a theatrical education, was modeled on the practice of reading other texts that also told stories and, despite minor differences, used the same verbal forms, and required the same competence—I am referring to fictional or historical narratives. The verbal text of theatre, handled and perceived as a reading text, was logically co-opted as a literary genre, called "drama" in English but still *théâtre* in French, to be taught in schools as literature and surveyed in literary history. Accorded this prestige of literary status, dramatic texts enjoy today a surprising popularity as meaningful reading material. Whether that success in turn encourages attending theatre performances is debatable. There is no evidence that literary reading actually promotes the interests of theatre. It has nevertheless a direct effect on transformational processes that lead to theatre performances.

In the first place, the status of dramatic texts as texts to read can subtly influence their textual production. No doubt playwrights principally want "to write for the theatre," that is, to have their texts performed; but how many of them, tempted by success and financial rewards, also want to be published and benefit from prestige and sales? To what extent, perhaps unconsciously, does this new perspective affect the structure, language, and story of a dramatic text? Has it contributed to the evident evolution of theatre writing in the nineteenth century? Perhaps the literary character of that evolution can be matched with progress in literary reading of theatre. However, many factors have contributed to changes in theatre writing, and it would be hazardous to single out among them the emergence of theatre as literature.

On the other hand, the growing practice of literary reading may be safely expected to have an impact on the various phases of reception in theatre. Many spectators today know the text of a play, especially a classic, before they attend its performance, and their response cannot help reflecting their literary experience. More interesting is the likelihood that literary reading contaminates the reception of the dramatic text already during the first phase of the total theatre process. How many producers, directors, performers, when they first approach the text of a play, read it as literature rather than as theatre? Eventually, of course, they reread it as theatre for the purpose of transforming it on the stage. But not innocently, not without some memory of the initial literary reading. To that extent, literary reading must be taken into account as a latent influence on properly theatrical reading, as a potential source of its transformations.

## 2. Textual Transformations of the Text

### Literary, Theatrical, and Staged Texts

The role played by the dramatic text in the total theatre process cannot be fully grasped if the notion of *text* remains unclear. Part of the confusion that surrounds it today stems from the recent use and abuse of that term in all sorts of scholarly writings. Modern criticism started the trend by proposing that all written statements, whatever their nature, be called texts—a practice which in turn generated fashionable catchwords such as textuality, intertextuality, intratextuality, supratextuality and the like. The concept of text as a set of signs soon also became applied to other categories of statements, yielding references to graphic texts, film texts, music texts and, initially in Italy, the *testo spettacolare*, a "spectacular" or "performance" text comprising all signs that appear on the theatre stage. Such neologisms are sometimes useful. In many instances, the *testo spettacolare*, or its French version, *texte spectaculaire*, can conveniently replace the simpler if less precise "performance." But its use would cause ambiguities, or awkward formulations, in a study that stresses the distinction between the fixed dramatic text and the live performance, between verbal and nonverbal signs. The term *text* then will always refer here, unless otherwise specified, only to the verbal text of a play, whether in a printed form, or as a manuscript, or on a computer screen, or as an orally transmitted text, that is, as the fixed textual support of a dialogue delivered on the stage.

Yet, even in this restricted sense, the text can be understood in at least three different ways, corresponding to different ways of approaching and processing it. In its most usual meaning today, as we have seen, the dramatic text is handled as a literary work to be read (or heard), that is, as one of the possible forms in which a story is told with words, most usually in a book form. Viewed from that perspective, the dramatic text is often referred to as drama, but I prefer to call it the *literary text*. It is received as literature is supposed to be received, as a set of verbal signs produced by an author in order to communicate to the reader the vision of a fictional or historical world. All components of this text, whether dialogue or stage directions, or even titles, are considered to be equally valid signs, intended to yield that vision through their combined contribution. They tell the readers who the characters are in the story, what they do and what they say, and where and when the action takes place. When we begin reading a literary text titled *Hamlet*, we expect to be told Hamlet's story; and, informed in italics or parenthesis, that Hamlet picks up Yorick's skull, we concretize that action in our imagination with the same suspense of disbelief as we concretize him saying, in a soliloquy offered in normal print, "Alas poor Yorick!—I knew him, Horatio." To that extent, despite some formal differences, we treat the signs of a dramatic text in the same way as we treat the signs of a narrative text. In both cases, we move directly from the author's words to the imaginary world.

True, that world is not quite the same as most fictional or historical worlds evoked in literary narratives. As a rule, time moves in it in a different manner: instead of following a linear development, including flashbacks, it is fragmented in several segments, corresponding to acts, scenes, or tableaux, all progressing at the same pace, but leaving gaps between them. We may try to fill them out, reconstructing a linear time; but somehow the lost sections thus mentally recreated never match the feeling of immediacy of the ongoing temporal sequences. Things seem to happen only at selected moments.

Space also presents problems. Unlike most narratives, dramatic texts contain minimal references to specific spaces. Their worlds do not lack a spatial dimension; in fact, as has been repeatedly pointed out, they contain various types of spaces, close and remote, concrete and mental, and their relations play often an important part in the story. Yet the visualization of these spaces depends much more on the reader's imagination than in traditional narratives. The scant reference to the walls of Elsinore will rarely fail to trigger a vision of a medieval castle and, by extension, the culture of a feudal society; but that vision, without concrete features that narratives usually provide, will totally draw on personal memory, and vary in kind, detail, and clarity with each individual's power of imagination and stored images of the Middle Ages. The space evoked by dramatic texts risks merely to suggest a rough outline of a world, incomplete and fluctuating.

But the most significant difference concerns the concretization of characters. That people in the worlds of dramatic texts generally talk much more than people in the worlds of novels is rather secondary. That they are slower to act and usually engage in fewer decisive actions also has a small impact on an interested reader. The fact that their actions, like spaces, lack precision, and require more imaginative concretizations, is partly compensated by their own protracted commentary on these actions. Still, unimaginative or simply lazy readers may visualize a world where, between outbursts of violence, people barely move while they talk. The real problem, however, lies in the perception of motivations, and the formulation of judgments of value. To be sure, people in worlds of dramatic texts offer their own reasons for their actions, and tell how they should be judged. But their statements are always suspect: they may be self-serving, or honestly mistaken. For the reader, they never have the authority of the authorial voice of a narrator who can be trusted to tell what is true or false, right or wrong. To understand and judge, the readers must substitute their own individual wisdom, contribute their own meaning to the fictional world. Which demands a sustained mental effort, and a personal commitment to fictional issues. No wonder then that, read as literature, dramatic texts yield only surface events to superficial readers; and that, among readers who care for meanings, they tend to generate more controversies than controversial novels.

In all these ways, as a general rule (for one always can cite exceptions), dramatic texts constitute a more open literary form than narratives. By the same token, for serious readers, reading plays as literature is always somewhat frustrating, and perhaps more demanding than reading novels. Discounting "classics," old or new, required to be read by students, most published dramatic texts, despite their surface simplicity and appealing brevity, are less popular among readers than short and long fiction. But they *are* read. And their vision of an imaginary world has the same lasting power, the same power of retrieval and reinforcement, as have all worlds of literary fiction. Once read, and even more so when it is reread, the *literary text* thus always projects some of its meaning on its eventual theatrical transformations.

In fact, by dint of a *literary fallacy*, many naive theatre readers still assume that the literary text is identical with the text that is transposed on the stage. For them, all nonverbal signs added during the performance are only intended to "flesh out" the literary story, somewhat like illustrations in a novel. Many such readers, trusting in the inventiveness of their imagination, are satisfied with their own "fleshed-out" mental vision of the imaginary world, and dispense from seeing it staged. Or, when they do attend a performance, they mainly want to be thrilled by its performant function, in the form of acting, aesthetic or erotic *performances*, or to be moved by a live display of passion, or to participate in a social ritual. And they are disappointed or offended when the story they are offered diverges from the story they had read. The producers of a performance are often sensitive to the negative reactions of such readers/spectators, and try to minimize them by keeping close to the literary text. Indirectly, literary references thus seep into the production of performances.

A properly theatrical process, however, involves a different reading of the dramatic text. As its ties to literature are severed, the text recovers its primary function as a set of fixed notations of past and future performances. It is treated deliberately like a textual matrix of theatre, a text to be staged, a source of theatrical transformations. Read as a feature of theatrical process, the dramatic text becomes indeed a *theatrical text*, demanding a different type of visualization than the literary text.

To be sure, a proper reading of the theatrical text involves, like any reading of a story, a mental concretization of an imaginary world outside the text. In the case of the theatrical text, however, that world is always concretized as a stage. All spatial and temporal indications are understood to refer to space and time on the stage, all actions are placed on that stage, and characters are visualized as actors on the stage, not as imaginary people in a real or fictional world. The name "Hamlet" refers not to a prince of Denmark, but to an actor acting out the part of Hamlet; the mention of Elsinore's walls communicates the vision of sets intended to stand for such walls. No doubt, as shall be seen, this concretization may take into account the vision of a world that the imaginary stage could communicate to a potential imaginary audience, but such concerns are peripheral, whereas the vision of the stage stays central in the mind's eye.

This type of reading offers less excitement than a literary reading: action on a stage lacks the appeal of stories about fictional or historical characters. A theatrical reading is also quite difficult: it requires familiarity with staging techniques and styles. It is little practiced outside a small number of theatre professionals or amateurs. Theatrical reading is essentially an individual, very private experience that, while it takes place, is rarely shared with others. Yet it forms an essential link in the total theatrical process. A dramatic text cannot be transformed into a performance without being first processed as a theatrical text.

The pivotal operation of theatrical reading takes place during the first phase of transformations. On the one hand, coming close after a literary reading, and often overlapping with it, theatrical reading is still contaminated by the vision of the imaginary world conveyed by the literary text. In that sense, it contributes to a tension between two competing goals of staging: to tell the literary story as faithfully as possible, and to explore all possible ways of telling the story on the stage. On the other hand, theatrical reading also already lays the foundations for the next phase in the transformational process: elaboration of successive *virtual performances* during a third type of reading—a reading that produces the *staged text*.

The *staged text* provides a textual mediation between the written text and the oral text delivered on the stage. In that function, it generates a first material alteration of the total dramatic text. Among all the verbal signs in the dramatic text, the staged text only retains those which will reappear during the performance in an oral form, as the staged dialogue. The other signs, that is, all types of stage directions, may be taken into account during the reading but may be also disregarded, in part or entirely; in extreme cases, even identifications of speakers can be bypassed. Besides, when stage directions are processed during the reading of the staged text, they are transformed into nonverbal signs in the visualized performance, lost among many other nonverbal stage signs supplied by the reader's imagination, and subordinated to the compelling authority of the dialogue. In short, whether totally dismissed or tentatively accepted, they are not treated as an integral part of the dramatic text.

The staged text could thus be defined as a transformed theatrical text, cut down to the lines of dialogue. There are many reasons for this first dramatic transformation; they will be discussed in the next section. Yet even thus reduced, the staged text is basically read in the same way as the theatrical text, with the goal of generating a mental vision of a stage. There is, however, one important difference: the theatrical text usually receives a single full reading, yielding a stable vision of the imaginary stage, whereas the staged text may involve many complete or fragmentary readings, yielding many unstable versions of the stage. Each reading, or rereading, brings more precision to various imaginary stage features, adding or changing them, playing with the entire repertory of nonverbal signs, carrying out all manners of transformations. Even the dialogue, assumed to be stable, can be transformed during that mental process: indirectly, when nonverbal signs, especially intonations, gestures, or facial expressions, are brought to modify the normally coded meaning of words; and directly, when the words themselves are altered in the reader's imagination.

At some point, successive readings reach a high degree of coherence and provide a great precision of details. The fluctuating vision of the stage takes on the density of a virtual performance, becomes a project of a real performance. A staged text can generate many such virtual performances, endowing them with separate existences in the imagination. Stored in memory as mental structures, they undergo further changes that carry them over to the actual staging phase. However, up till the conclusion of the rehearsal sequence, and often during the initial run of a show, fluctuating virtual performances can keep on inspiring new transformations in the real performance.

## Conventional Transformation: Discounting Stage Directions

When the dramatic text is turned into a staged text, the most radical transformation concerns stage directions. All dramatic texts, both in literary and in theatrical readings, contain at least the identification of characters who are speaking. As a rule, this basic form of stage directions retains its function in the staged text. Many texts, particularly Greek and French classic tragedies, contain no additional directions, or very few: their conventional transformation is minimal. Most texts, however, provide a great many more indications, not only about crucial activities such as entrances, exits, violent physical action, exchanges of objects, telling gestures, or facial expressions, but also about detailed features of the space in which these activities take place, their social or psychological background, secret intentions and reasons. Expanded even farther, as in Bernard Shaw's plays, these directions offer the author's direct commentary on the meaning of the text. It is this general type of stage directions, whether concise or extended, that bears the brunt of transformations carried out by the staged text: eliminations, reductions, or alterations.

There are several reasons for such discounting of stage directions. First, the power of tradition. For at least a hundred years, since the emergence of staging as a central feature of theatre, playing with textual directions has become an accepted practice, not only tolerated but acknowledged as a privilege of great directors. By tradition, it has become one of theatre's tacit conventions: not that stage directions *must* be transformed, which would be a constraint, but that they *may* be bypassed in the staged text. Obviously, many directors do not take advantage of that convention, although they are aware of it. Their claim to show respect for the author's intentions, that is, for the literary text, should not be regarded as an alibi for lack of originality; it rather expresses a social attitude toward the past that will be discussed later, together with other social factors affecting theatrical forms. Other directors, however, have no such qualms. And their number and success indicate that the conventional discounting of stage directions is grounded not only in tradition, but also in the very nature of stage directions, always somewhat vague, unstable, fragmentary, and dispensable.

They are vague because, in contrast with dialogue signs, they cannot be reproduced exactly on the stage. They require being transposed into a nonverbal system of signs, such as facial expressions, or transformed into action, or provided a material shape: operations that rely on suggestions rather than on information, and involve wavering interpretations. How to show with precision that a character *is lying*? What sort of kiss will best meet the direction: *he kisses her* ? And will that direction have the same meaning each time it occurs, or will it suggest different kisses and different feelings at different times? Because they are vague, stage directions are thus also unstable, leaving many open options. Besides, none of these options can be particularly compelling on its own merits. For even extended stage directions are always fragmentary. Focusing on a limited number of selected exchanges, and highlighting only some isolated features, they do not support each other, do not refer to a coherent network of meaning. In fact, when the staged text generates a virtual performance, and coordinates images of action on the mental stage, the overall coherence of that vision has a clear priority over suggestions of fragmentary stage directions. If they fit the grand design, they may be retained; but if they disturb it, they will be dismissed. In other terms, followed or discarded at will, they have no stable influence on a theatrical reading of the text.

More generally, in the ideal scheme of theatre as total process, textual stage directions have no proper place. They challenge the principle of strict separation between the authorial and the directorial functions. The two functions, let us repeat, involve clearly differentiated activities, regardless of who performs them: two different people, or a single individual, or collectives. The authorial function, limited to the production of the fixed dramatic text, has been traditionally the responsibility of creative "authors"—sometimes groups, but usually playwrights, anonymous or not. In contrast, the directorial function, centered on staging concrete performances, has been initially carried out by impersonal conventions of theatre, ritual rules or formal performing styles, offering few opportunities for creative innovations. When directorial activities were thus regulated by custom, there were few tensions between the two functions, and hence few reasons for "authors" to seek to influence performances with stage directions inserted in their texts. No doubt many playwrights, who did not do their own staging, have been occasionally unhappy with the performance of their plays; but their displeasure surely concerned failings in execution rather than a transformation of meaning.

Why then, in modern texts, have stage directions proliferated? Why has the functional separation between the roles of author and director been systematically transgressed? The principle of a division between the two functions is not in question. But the contingent relation between people who perform these functions has dramatically altered. At the end of the nineteenth century, when staging emerged as a central feature in theatre appreciation, the role of human agents of the directorial function grew in proportion. A new prestige accrued to the *metteur en scène* who, as an original artist, claimed to be responsible for the entire performance, and hence to have the right to give it its meaning. Transforming textual references with their own staging signs, modern directors seemed thus to usurp the "author's" authority over the meaning of the text. Authors in turn, to protect their texts against directorial transformations, reinforced and multiplied textual stage directions. Transgressed by the practice of both authors and directors, the overall distinction between authorial and directorial functions became somewhat blurred. But only on the surface. For, as shall be seen, while they feel free to transform the meaning of a text, modern directors still claim to keep intact the author's dialogue; and, while they disregard authorial stage directions, viewed as constraints on an independent directorial function, they still accept constraints of fixed authorial verbal exchanges, that is, the staged text.

Only in one case can stage directions not easily be dropped from the staged text: when they replace a missing or deficient dialogue. The best-known example is Beckett's *Acts Without Words*, wherein the dramatic text offers a continuous sequence of stage directions, without a single spoken word. Beckett's text surely qualifies as theatre, if marginally. It can be read as literature, but also as a theatrical text; it is intended to be staged as theatre; it contains a set of fixed verbal signs that must be retained in all performances; and it can inspire at least some directorial transformations by the means of added stage signs. But it has one strange feature: its verbal signs refer exclusively to action on the stage, not to any dialogue. As a result, however, this extended stage direction is not fragmented like the usual stage directions, nor does it compete with directions suggested in the dialogue. It forms a coherent network of basic images that ensure some coherence of meaning. In that sense, it has the same function as dialogue in other plays. In fact, somewhat paradoxically, Beckett's text both asserts and undermines the claim that stage directions form a part of the staged text: on the one hand, stage directions play in that text the role of the staged text, but, on the other hand, they play that role only because there is no dialogue at all, and hence stage directions must substitute for it. In other terms, when dialogue on its own cannot generate a satisfactory staged text, then stage directions exceptionally gain the full status of an authorial text, that is, they are attributed the power of a fixed dialogue. One should add that such cases are extremely rare.

## Covert Transformation: Altering the Dialogue

By convention then, since stage directions can be discounted, the fixed authorial text is reduced to the dialogue. However, the same convention also postulates that this dialogue, when it functions as a fixed text, can be somewhat altered in its form. It is generally assumed, when a production claims to stage a specific text, that only the words of the original dialogue are retained, but not necessarily all the words. As a rule, a performance of *Hamlet by* Shakespeare must contain enough of unchanged Shakespearean dialogue to justify its attribution to Shakespeare. Cuts are acceptable, but any overt *change* in that dialogue, by the same tacit rule, requires a change in the performance's description, transforming it into a production of *Hamlet* as *adapted* from Shakespeare. At least, in theory. In practice, there are problems with that convention, and many supposedly fixed dialogues receive many covert textual alterations.

One type of alteration occurs inevitably when the staged text is performed in translation. A staging of Sophocles in English can never claim to reproduce the original dialogue: not only are the words and syntax different, but also their denotations and cultural connotations. There are several English versions of *Oedipus Rex*, offering quite divergent staged texts. When we read them as theatre, we get similarly divergent virtual performances, potentially leading to divergent productions, none of which ought to claim to be a play *by* Sophocles. Yet most performances of *Oedipus Rex* make that claim, as if no textual transformation had taken place. True, the translator is often attributed part of the authorial function, so that the translated rather than the original dialogue becomes the fixed text to be staged without formal changes. But even an authoritative translation never enjoys the full authorial authority of the original: readers of a translated text, working on its virtual performance, feel encouraged, and indeed justified, to carry out their own personal transformations on a dialogue that they know to be already transformed. Nevertheless, performances that include such changes are rarely acknowledged as *adaptations*. The alteration of translated texts is never denied, but it is not highlighted; for most people, it does not undermine the convention of the textual integrity of the dialogue.

The second type of alteration is less innocent, more selective, and usually secret. It involves cutting out, switching, changing, and adding parts of the dialogue. When it is textually recorded, this practice can generate, as it did for many classics, several competing versions of an often problematic Ur-text. More generally, such alterations take place in the secrecy of a reader's mind when, acting as a potential director, and building up virtual performances, he or she modifies the text of the dialogue while imagining it delivered on the stage. This process may spill over to concrete rehearsals, and sometimes to actual performances, without leaving recorded textual traces. Only spectators familiar with the text are able to detect and note it.

The resulting textual transformations, especially cuts and switched lines, are often dictated by pragmatic considerations: size of the stage, number of available actors, time or budget constraints, and so forth. These are considered to be inconsequential changes, and they are readily accepted by the public when it is informed about them. Other changes, however, reflect ideological goals, leading to controverted modifications of meaning. Thus Shakespeare's dialogues have been considerably altered to meet the demands of successive English regimes. Today such practices are frowned upon, but no doubt still occasionally take place without being advertised. In contrast, we are quite indulgent about transformations of dialogue that are motivated by artistic considerations: shortening exchanges for the sake of a faster rhythm, changing words to achieve a greater dramatic impact, adding lines that might enhance directorial or acting *performances*. But even then we tolerate textual alterations only when we judge them to be so minor that, by convention, the play in which they occur can still be attributed to its original author; otherwise, we want to call it an adaptation.

But can one firmly rely on a convention? Two recent French productions of *Hamlet* indicate that, at least in some cases, practical paradoxes can in fact undermine the conventional notion that there can be a relatively stable fixed dialogue.

In 1985 Antoine Vitez claimed that his performance of *Hamlet*, discussed above in Part II, offered "for the first time" a staging of the *complete* text of the play. This claim, perhaps true for France, has some arresting implications. Visibly Vitez, a seasoned director, believed that a venerable classic, quite well known in France, could have achieved its reputation without ever having been performed in its totality. Perhaps *Hamlet*'s popularity reflects the power of its literary text; but it must have been sustained by all previous performances which, Vitez claimed, were based on a radically cut down dialogue. In other terms, *Hamlet*'s fixed dialogue which, by convention, in order to be attributed to Shakespeare, can only present minor alterations, in fact has always been considerably transformed in many different ways. Which means in turn that there has never been, at least in France, but probably also in England, a stable text of *Hamlet*, and that all of its versions, however incomplete, can have an equally valid claim to Shakespeare's authorship. It is significant that Vitez himself did not offer his performance as being "truer" to Shakespeare than past performances; actually, using a new translation, poetic but quite free, he probably thought he was bringing out a new *Hamlet*. It is secondary that his staging lacked a strong personal vision. It did demonstrate, by its own claims, the basic instability of a conventionally fixed dialogue, and the relativity of limits beyond which covert transformations of the staged text must be identified as an adaptation.

Daniel Mesguich's production of *Hamlet* at the Théâtre Gérard Philippe in 1986–1987, only two years after the Vitez show, raised a similar problem about acceptable limits of textual transformation. Mesguich also used a new translation, and also claimed to be staging Shakespeare. Yet his dialogue deviated radically from the original text, in fact much more than in any other performance of *Hamlet* that I have seen. A lot has been cut out, but within usual conventional limits; and most of the remaining lines seemed to stay close to their model in Shakespeare. But there were also several major changes. A most radical transformation occurred when, during Hamlet's instructions to the acting company, one "actor" suddenly stepped forward and, interrupting the Shakespearean text, expounded on Mesguich's theories about theatre, and told a personal anecdote. Another type of alteration carried out a redistribution and/or repetition of lines, leading to exchanges between two Hamlets, two Horatios and two Ophelias, and the splitting of some speeches between Hamlet, a series of prompters, and a mysterious philosopher figure. Some of these textual transformations relied upon innovations in staging, quite inventive and very effective. But the question is not whether Mesguich's openly avant-garde *Hamlet* offered an excessively provocative version of the play. The question is whether his production, in terms of its textual content, justified its attribution to Shakespeare or ought to have been called an adaptation.

Which raises another question, also difficult to answer: Who can claim to judge, outside of the producer of the play, whether its textual transformations in fact overstep the boundaries of conventional changes and turn the performance into an adaptation? Professional or amateur critics? No such judgment was made in critical reviews of Mesguich's *Hamlet*, nor by public comments I heard around me. Perhaps most spectators, delighted by a stunning directorial *performance*, were willing to accept even a tortured staged text. But does that mean that all textual alterations, however radical, are discounted as long as the show is a success? That the public acknowledgment of adaptation has no stable conventional meaning? That it simply serves to announce that no original text will be produced? I must confess that, even at this time, my own response to Mesguich's performance remains ambiguous on this point: I have trouble accepting it as a version of *Hamlet* by Shakespeare, and yet I like it as a version of Shakespeare's *Hamlet*.

The problems raised by textual alterations in the two French productions lead thus to an impasse, undermining the very notion and convention of meaningless changes. But most alterations are less problematic. As a rule, the convention operates reliably: unless it is specifically identified as an adaptation, a performed play can be expected to retain the dialogue of the original dramatic text. In other words while remaining aware of potential transgressions of that rule, we must assume that a verbal text delivered on the stage can be *practically* equated with the staged text processed during a theatrical reading and concretized mentally in the form of virtual performances.

## 3. Referential Transformations of the Text

### Referential Tensions in Virtual Performances

In virtual performances, first imagined during a theatrical reading of the dramatic text and then progressively transformed during rehearsals, written dialogue is concretized as an oral dialogue, uttered by actors on the stage and supplemented with various other stage signs: intonations, facial expressions, gestures, movements, costumes, sets, and so forth. The number and detail of these additional signs will obviously vary with the power of individual imagination. Most amateurs will construct indistinct and fragmentary performances, with vaguely outlined actors delivering their lines on a misty stage; they will rely on the support of stage indications; and likely will be tempted to relapse into a literary reading. In contrast, a director (re)reading the text with an eye toward a real performance, will endow the actors with precise physical attributes, adjust their expressions and moves from line to line, build up the environment with sets and props, manipulate lights and sound effects, try out in his mind all sorts of details. Most theatrical readings no doubt oscillate between these two models. But, whatever their degree of specificity, all virtual performances must always resolve a fundamental tension that is created by two different semiotic goals of staging that compete in transforming textual referents.

On the one hand, as it is generated by reading, a virtual performance aims at creating a mental vision of a stage on which the dialogue is taking place. Viewed from that perspective, a virtual performance is a direct referent of the dramatic text, its first (imagined) concretization. When it takes a form in the reader's mind, it is principally related to information found in the text, that is, in the dialogue. Ideally, the objective of such a virtual performance is to fit as well as possible with the indications of the staged text. The reader seeks to supply the mental stage with those nonverbal signs that best correspond to verbal signs. For example, he or she visualizes angry intonations and facial expressions to match words referring to anger. True, no segment of the dialogue can be sufficiently precise to yield only one referent. A number of choices must be made, which entails changes in transformations and, as will be seen shortly, raises new problems of textual stability. Still, even the most original virtual performances, as long as they are related only to the dialogue, merely need to offer the best possible referent of the staged text. In terms of this goal, all referential changes can be practically equated with changes that any concretization must bring to any complex text.

In reality, however, especially when they are constructed by professionals, few virtual performances are considered to constitute the final goal of theatrical reading. As a rule, they are viewed as an intermediate step—first mental versions—leading to the production of real performances. Approached from that perspective, the main mission of a virtual performance is to explore and develop semiotic objectives of the real performance, that is, to communicate an original vision of an imaginary story world. To achieve that goal, the virtual performance, like a real performance, creates a set of stage signs, verbal and nonverbal, intended to generate the concretization of a novel referential world in the minds of spectators. In that process, the virtual performance no longer directly relates to the requirements of the dramatic text as in its pursuit of its first goal; it is solely oriented by the requirements of the particular imaginary world. The two goals can be contradictory.

For example, an actor mentally visualized as playing the part of Hamlet could be given, to achieve the first goal, traditional gestures of hesitation that match and confirm a hesitation suggested by his lines in the text. But, to meet the second goal, he could be given gestures showing decisiveness in order to suggest, to future spectators, that Hamlet knows what he is doing. The two images are mutually exclusive, corresponding to two contrasted interpretations of Hamlet. The virtual performance must make a choice, and that choice entails two different alterations of textual references in the dialogue.

The two goals thus involve two different semiotic strategies. In its function as a mental referent of dialogue, the virtual performance is based on the reader's reception of a given text; its transformational processes are limited to the reader's understanding of the text. In its function as a mental first version of stage signs, on the other hand, the virtual performance is based on the reader's vision of the world he or she might want to communicate to the spectators; and transformational processes are oriented by personal and ideological concerns that, originating outside the text, may have little to do with textual suggestions. Different teleologies, different approaches, different problems: a virtual performance cannot accommodate them easily. Hence the tension that always underlies all virtual performances, and threatens the stability of textual references.

In practice, that tension rarely leads to dramatic decisions. The competing objectives are usually reconciled in the form of a give-and-take compromise. Since the importance granted to textual referents is inversely proportional to the importance granted to a future real performance, most decisions only involve relative preferences. If the reader/director, moved by personal reasons, is strongly committed to a message originating outside the text, a philosophical, moral, social or political cause, then properly textual references, based on the dialogue, will be considerably but never totally eliminated. Conversely, a reader/director fascinated by the text will try to remain faithful to the dialogue's meanings but will also give at least some thought to changes that a future performance might require. In either case, the final decision will in fact be postponed until the phase of virtual performances, after various rehearsals, merges with the phase of actual staging. A number of more specific factors will contribute at that time to final referential transformations: they will be discussed below in the section "From Text to Stage."

## Altering Virtual Performances: Wild or Probable Referents

Let us first examine what happens when a virtual performance focuses exclusively on a mental staging of the dialogue. In such an ideal situation, unlikely but imaginable during an early reading, its sole task is to propose an animated vision of the staged text on an imaginary stage. But it is not a simple task. It must deal with a disturbing feature of any text reception: the instability of many textual references. This instability perturbs much more the visualization of a staged text than of a literary text. In literature, most references concern notions that are assumed to be similar for practically all readers, and hence to yield referents that follow general models. When a dramatic text is read as theatre, however, referents to be placed on the mental stage will unpredictably vary from reader to reader, without any stable common model. When we read *Hamlet* as literature, for example, we may visualize different Hamlets and Elsinores, but we assume that these Hamlets and Elsinores are always versions of shared stable concepts more or less well defined in the text: an Ur-Hamlet and an Ur-Elsinore. But when we visualize a staging of *Hamlet*, we have no general image of the actor playing Hamlet nor of sets referring to Elsinore. Costumes, lights, gestures, facial expressions, or props similarly lack precise definition in the dialogue, and hence are always largely unpredictable.

One might object that dialogue itself often contains clear references to various features of a mental stage. Dialogue allusions to doors, chairs, light, swords, specific actions, or physical traits operate, in that sense, as if they were stage directions incorporated in the staged text, and hence help to determine the nature of referents. For example, the skull picked up by an imaginary actor playing Hamlet will not be visualized at random as any possible skull: it will be conceived by all readers as a particular version of a shared model: a skull that can fit its iconic function as a sign standing for the specific skull of Yorick, a jester and Hamlet's mentor. Similarly, one could argue that a certain number of verbal signs in the dialogue will always yield a number of quite precise referents on the mental stage, creating a tiny enclave of predictability within the general instability.

But this argument has two major weaknesses. In the first place, no compelling obligation ensures that readers/directors will follow staging suggestions made in the dialogue. Treating them as a variant of stage directions, they may choose to visualize them on the mental stage, but they also can disregard them at the price of a small incoherence compensated by a much greater coherence of general meaning. In the second place, the formulation of such indications often lacks precision; a sword may be claimed to be drawn, or a gauntlet to be thrown down, but there are many types of swords and gauntlets, and many ways of performing such actions, each variant altering drastically the mental picture.

It is better therefore to posit that nothing in the dialogue can generate stable forms on the mental stage. At the same time, however, it is important to remember that the same dialogue, in order to yield a virtual performance, must always somehow suggest many mental stage features that are not mentioned in the text. Like a real performance, any advanced virtual performance, in addition to verbal signs must always contain certain *compulsory* nonverbal signs: features without which words can be neither imagined nor produced on the stage. Thus dialogue lines cannot be delivered without some intonation, and the actor who speaks the lines must display a facial expression (be it blank), wear some sort of costume (be it nudity), perform some gestures and moves (or be motionless), appear in a certain light (be it darkness) and be surrounded by some sets (at least a bare floor). Each of these signs, as shall be shown later, always somehow affects the referents of the dialogue. But the dialogue does not indicate exactly what these signs should be, nor how they should modify referents.

When we read Hamlet's words: "Alas, poor Yorick!" and try to concretize in our mind an actor who delivers them, we are not informed as to the intonation of that actor's voice. Yet, on our mental stage, we must imagine some intonation, while aware that our unavoidable choice will turn the statement into an expression of nostalgia, or amusement, or despondency, enriching in different ways the referent of the line. Whatever we decide, then, we necessarily create a referential transformation of the staged text. In other terms, with their compulsory nonverbal signs, all virtual performances demand a constant alteration of referents suggested by the dialogue.

Hence the following questions: Are these transformations really unpredictable, leading to wild referents, or can they be predicted with some degree of probability? Is there something in the staged text, or outside it, that controls referential alterations in virtual performances? What goals can influence choices of referents and intended meanings?

It would seem that there are three main sources of referential choices. The first, and perhaps the most influential, derives from the literary reading that usually precedes, and often accompanies, a properly theatrical reading. When the dramatic text is read as literature, let us repeat, it yields an imaginary world that is much more stable than a mental stage. To be sure, individual readers visualize that world with different details, and deduce different meanings, but each vision increases its coherence as the reading progresses or is repeated. Even an "open" text, say, *Waiting for Godot* read as literature, while requiring some interpretation, eventually conveys a well-integrated story about two bums who, on a country road with a tree, are compelled to wait for a symbolic object of desire, God, or Change, or Death, and so forth. For each individual reader, such a coherent vision then provides, consciously or not, a model for subsequent properly theatrical readings, and inspires virtual performances where compulsory features, added on the mental stage, are chosen to support the referents yielded by the literary reading. The fact that most productions of *Godot* are quite repetitive suggests, in that sense, that they have been inspired by such similar literary readings, generating "faithful" but unimaginative performances.

The second possible source of referential choices lies in the message that a reader/director wants to communicate. In that case, the literary reading of the text is disregarded, and the virtual performance is built up directly during a theatrical reading. The reader/director is not trying to visualize a mental stage that best corresponds to dialogue signs: say, a virtual performance of *Godot* where added nonverbal features would support the lines delivered by the actors. Rather, regarding the virtual performance as a model for a real performance, a reader/director focuses on the way that signs placed on the mental stage might be received by future spectators. In other terms, when it is inspired by a personal message, all features of the virtual performance are determined by their ability to convey the desired message and not by the requirements of the dialogue. A virtual performance of *Godot* seeking to censure U.S. policies in Central America thus might, on the mental stage, visualize the actors who play the bums as wearing sombreros, and actors playing Pozzo and Lucky as looking and moving like

American soldiers. Outside motivations usually justify quite radical and inventive referential alterations. However, directed to potential spectators, such virtual performances lack stability since the reader/director cannot be sure of the audience's reactions. The full impact of outside messages can be only evidenced by transformations carried out in real performances.

The third source of choices in visualization could be defined as the internal logic of the staged text. Rejecting both the literary model and outside concerns, many readers/directors believe that the dialogue itself, unraveling the network of its verbal signs, somehow always produces a coherent pattern of meaning, suggesting precise referential strategies. During the theatrical reading, such readers/directors build up their virtual performances with tentative touches, playing with a variety of nonverbal features in order to support verbal references, changing them as the reading progresses, and reshaping the mental stage till it stabilizes in the form of a satisfactory vision. In theory, this constant adjusting and readjusting of referents is oriented, and hence justified, by a coherent meaning of the story that the virtual performance conveys to the reader who acts both as its imaginary director and its imaginary spectator. Formulated in these terms, this approach is extremely popular, leading to real performances which, as is so often claimed, are dictated by the text.

Yet *praxis* demonstrates that even very coherent dramatic texts yield many different meanings and hence many different virtual and real performances. Faced with that diversity, students of theatre may be tempted to survey it systematically: measure the gaps between staging variations, note extreme boundaries of deviation, and draw the map of "semiotic fields" that would include all the potential performances of given texts. But such a study, even restricted to a single text, would be beyond the power of the most dedicated scholar. Logically, giving up the hope to bring order to chaos, many theatre students then prefer to acknowledge that the "semiotic field" of a text cannot be explored, and that it has no definite limits. They are encouraged in that opinion by claims of deconstruction that signs cannot have stable meanings, or swayed by post-Lacanian arguments that no sign can resist the uncontrollable impulses of the "desiring subject." Indeed, from either of these fashionable perspectives, no virtual performances derived from verbal signs can have any solid source; and, which comes to the same, all performances of a given dramatic text are always somewhat "wild."

These arguments are quite persuasive and supported by the evidence of many "wild" performances of canonical texts. However, both deconstructionists and theoreticians of the "desiring subject" demonstrate, in their own writing practice, that the fragility of verbal signs, and the instability of textual referents, must not be taken too seriously. While theorizing the "wildness" of all receptions of texts, these writings clearly assume a stable reception of their own statements. And their success indicates that this expectation is generally met. No doubt there always will be some "wild" readings of Derrida and Lacan; but, within the sociocultural group that normally can be expected to read Derrida and Lacan, most readers can be expected to draw from their texts at least the most basic of their intended meaning, getting a core of *probable referents*.

For similar reasons, it can be expected that readers of a dramatic text, when they belong to a specific sociocultural group, will also assign *probable referents* to its verbal signs, and build up *probable virtual performances* on the basis of these probable referents. In many cases, these probable responses will eventually affect real performances. To be sure, some individual readers will always imagine various "wild" virtual performances. Idiosyncratic reactions to a text cannot be predicted, nor safely explained. Only an aberrant "wild" virtual performance could have inspired, in a production of Sartre's *Les Mains sales*, a transformation of its final line "Non récupérable!" into its contrary: "Non! Récupérable!" But there remains a high probability that readers/ directors with the same sociocultural background will normally visualize, for the same dramatic text, very similar mental stagings, associating similar nonverbal features with verbal statements in the dialogue.

In such probable virtual performances, the referential transformations of the staged text can then be expected to follow quite predictable directions, tied to the culture of a given group. For a prison inmate, for example, the entire network of references in *Waiting for Godot* will probably be oriented by a commanding desire for freedom, entailing appropriate alterations in textual referents: country-road sets changed into prison-yard sets, actors costumed in prisoner outfits or in guard uniforms. Whether a real prison performance of *Godot* would retain such transformational features of the probable virtual performance is unpredictable: too many other factors are at work. But we are dealing now with virtual performances that modify textual references *before* an actual production.

There is one practical problem with the notion of probable virtual performances. In order to predict them, or to explain them when they are documented, one needs to have a good knowledge of the sociocultural group of readers/directors. And such groups are hard to define. The general milieu of theatre people includes many national, social, and cultural groups that interact and change at a rapid rate. How can one identify with any precision the probable group of a given reader/director? Or estimate, within that group, which of its various subgroups has inspired a given reading, and at what point in its changing outlook? A recent performance of *Godot* placed it on the rooftops of an industrial city, no doubt reflecting an earlier referential transformation of the dialogue in a virtual performance. For what group, and hence for what type of reader/director, was it a probable transformation? Perhaps the notion of probability has only a theoretical interest for virtual performances, always visualized only by individuals, and should be reserved for the reception of real performances by concrete groups of spectators.

But perhaps pragmatic concerns are here secondary. Virtual performances constitute an essential step in the theatrical process and must be well understood. Whether influenced by a literary reading, or an ideological commitment, or a *probable* visualization of the dialogue, they account indeed for a first referential transformation of the dramatic text, the first alteration of its meaning. The theatrical process cannot be fully appreciated without an acknowledgment of that function, regardless of the fact that virtual performances are always secret, at best recorded in secondary documents. The real pragmatic impact of virtual performances is felt during the transition from text to stage.

## 4. From Text to Stage: Parameters of Transformation

### Open and Closed Texts: Textual Transformability

Implementing the transition from text to stage is the proper responsibility of the directorial function. It may be carried out, as noted previously, by an author, an actor, a group, a single director, or any combination of the above. Whatever the case, however, here as elsewhere, the agent(s) performing the directorial function always will be referred to as the director. The director's specific role is thus to direct the transformation of a dramatic text into a staged performance. This process begins with the reception of the text, usually through literary and theatrical readings, continues with the creation of a virtual performance, then reaches its central phase with the supervision of actual staging.

In all these phases, in addition to providing a general leadership, the director is involved in a constant interaction with the verbal signs of the text. During that process, some signs can be cut out or changed, but—by a tacit convention—the dialogue is expected to remain stable, reflecting its historically privileged status. The director's contribution, and claim to original creation, rests on the production of nonverbal features that the performance adds to the dialogue. Some of these features may be designed to serve the performant rather than the referential function, but, once displayed on the stage, they also operate as signs and combine with all the other signs, verbal and nonverbal, in evoking an imaginary story world. The overall activity of the director thus always results in some referential transformations of the text. The orientation of these changes is dictated by the director's goals, whether artistic or ideological. But the scope and concrete features of change also reflect the specific nature of the text, which can be more or less suitable for transformations.

In theory, all texts can be transformed. In practice, there are many reasons why a given text is selected to be transformed. Some texts appeal to particular directors because they fit their personal goals. Other texts are revived, and transformed, on special occasions, such as anniversaries and commemorations, or because they have been recently "rediscovered," or because they are taught in schools and form the repertory of "classics." But, all other things being equal, some texts seem to encourage transformations, as it were, on their own, that is, by certain features of their verbal signs. These texts, as a rule, inspire innovative performances whatever the specific reason for their staging.

The usual explanation of their appeal is that they carry a universal message. They are supposed to deal with eternal issues—love, death, anxiety, hatred, envy, guilt, and so forth—and hence to remain always relevant. But such a general relevance does not suffice to trigger transformations. Many texts that deal with universal topics fail to generate original performances. And some of the most original performances minimize the universality of the text, focusing instead on a contingent issue. In fact, any dramatic text can be staged to stress universal or particular themes, depending on the director's inclination rather than on its own message.

Not the topic, then, but rather the malleability of the text accounts for its appeal to innovative directors. Such directors, seeking a creative role in the production of the performance, know that they have to transform the traditional meanings of the dialogue. They are therefore naturally drawn to texts that have a high potential of transformability, texts wherein verbal signs can be easily manipulated in order to generate new meanings. And indeed some dialogues lend themselves to manipulation whereas others appear to resist it; whatever their topic, some dialogues invite transformations while others discourage them. From the perspective of a creative director seeking to bring in a new meaning, these two types of dialogue operate as open texts and closed texts.

The degree of referential transformability, determining the openness or closure of a text, obviously involves many factors. Any particular text reflects the impact of several of them, including some that are specific to it. It seems, however, that three factors are general enough to deserve special attention. They concern three formal features that any dialogue must display with varying degrees of intensity: (1) frequency of verbal references to nonverbal stage signs, (2) degree of referential integration, and (3) precision in the use of the linguistic code. Though they combine and interact one with another, they will be examined separately.

First, then: frequency of verbal references to nonverbal stage signs. Statements made in the dialogue about material features of the stage (sets or props) and events that take place on it (movements, gestures, expressions or intonations) have been discussed above (Part III, third section). We have seen that, like formal stage directions, these references are not really compelling, though they tend to be followed in most staging practices. When, in *Richard II*, York tells Northumberland that, in the past, had he lacked proper respect, the king "would / Have been so brief with you to shorten you, / For taking so the head, your whole head's length" (III,3), the actor is usually made to suggest decapitation with a hand gesture cutting across his throat: a logical interpretation of a relatively minor ambiguity. But other gestures could have worked as well: measuring the length of the head, or cutting across the throat of the actor playing Northumberland, or—in a bold staging—pointing to a decapitated body brought on the stage for that purpose as a part of the background. However, a director could also decide not to have any clarifying gesture at all, maintaining the ambiguity of the text. Similarly, in same play, a reference to a gauntlet challenge need not be matched by the display of the gauntlet; coherence demands its presence, but a director may chose to disregard strict coherence. No dramatic text is totally devoid of ambiguities and incoherences, and hence no performance can be expected totally to avoid them.

Yet clarity and coherence are powerful magnets, especially with regard to truly important stage features: decisive events, violent actions, fatal weapons. A heavy accumulation of such major textual references contributes to the closure of the text. It restricts the freedom to change meaning: even partial transformations, resulting from an innovative staging, must be carefully weighed lest the entire performance turn into parody. Conversely, a dialogue with few references to stage business has a high transformability potential, opening vast areas of the text to the director's own meanings.

Second factor: degree of referential integration. All dramatic texts juggle a large number of signs which, decoded by a reader/director, communicate a heterogeneous mass of referents. To that extent, the mentally visualized story world, or stage, reflects the chaotic appearance of the real world. And, like our vision of the real world, it requires a structuring activity during the reception process in order to make sense of fragmentary, discontinuous, and uncoordinated networks of meaning. A well-organized dramatic text, anticipating that need, manages to integrate in a tight structure the largest possible number of meaningful references to action, ideas, feelings, appearances, message, history, space, and so forth. Together, they combine to make a certain sense. In contrast, a loosely structured text has few specific references, and leaves them dangling without clear connections. Their combination yields no commanding overall meaning; at best, it rather suggests a multiplicity of possible senses.

In either case, the required restructuring of meanings in theatre performances, virtual or real, must be carried out by directors, moved by their vision of the story world. But they always work with an initial structure received from the author's text: a dialogue that is either constraining when it is well integrated or stimulating when it is loose. Obviously, there are no totally integrated or disorganized dialogues, no absolutely closed or open texts. But the degree of integration may vary considerably, in proportion to the power of various integrating devices: strict causal relations; formal patterns of circularity; parallelism or antithesis; redundancy and echoes; clockwork construction, as in Feydeau's comedies.

A text well fortified by these devices will seem to the director to be closed to partial transformations: changing one set of references might bring the collapse of the entire structure, an intimidating prospect. It is well known, for example, that Sartre's *No Exit*, while often performed, is generally staged without significant variations; even innovative directors appear unwilling to transform its tight pattern of a closed room, three couches, and circular exchanges between three characters. Other Sartre's plays display other forms of closure; and they are rarely staged.[2] And no wonder, since Sartre took special care to integrate his texts on all levels, adjusting location to plot, temperament to action, vocabulary and syntax to temperament, and everything to his philosophical message, so that nothing can be altered without endangering the whole. In short, in order to protect the authorial meaning of his works, he keeps to a minimum their transformability potential.

*Waiting for Godot* relies on a more subtle strategy. It is quite evident that its structure displays a pattern of integration based on a strict binary principle: two dramatic situations, two characters in each situation, two acts, and a systematic equivalence/opposition relation between and within each dual unit[3]—telling marks of a closed text. Yet, paradoxically, *Godot*'s performances have multiplied throughout the world, yielding often a surprisingly original staging and an innovative directorial meaning. The reason for this paradox lies in the nature of the binary integration that concerns only the macrostructure of the play. In contrast, most of the actual dialogue verges rather on disintegration: disconnected and repetitive exchanges, inviting arbitrary interpretations. *Godot*'s transformability potential is heightened by that openness. But it also benefits from an additional factor: the imprecise meaning of many of its textual statements.

Which leads to the third factor: precision in the use of the linguistic code. One recalls that, in contrast to a literary text, where ambiguities are usually clarified with increasingly precise references and paradigmatic confusion is dispelled by syntagmatic checks carried out by readers at their own pace, stopping and moving back when needed, a theatrical text tends to be elusive, slippery, and vulnerable because of the fragility of verbal exchanges. Delivered on the stage, a dialogue is constrained by time limitation, and its words, not always distinctly perceived and subject to vagaries of voices, can never be retrieved or elucidated. Authors of dramatic texts intended to be staged are well aware of this vulnerability of verbal signs. They also know that several textual strategies can serve to achieve a more reliable communication. A precise vocabulary, a logical syntax, and explanations of equivocal terms or notions may not enhance the literary quality of a dramatic text, but they ensure that its references will have a better chance to reach the future spectators, regardless of interferences by directors who, in fact, are thus discouraged from interfering. But not all texts attempt to build such a linguistic closure and weaken their transformability potential. Some seem to be deliberately open to transformations. They indulge in poetic images and/or words with an imprecise sense, and avoid clarifications that could hamper directorial initiatives.

A good illustration of the first category can be found in Sartre's *Les Mains sales*, which heavily stresses the linguistic closure. Like most other Sartre plays, it is protected by many references to stage features and by a high degree of integration; but, more than the others, it relies on a textual clarification of its key terms and/or ideas. Thus *role-playing* is mentioned, within one short scene, more than twenty times, by the means of a rather brilliant variation on forms of "jouer"—in the infinitive, first, second and third person, and in the affirmative, interrogative, and negative; the meaning of self-respect is explained in simple terms to characters conveniently assigned very simple minds; and the abstract notion of commitment is elucidated by the characters themselves when they argue about their personal problems. There is no need nor opportunity to reinterpret, hence to transform, what Sartre has set down so firmly. The transformability potential is minimal.

*Godot*, and partly *Hamlet*, evidence the opposite approach. The lack of verbal precision in *Godot* needs few comments. As has been often noted, the very name of Godot, featured in the title *and* in the plot, obviously has been intended to have many possible meanings, while nothing in the text helps to chose among them. And Lucky's monologue, though less meaningless than one may think, certainly makes no evident sense, while nothing in the text indicates how it could/should be delivered to acquire at least some clear meaning. Most of the dialogue is similarly vague. As a result, the director is not only free to project a personal meaning, but drawn to do so by the textual vacuum. To a large extent, the poetic quality of *Hamlet* derives from a comparable verbal imprecision. The celebrated interrogation, "To be or not to be," while well conveying a philosophical questioning of life, actually raises very vague points and relies on quite vague terms. At the end of the monologue, the reader/director may still wonder what "to be" really means, or what is the proper sense of "that is the question"— doubts that encourage supplying one's own meaning. Both *Godot* and *Hamlet* are wide open to transformations, and indeed have been generating a remarkable stream of original performances.

My examples obviously illustrate extreme cases of high and low transformability. For most texts, matters are more complex. Many open texts fail to be staged frequently or with originality. Some very transformable French classics have not yet escaped from the hallowed stage of the Comédie Française, and Shakespeare still breeds, as Peter Brook noted, the most persistent manifestations of *dead* theatre. Conversely, well-closed texts, such as Marivaux's *La Dispute*, have been boldly transformed by determined directors. In most cases, openness and closure have no truly predictable impact on future performances of a dramatic text. However, they can help to explain, after the fact, and all other things being equal, why some texts evidence more staging appeal than others. Their contribution to transformability, within the limited scope of its goals, can at least make claims to some degree of objectivity.

Other approaches offer few concrete answers to the initial question: Why do some texts, and not others, inspire fertile stagings? We have seen that the content has little to do with that issue. It is not much more helpful to state that, in order to generate repeated revivals, a text must be attractive, that is, it must seduce directors by an exceptional promise of future referential interest. How can one grasp what generates that promise? What features of the text account for the elusive quality that, instinctively, we attribute to "a great text"? Surely this "greatness" and hence a text's appeal cannot be reduced to a formula. Analyses of past great theatre successes may bring into the open some of their secrets, but much remains mysterious. The matching of individual talents of playwrights and directors, their emotions, or ideologies, or artistic sensitivities, cannot be fully explained nor anticipated: there will always be only a few masterpieces.

At best, we may try to formulate probabilities. For example, in the spirit of sociocriticism, we can propose what *type* of text expresses or satisfies the expectations of a sociocultural group, what *type* of production and/or reception fits the past, the present, or a predictable future. But our best efforts will never fully account for the fortune of a concrete text, for wild reactions of talented directors. We are bound to the limited area of probable production and reception and to the limited observation that it can offer. Within these boundaries, nevertheless, the notion of textual transformability is indispensable for a full understanding of the transition from text to stage.

## Types of Transformed Performances

Each performance, we have seen, always somewhat transforms the meanings of the verbal text by the means of added stage signs. The scope of transformations, as shown above, can be partly related to formal features of the text, more or less transformable. But, whatever the text, the actual extent of transformations and their direction depend ultimately on the decisions of directors responsible for the performance.

Several factors are each time at work. Some escape any rational discourse: fleeting impulses, uncontrolled obsessions, secret complexes, inchoate feelings of anxiety, or desire, or hatred. They move individual directors without their full awareness; and, while one can attribute to them many strange transformations, they cannot be predicted or clarified. Such factors generate truly wild performances, beyond the scope of this study.

Other factors concern a director's personality. Ambition, drive, and creativity surely have an impact on the scope of transformations. Yet, however decisive, these factors will also be here discounted; they may increase aggressiveness toward the text, but do not determine any special direction. Besides, the search for a purely formal excellence often drains the energy released by a powerful personality and thus protects the text from radical transformations.

In contrast, there exists a direct and focused relation between the manipulation of meaning and the role that directors want to play in the theatrical process, their attitudes toward both text and performance, and their conscious or unconscious goals when they carry out their directorial function. In that sense, three major distinct positions can be observed. The first ties the directorial function to the service of the text: the director primarily seeks to tell on the stage the same story that was told in the text, and holds serious transformations to a minimum. The second stresses the performant function of theatre: the director primarily seeks to bring about all potential *performances* that the text may generate on the stage. The third may be identified as an ideological teleology: the director feels compelled to promote some strong personal ideas, and tells on the stage a story that uses the text as a support for these ideas. Some performances try to combine all three goals, in an attempt to serve a classic text with great *performances* while conveying a contemporary committed message: Planchon attempted it in his staging of *Tartuffe*, which will be discussed below. Others focus on one goal only: thus, as we have seen, Mnouchkine's *Richard II* practically sacrificed text and message to the performant function. Regardless of their interaction, it is better to take each approach separately, and see how it operates in transformed performances.

## Text-Oriented Performances

The first approach yields performances oriented toward the text. It is the most traditional approach: in fact, respecting the text has been long believed to be the only proper attitude in theatre, and even today most directors are expected to conform to it. The main justification for such a respect is that a performance ought to display the same qualities that made the text "attractive" in the first place, that is, those that inspired the desire to stage it. As a result, a text-oriented performance ideally follows as closely as possible the story told in the dialogue and, by the same occasion, strives to convey to the public the major meanings and messages that the dramatic text communicates to its reader/director.

A text-oriented performance, however, must not be naively conceived as a mere animation of the dialogue, offering a strictly "faithful," three-dimensional version of the story already told in the dramatic text. In fact, even in performances most deliberately oriented toward the text, references made on the stage can never be identical to references made in the text. For, as will be shown shortly, once stage signs are added to the verbal signs, the story world communicated by the performance will always deviate from the story world visualized directly in the process of literary reading; in fact, it will also deviate from the story world that could be communicated by the tentative virtual performance produced during a theatrical reading. In short, a referential gap between text and stage is inevitable. But there are various ways of dealing with it: reducing it to a minimum, or enlarging its scope, or filling it with new material while taking care not to alter the text's major meanings.

That nonverbal stage signs, always somewhat in excess of verbal signs, are the first cause of all referential gaps needs no long demonstration. The world evoked on the stage with sets, props, costumes, physical appearance of actors, their intonations, gestures, and facial expressions, has no chance to correspond to the world imagined by individual readers of the text: it will be more detailed and complex, or, on the contrary simpler, but always different. And, let us repeat, most stage signs are compulsory, so that a director cannot try to eliminate them in order to minimize the prospects for referential differences. On the other hand, relying on probable rather than individual receptions of the text, a cautious director can at least minimize the impact of unavoidable differences so that they would not affect understanding the story or drawing intended meanings. There is, for example, a vast range of probable visualizations of a pair of bums, their outfits and behavior, all of them equally well serving on the stage to communicate the textual references to bums in *Godot*. In terms of probable readings, then, the referential gaps created by nonverbal stage signs do not have to undermine the goals of text-oriented performances: they can be made to conform to the overall probable reception of textual story and meaning.

Two other causes of referential gaps have more serious effects. In the first place, a director's reception of a complex dialogue inevitably yields, as shown above, a considerable number of possible or even probable meanings. These meanings can easily coexist and compete one with another in any verbal text that, as is usually the case, contains various vague, equivocal, or contradictory statements. It is difficult, however, if not impossible, to convey all of these meanings simultaneously on the stage. Indeed, the stage can only display selected concrete stage signs that point to specific referents. One may wonder, for instance, whether *Godot*'s bums are happy or sad, hopeful or resigned, noble or trivial, or simply indifferent to what might happen to them. A reader will hesitate between the answers, but a director must make a choice that will determine the selection of appropriate stage signs: happy or resigned or flat intonations, but not all three at the same time. By the same token, of course, supporting a particular meaning of the story with carefully selected signs, the director will necessarily mask all other competing textual meanings. The very open text of *Godot* is always transformed on the stage into a closed performance.

Second: a similar referential gap occurs when performances clarify textual ambiguities in their natural drive toward coherence. Some

directors, particularly attached to clarity, may believe that they serve
the text when they remove, with appropriately slanted stage signs,
disturbing manifestations of verbal obscurity. For instance, one could
claim, if *Godot*'s bums really trust in Godot's coming, then they have no
good reason to attempt suicide; and, persuaded by that logic, a director
might want to set things straight by turning the hanging scene into a
joke. Without altering the story, nor any major meaning, he or she will
cut out a textual invitation to ponder about the sense of an ambiguity.
As a rule, however, such changes take place without a conscious intention to promote coherence. Indeed, any stage sign connected to a
verbal ambiguity cannot help but somewhat clarify it. In a faithful
staging, the failed suicide in *Godot* must be *shown* on the stage and,
through their movements, gestures, expressions, and intonations, the
actors playing the bums will always narrow down the open meanings of
the text to one probable coherent meaning. The resulting referential
gap between text and stage will be beneficial insofar as it sharpens our
vision of the story world, but it will also impoverish that world.

In other cases, however, awareness of the inevitability of referential gaps can stimulate an enrichment of the story world. Truly innovative directors, while firmly dedicated to producing text-oriented performances, find inspiration in the knowledge that transformations are
unavoidable but acceptable as long as they do not change major features of the textual story. Without reaching beyond the probable referential field, they expand that field from inside, exploring its possibilities and inserting new but compatible features in the staged world. To
squeeze discreet minor meanings from the text, they resort to close
readings, structural analyses, historical reconstruction of the verbal
code—in short, all orthodox means of recovering lost or hidden references. And sometimes they are inspired by an intuitive vision of a
missing feature that rounds up the story. There are enough textual
suggestions that Godot stands for God, for example, to motivate such
directors to have the two bums kneel in deep prayer at the end of
*Godot*'s performance. The religious note thus added with stage signs
would contradict textual stage directions, a permissible strategy, but
would mesh creatively with one of the probable meanings of the text.

That a text-oriented performance can easily accommodate many
such staging variations should not be surprising. No text can be declared to be firmly closed, especially when it is viewed from a historical
perspective. At any particular time, and for any particular group, it
offers new openings as its verbal signs generate different probable
receptions. Caught in the diachronic flux, successive readers change
textual meanings in accordance with their own change brought about
by History. And successive directors, both traditional and innovative,

caught in the same process of change, approach their staging strategies with the same changing sociocultural bias that determines new reading receptions. As a result, when they perceive textual openings, they tend to produce nonverbal stage signs with references that are naturally compatible with textual references of verbal signs. An innovative approach will exploit more openings than a traditional approach; it will endow meanings with a greater subtlety; but its performances will display a similarly concerted combination of all signs, evoking a harmonious vision of the story world first proposed by the text.

The specific directions that innovation may take in text oriented performances will be discussed in Part IV. Some of these directions are also followed in traditional staging. Indeed, it bears repeating, whatever its exact strategy, a text-oriented performance always carries out enough transformations to give it some originality. This originality is an essential factor in theatre's appeal; it is expected from the most conventional productions of a "faithful" performance. Each "faithful" performance, however original, asserts in priority its dependence on the text it serves, offers the reassuring demonstration that the text is its fixed support. Yet it is not the text, always the same, but the originality of each staging that creates interest in the performance. In that sense, though rarely very exciting, text-oriented performances constitute exemplary manifestations of the basic destiny of theatre: a constant revival of old texts in new stage productions.

## Performances Inspired by the Performant Function

Quite different, in a sense, antithetical, is the role of the text in performances inspired by the performant function of theatre. Instead of serving the text, these performances treat it as a pretext: a source of inspiration for a staging that seeks to display extraordinary achievements by performers, that is, *performances*. The director's stage signs, while keeping their referential status, are primarily intended in such performances to offer various exceptional features, related to properly theatrical or to nontheatrical interests: superior acting, set designs, costumes, or a striking aesthetic or erotic appeal, or the prestige of a celebrity. This search for a *performance* can also lead to an enhancement of the appeal of verbal signs at the expense of their referential function: thus, as discussed above, in Mnouchkine's *Richard II* the poetry of the text had an exceptional impact largely because its references to the story were often lost. The variety of ways in which the performant function can operate in a performance has been discussed at length in Part I above; there is no need to go over them here.

It bears repeating, however, that *performances* as such contribute very little to the referential story. In fact, when they are perceived, they desemiotize the stage, and interrupt for a while the vision of its mental mirror-image world. Nontheatrical *performances*, say, exceptionally beautiful sets or exciting bodies, actually urge a recall of norms in the world outside theatre. And theatrical *performances*, while they increase the overall interest in the performance and hence improve the conditions of its reception, tend to limit their referential contribution to the discrete features that support them. For instance, in Chéreau's version of *La Dispute*, a cleverly designed backstage garden seemed to have an unbelievable depth: a *performance* that certainly enhanced the reception of the play but added only a small touch to the meaning of the story by its allusion to the Garden of Eden. And, in Mesguich's *Hamlet*, when rotating prompter boxes suddenly were slammed down at the end of Hamlet's monologue, most spectators applauded the director's inventive *performance* but could hardly draw from it any precise meaning related to Hamlet's story. As signs, garden and prompter boxes referred in fact much more effectively to the theatrical nature of the performance than to any feature of its imaginary world.

In that sense, Mesguich's prompter boxes, though quite unexpected in the setting of Elsinore, contributed very coherently to the general theatricality of his somewhat surrealist staging. In some cases, however, the performant strategy may lead to incoherence, especially when a performance is well structured. To suggest the innocence of a young couple in *La Dispute*, Chéreau placed them naked in a nature setting—a logical referential device that, however, was surely also expected to create a *performance* by its boldness and/or erotic appeal; as a result, when the verbal text called for the girl to discover her beauty in a mirror, no mirror could appear on the stage. Nor did the boy's eyes substitute for it. But the audience did not seem to mind, noticing but justifying the minor incoherence by the overall coherence of the directorial *performance*.

There remains that most effective *performances*, at least in my experience, are carefully matched with referential goals, and while they always strain the coherence of the story world on one level, they sometimes manage to reinforce it on another level. When Planchon staged *Tartuffe*, its extraordinary success was partly attributed to startling sets, props, and costumes: a half-crumbling baroque facade with a giant eye on top as an improbable mirror image of a staid bourgeois dwelling, a Christlike figure and a king's statue within it, and actors in long underwear. Each of these apparent incongruities was striking, if not shocking, and hailed as a *performance*; but together they could claim to project a coherent symbolic meaning on Tartuffe's society: a decadent world of religious and political rituals wherein, in the absence of a manifest royal authority, an awkward middle class was trying to determine what could be its new place.

At the end of the play, however, Planchon broke with this historic coherence. He added an anachronistic episode of modern police brutality, evoking Gestapo troopers breaking into a victim's home: a powerful scene, expanding Molière's short verbal conclusion into a long sequence of violence. Hailed as another directorial *performance*, this open intrusion of totalitarian terror had no obvious relation to the conventional spirit of Tartuffe's world. In 1966 France, it brought to mind rather the horror of World War II, Indochina, and Algeria. At the last moment, the hidden flawed structure of the global performance was illuminated by a dazzling flash of incoherence. It seemed as if, in the final scene, Planchon lost his control of the performant function, misjudged his ability to integrate in the total performance his boldest attempt at a *performance*.

But was the police episode really intended by him to offer a *performance*? My feeling is rather that Planchon, like many French at that time, was deeply committed to an antitotalitarian ideology and used *Tartuffe*'s last scene, quite deliberately, to expose the threats of all police states, even those masquerading as democracies. The referential incoherence of his staging derived from that ideological commitment, and its basic incompatibility with Molière's dialogue. To combine a classic text and a modern message is always a daring project; by pulling it off in the last scene, at a small price in coherence, Planchon did achieve a *performance*, but without looking for one. In all other respects, his *Tartuffe* served well the performant function, and was well served by it, a near perfect example of harmonious coexistence of referential meanings and outstanding stage accomplishments.

## Ideologically Oriented Performances

The ideology that inspired Planchon to transform the end of *Tartuffe* was clearly political. But there are many other types of ideological positions that inspire referential transformations. As understood here, *ideology* refers to any set of strong ideas that shapes a director's vision of a performance's goals. These ideas may take the form of a philosophy, a social policy, a cultural concept, a theory of psychology, a trust in an absolute value, or any other belief that compels the director to alter, by the means of stage signs, the textual meaning of the story.

Most such compelling ideologies, like Planchon's antitotalitarian views, reflect critical issues of the contemporary society. Some, to be sure, first originate in individual experiences, but they acquire their full transforming power only when they become conceptualized and recognized as a general ideology. A director victimized by racial or sexual prejudices will have personal reasons to object against discrimination; but his or her concerns need to receive an ideological form in order to motivate a conscious transformation of a dramatic text into a manifesto against discrimination. Or, in a less focused way, personal reasons to question a stable meaning of life need to be formulated as an ideology of the absurd in order to generate a deliberately absurd staging. True, individual obsessions that do not, or cannot, take the form of an ideology can also influence staging, and sometimes lead to startling transformations of meaning; but, as noted above, they usually result in wild performances that elude rational explanations.

General ideologies present no such difficulties. They have a high degree of visibility in the sociocultural group that promotes and debates them. Whether grounded in contingent political issues, such as the Vietnam War in the United States, or in endemic problems such as racism, sexism, or social and economic injustices, they inspire passion, strong commitments, and dramatic texts written specifically for ideological purposes: Megan Terry's *Vietrock* or Sartre's *La putain respectueuse*. Referential changes in performances oriented by these powerful ideologies are easy to detect and explain. Planchon's manipulation of *Tartuffe*, or Peter Brook's stage signs that gave an antiwar slant to his version of the *Mahabharata*, a basically epic text even in its theatrical adaptation, can be matched with many other examples of ideological staging: no point multiplying them here.

More diffuse issues have less evident ideological effects. The erosion of humanist values in a technological world, the alienation of creative minds in a society dominated by mass media or by a corporate culture, have inspired as yet few fiery debates, few committed ideologies. They create nonetheless a basic anxiety among the most concerned groups, principally intellectuals and artists, and anxiety breeds ideological reactions. The current trend of art toward self-referentiality, that is, art about art, and the inward-directed interest in a human nature severed from History, clearly manifest an ideology that promotes individual withdrawal from an increasingly indifferent society— an ideology that claims that art is more important than reality, and that inner truth is more valid than socially determined values.

Influenced by that ideology, various directors have been altering the meaning of dramatic texts in order to illustrate, denounce, or compensate their feeling of alienation. Their transforming strategies can be best detected in performances by groups that are particularly sensitive to social and cultural estrangement. Grotowski's work with the Wrocław Laboratory offers a good example.

Grotowski's most telling experiment, in that sense, was probably his radical transformation of Corneille's *Le Cid* into a fragmented performance where stage signs had no apparent relation to the text.[4] The scene where Rodrigue's fate is hotly argued by two characters trying to influence the king was staged like a corrida, with two actors/bulls running at a toreador. Grotowski based that staging on primordial images generated by Corneille's text in the mind of actors, trusting that their semiconscious associations could reveal universal myths that are concealed in great works. But this belief in the individual unconscious as a source of truth surely was inspired by an ideology influenced by contingent social conditions. Working in a communist Poland that encouraged artistic innovations but no political dissent, Grotowski responded to these mixed signals with a mystical ideology of aesthetics, denying importance to History, hence to politics, and sanctifying an art emerging from the recesses of a secret self. By this ideological logic, the clearly political meaning of *Le Cid* was dramatically replaced by the celebration of a sacrificial ritual.

A comparable position was taken by the Living Theatre when, disappointed by the public response to its politically committed performances, it decided to stress the release of individual emotions. But the ideologies of the two groups were not quite the same, reflecting differences in situations. Grotowski, facing a censorship forced upon his society by an outside power, turned with hope to universal values while waiting for a return of freedom in Poland. The Living Theatre, in a democratic country, had only its own free society, perhaps its own hopes, to blame for the failure of its call for individual liberation; hence its more radical discount of humanist concerns, and a deeper feeling of withdrawal that, gradually, led the group to disband itself. Grotowski's ideology also became with time more sharply focused on individual self-expression. But then his working conditions had changed, leading him first to a secretive "retreat" in Poland and later to exile in California.

The ideology of withdrawal, which inspired early performances by Grotowski and the Living Theatre, lost much of its appeal at the same time that radical avant-garde companies went into a decline. But the rejection of History can be also detected in performances offered by better established companies that serve a more general ideology of Art. Mnouchkine's *Richard II*, we noted, transformed Shakespeare's story into a theatre performance about a theatre performance, demonstrating that art is the proper topic of art. Mnouchkine was also seeking to produce a *performance*, but the two goals are not incompatible. More to the point, Mnouchkine and other popular directors who eschew History for the sake of Art, and thereby promote an aesthetic ideology in fashion in artistic circles, no longer seem to believe that artists must withdraw into their individual psyches. They may be frustrated with social or cultural changes around them, but they appear to have made peace with their society. In fact, few radical ideologies, whatever their direction, are now at work in theatre.

By the same token, ideologically oriented performances have become moderate and predictable. It was to be expected, for example, that the Avignon festival would offer, in 1989, at least one major celebration of the Revolution: a revival of the now respectable *Marat/ Sade*. It was equally predictable that, respecting the conciliatory mood of the bicentennial, its staging by Gelas would make only tame changes in the textual meaning. Also predictable, though inconclusive, were the results of an experiment carried out, in the mid-eighties, by a group of American theatre students.[5] Each proposed a totally free "personal" staging of *Godot*. It was quite telling, but not unexpected, that the suggested ideological transformations of meaning reflected a very limited range of concerns and, hence, few corresponding ideologies. Many proposals referred to racism and apartheid, and several to sexism, unemployment, theatre as theatre, conformism, entrepreneurship, computerized environment, and inner-city decay. All of these themes could have been predicted: they matched hot issues debated on the campus at that time. Truly "personal" or original contributions were extremely rare.

Not all ideologies of a group of students can be assumed to be shared by other groups. But their very high degree of predictability, as well as the narrow scope of their topics, suggest that, in other groups, ideological choices are probably similarly restricted; that a culture polarized by a limited number of tensions generates few focused ideologies; that directors inspired today by ideological issues must not be expected to show much variety, neither in their change of meaning, nor in their staging strategies. As a source of innovation in theatre, ideological transformations seem to have reached an impasse, even though they can be enhanced, as in Gelas's *Marat/Sade*, by a grafted display of *performances*.

We shall examine in Part IV what social factors encourage or, as is the case today, discourage the staging of ideologically oriented performances. Visibly, the general appeal of an ideology plays an important role. Serious directors must be strongly motivated by an ideology in order to feel compelled, and justified, to make deliberate changes in the meaning of a dramatic text, to seek out approved texts that lend themselves to these changes. Their loyalty, to that extent, is first to their ideological goals and second to theatre. In extreme cases, no doubt, they engage in theatre production primarily in order to promote ideas, feelings, and action. In the spirit of the "speech act theory," they conceive their performances as a way of acting on their public rather than serving theatrical art. Ideally, together with their performers, they are committed to public service, placing what happens to "others" above their personal, professional, or staging concerns. In an age dedicated to the "me first" mentality, they tend to be viewed as disturbing oddities.

## 5. Transformational Strategies of Stage Signs

In previous sections, we have been mainly concerned with the transformation of meaning. Some types of texts, called transformable texts, were found to encourage such changes, others to resist them. We have also seen that directors follow their own goals when they deliberately transform textual meanings with nonverbal stage signs. However, not all referential changes have a direct influence on the meaning. For, let us repeat, any sign placed on the stage, for whatever purpose, always somewhat recasts the story told in the dialogue, alters something in the imaginary world, transforms verbal references. And most of these changes are not intended to affect a major meaning of a performance. They merely modify a particular feature of the story world—a referent of a verbal sign on which a nonverbal stage sign has been grafted—or add a new feature: a referent of a nonverbal stage sign that is operating on its own. The story world is thus enriched with an expression on the face of a character, or an intonation of a statement, or a chair in a room. These discrete referential changes, however minor, contribute to the transition from text to stage as much as do transformations of major meanings. It is therefore advisable, in order to explore *all* transformational strategies on the stage, to focus not only on what happens to textual meanings in a performance, but on the more general problem of what happens to all textual referents, including meanings.

First, however, we need to clarify the exact nature of textual referents, and how they can be grasped. We know, of course, that they are communicated by verbal signs, by the words of the dialogue. But we also know that, as such, words have no referents; they are pure signs with a recognizable form (signifier) that is associated by code with a general definition (signified). In a dramatic text, we rely on the context given in a specific dialogue, telling a specific story, in order to concretize the general definition of a word, that is, its signified, in the form of a specific referent in the story world: a particular person, object, feeling, idea, institution, and so forth. Which means that, to release their referents, words must be processed in the way they operate in the dialogue; they must be read as parts of the dialogue.

But what type of reading will yield such "pure" textual referents? Clearly not a theatrical reading. A dramatic text read as theatre, as we have seen, first generates the mental vision of a stage, and only then, if at all, the vision of an imaginary story world that this stage could communicate to an audience. And the mental stage always already includes a considerable number of nonverbal stage signs: initial images of sets, actors, action. There follows that, in the virtual performance that animates the mental stage, these nonverbal stage signs necessarily combine with the purely verbal signs of the dialogue. When directors, reading the text as theatre, attempt to imagine what kind of story world could be communicated on their mental stage, they always already combine the referents of verbal and nonverbal stage signs. In other terms, during a theatrical reading, directors cannot separate the operation of verbal and nonverbal signs, and hence cannot imagine what could be purely textual referents of the dialogue. Any change they might want to bring, then or later, to the imaginary story world, can only transform a world that always already somewhat deviates from the world evoked in the dialogue. A theatrical reading, in short, offers no "pure" textual referents that can be identified as objects of transformations on the stage.

Only a literary reading can inspire directors to change, in their performances, properly textual referents. When it is read as literature, a dramatic text generates a direct vision of the story world, not mediated by a mental staging nor influenced by mental stage signs. In that imaginary world, readers visualize truly "pure" referents of verbal signs: they concretize the general definitions of words within the strictly textual context of a specific story. True, each reader pictures a different world, but, as a rule, variations are minor. Whether vague or precise, referents drawn by different individuals from the same dialogue tend to be compatible, yielding similar stories. As individual readers, directors instinctively assume that their own genuinely literary reading is typical for their sociocultural group, hence that the world they visualize will be probably visualized in a similar way by other readers in that group. The referents they obtain from verbal signs become, in that sense, *probable* textual referents: what the text may be expected to convey when it is only read, or what it could convey if, against all odds, it were to be staged without any referential changes.

Transforming, on the stage, textual referents means thus altering, in one way or another, referents that are communicated by a literary reading. It matters little, in that process, which one of the two basic systems of theatrical semiosis are involved: the primary system whereby all signs, including verbal signs, merely refer to their mirror image in an imaginary world, say, when an actor's declaration of love refers to a character's declaration of love; or a cultural system whereby some features in that imaginary world operate there as secondary signs, referring to something else, say, a character's declaration of love standing for his or her feelings of love.

Indeed, since any cultural sign, as we have seen, must always also be placed on the stage in the form of a primary sign, any transformation of cultural referents entails automatically a transformation of the corresponding primary referents: in order to alter, with a derisive sneer on a character's face, the probable textual meaning of that character's declaration of love, the director must alter the probable textual vision of the character's face with a visible derisive sneer on his or her face. Modifying a declaration of love will always modify simultaneously both primary and cultural textual referents. The reverse, however, is not always true. Changing a primary referent does not necessarily result in a change in a cultural referent. As we have seen, many features of the story world do not operate there as cultural signs and, when they are transformed from their literary probable vision to the mirror image of their appearance on the stage, nothing is changed in the commentary on the meaning of that story world. When an actor puts his hand in his pocket, and hence alters our vision of a character whose gestures, in a probable reading of the literary text, are left indistinct, our understanding of that character's psychology is hardly altered.

There remains that both types of textual transformations, combined or not, are constantly taking place on the stage. They are partly inspired by the nature of a given text, partly by a director's personal convictions, partly by stylistic and ideological expectations of the public, but most frequently by chance decisions made during the staging process. It is impossible to formalize in any precise way all their concrete manifestations. However, there are only a few variations among the types of overall impact they have on textual referents, corresponding to a half-dozen clearly distinct staging strategies. For, whatever their specific occasion and technique, all manipulations of verbal referents with nonverbal stage signs, carried out deliberately or not, have only a few general types of consequences for literary references: confirmation, reinforcement, restriction, subversion, and diversion. Each corresponding strategy affects differently the process of theatrical production.

## Confirmation

Strictly speaking, a strategy which seeks a *confirmation* of textual referents need not involve any significant transformation. It tries to evoke, on the stage, the same story world that is evoked in the dramatic text: a simple task that, it would seem, only requires matching probable referents of the dialogue with similar probable referents of the nonverbal stage signs. Ideally, the statement "I love you" would merely need to be seconded by a facial expression and an intonation that are widely taken to express love. Similarly, the stage only needs to be darkened when someone observes that "it is getting dark." In fact, however, for several reasons, even the simplest confirmation tactics often demand a very subtle manipulation of stage signs.

A first difficulty results from the complexity of verbal references in practically all dramatic texts. Textual referents rarely appear separately: they combine and overlap during variable segments of time. Arranging them in harmonious patterns requires a fine sense of balance. But an even harder balancing act is needed to match these patterns with appropriate referents of nonverbal signs, equally complex. The "To be or not to be" soliloquy must first be subtly decoded to yield a well-structured probable sense; but then begins the more delicate task of supporting each segment of that global verbal referent with suitable nonverbal referents suggested by intonations, facial expressions, gestures, posture, or costume. True, not all possible nonverbal stage signs need to be put to contribution. Even the most consistent strategy of confirming references never exploits all features of the stage. As a rule, textual referents are adequately supported with only a small number of carefully selected nonverbal signs—which simplifies a director's work. However, selecting the supporting signs and assessing their impact raises other problems.

It is unwise, for example, to multiply nonverbal signs in order to confirm a verbal statement that is sufficiently clear on its own. Redundancy of signs risks, in that case, transforming the textual reference in the spirit of reinforcement rather than confirmation. When "I love you" refers, in a probable reading of the text, to a genuine but moderate feeling, a convergence of several nonverbal signs with the same reference to love—say, appropriate intonation, facial expression, posture, and gestures—could add up to evoke an overwhelming passion. Or, if a dialogue indicates that a young woman is a nurse, but the story only concerns her private life, a director who shows her in a nurse's uniform risks distorting her textual image with an excessive stress on her profession. In all such cases the question is: At what point does convergence become redundancy, and turn confirmation into reinforcement?

To elude that problem, or at least minimize redundancy, a director can try to reduce the total number of signs displayed on the stage. However, as noted above, certain categories of signs are compulsory, and several of them are directly linked to the delivery of verbal signs in the dialogue. Statements of love cannot be made without a choice among intonation, face, and body signs; and an actor must always wear some costume. Avoiding excessive redundancy of such signs, while serving the goals of confirmation, demands a delicate dosage of convergence, and an attention to detail that many directors are unwilling to give.

Compulsory signs that have no direct impact on verbal statements are easier to handle. To confirm the textual story world, many features of the stage—sets, sounds, light—need only to yield mirror images of visual or auditory features that can be integrated in the vision of that world: a relatively easy goal because most verbal references to physical environment are imprecise and can be supported by a wide range of nonverbal signs. Avoiding redundancy among them creates no difficulty. The question is rather, how to choose among all the acceptable signs. Often, no doubt, the selection results from a chancy combination of external factors: available resources, a designer's fancy, traditions of style. In some cases, however, nonverbal signs are deliberately selected to support *performances*; and, when they achieve that goal, their performant impact undermines their referential function as confirming signs, creating a tension between text and stage. A dazzling drawing-room decor is perceived, and applauded, as a designer's feat, not as a feature supporting the story world.

To deal with all these problems, and to avoid redundancy of optional as well as compulsory signs, there is one very simple method applied naturally, perhaps unconsciously, by all directors: taking advantage of the flaws in most nonverbal semiotic codes. Indeed, outside of specialized areas, very few cultural systems are systematic and complete. Only a few colors—black, red, and white—operate today in a reliable manner as signs in the color system; most other colors, particularly blue, brown, orange, and beige, convey no definite meaning. Similarly limited is the number of clothing styles that have clear cultural references: most uniforms, to be sure, a few typical garbs of a profession or age group, and outfits suggesting great wealth or poverty, erotic invitation, or challenging eccentricity. Most people wear clothes that tell nothing definite about them. A simple beige dress has no association with any particular concept, cannot refer to a specific personality or status. Worn on the stage, to be sure, it does operate as a primary sign in the properly theatrical system, referring to a mirror-image beige dress in the story world; but, in that story world, it has no function as a cultural sign. Its impact on textual referents is properly neutral.

The number of "neutral" features that have no semiotic function in the story world is limitless. According to recent research, there are only five or six "universal" signs in the system of facial expressions;[6] that is, only five or six types of expression that clearly refer to a distinct emotion. Which means, logically, that an overwhelming majority of our expressions, falling outside these few types, have no recognizable meaning. Comparably, in any particular sociocultural group, the body language code includes only a few of our gestures or postures, leaving much of our normal physical behavior without any particular cultural connotation. There are also some clearly "neutral" voice intonations. None of these countless noncoded features, once it is concretized in the story world, communicates a cultural referent apt to modify referents of the verbal text, weakening, reinforcing, or distorting them.

There follows that, as it were by default, all "neutral" features of the stage always offer a confirmation of the textual world. A director who wants to reduce redundancy can always substitute a nonsemiotic feature for a corresponding cultural sign. When the text refers to an old lady, but does not stress her age, a sufficient confirmation is achieved with a couple of nonverbal signs: for example, white hair and weak voice. Adding redundant signs such as a gray dress, a lace collar, high-laced black shoes, a bent posture, or a walking stick would reinforce rather than confirm the textual referent; the old lady would become a caricature of old age. It is more convenient to have her wear a "neutral" standard beige dress, and walk normally.

One could claim, to be sure, that in some situations a "neutral" feature can have a distorting effect. When it replaces a cultural sign that is normally expected to match a verbal sign, it risks weakening or changing the probable textual reference. A really "neutral" face or voice or gesture undermines the sense of a statement of love. In these cases, however, "neutral" features are not operating on their own. Their distorting action derives rather from the absence of the expected cultural sign, that is, from a special—negative—impact of that sign. Such expected but absent signs have been called *zero* signs: signs that convey the notion of absence rather than their own coded referent.[7] In reality, absence in these cases has each time a different meaning, tied to the meaning of the "missing" sign. A missing facial expression of love changes the sense of words of love because, in the textual story world, it is expected to serve as a sign that properly confirms these words. The "neutral" feature that replaces an expected sign operates no transformation by itself; it merely draws attention to the transforming power of the missing sign. The absence of such a sign is thus but a rare special mode of its normal semiotic operation.

One may conclude that most forms of confirmation, while requiring subtle manipulations of signs, lead to few innovations in staging practices. Their action, aimed at reducing the distance, and hence the creative tension, between text and performance rarely moves theatre into new territories. Confirmation strategy rather tends to fuel the literary fallacy, the belief that theatre is primarily a form of literature. Its richest contributions are made to the recreation of period pieces, requiring a fine adjustment of old texts to new linguistic or cultural codes. But, of course, no performance can do without a great deal of confirmation. It is the bread and butter of all staging activity, a strategy followed spontaneously when no other strategy is deliberately applied.

## Reinforcement

Among properly transformational strategies, *reinforcement* is perhaps the simplest since, in theory, it merely seeks to stress referents that are already given in the text. As seen above, redundancy often serves that purpose. More generally, reinforcement occurs when nonverbal signs, chosen to confirm referents of verbal signs, are also made to strengthen the impact of these referents, or to assign them a greater role in the total economy of the performance. In many cases, this strategy has but a minor influence on the textual story world. It highlights what the text intended anyway to show on the stage. In some cases, however, reinforcement can lead to important referential changes.

The actual scope of transformations resulting from reinforcement is not always easy to determine. Let us consider, for example, the treatment of Polonius in Mesguich's staging of *Hamlet*. None of his lines was altered, or subverted by incompatible stage features. But several nonverbal signs were obviously chosen to reinforce the image of Polonius as a bourgeois parvenu: a portly silhouette, a sober costume of good cloth, a pompous intonation, benevolent gestures, and affected mannerisms verging on drollery. Together they made out of Polonius a well-meaning but bumbling paterfamilias, a pathetic though amusing figure about whom one could hardly care. To that extent, the reinforcement of selected verbal indications yielded no doubt a major transformation of an important feature of the textual world.

Yet, while projecting this reinforced bourgeois image, Mesguich did nothing to downgrade other possible interpretations. In fact, now and then, his own nonverbal signs also reinforced, or at least confirmed, images of Polonius as a sly politician or a foolish clown. These fragments of reinforcement were neither as systematic nor as powerful as the reinforcement of Shakespeare's suggestions that Polonius was speaking, thinking, and behaving like a bourgeois, but they highlighted some traits of character that did not fit a bourgeois figure.

Hence, no coherent Polonius emerged from the performance. As such, specific incoherences were minor and did not directly undermine the image of a bourgeois Polonius. But the role of that image in the total vision of *Hamlet*'s world was certainly reduced. Mesguich's reinforcement transformed effectively the probable literary reading of Polonius, but had a minor impact on the probable literary reading of the entire story.

A more one-sided transformation occurs when, reinforcing one network of verbal referents, a director modifies the balance between that network and other networks. In *Godot*'s binary textual structure, the two contrasted units, Vladimir/Estragon and Pozzo/Lucky, are assigned a carefully balanced relative importance. With nonverbal stage signs, however, one can reinforce selected textual references in order to increase the power of the Pozzo/Lucky unit. The actor playing Pozzo, chosen for his dominant physique, could wear an impressive costume, move with authority, and raise his deep voice whenever he says "I" or "my." Even when blinded, he would behave with dignity. And a bright spotlight could underscore the importance of all his gestures and facial expressions. The text of *Godot*, staged with such a one-sided reinforcement, would generate a performance focused on the tragedy of Pozzo's deterioration leading to death. Vladimir and Estragon would be downgraded to the minor roles of witnesses: a major transformation of literary reading.

A different type of transformation is achieved when one category of stage signs, contrasting with all others, is made to reinforce a clearly ironic reading of the text. Thus, in a recent Broadway production of *Dracula*, while lights, sets, props, and costumes provided a straight confirmation of verbal signs, a parodic style of acting, reinforcing the silliness of the dialogue, called for its ironic reception. Exaggerated body postures and gestures, inspired by early silent films, composed a succession of tableaux that drew attention to the grandiloquence of the melodrama. The original text of *Dracula* was not intended to be funny; but, for the modern public, its partial transformation with nonverbal acting signs released a latent humor that was highly appreciated, while preserving with other stage signs most of the seduction of the story. Selective reinforcement offers in that sense a useful strategy for an ironic updating of old texts which retains their overall interest.

A selective reinforcement, however, can also misfire when, instead of altering textual referents, it serves as a support for the performant function. Any reinforcement, in fact, has a much greater potential as a source of a *performance* than does simple confirmation. Indeed, all nonverbal signs that reinforce the referents of verbal signs operate, as it were, somewhat in excess of what is needed to concretize the imaginary story world. In that sense, a reinforcing sign draws attention to its deliberate presence on the stage, and hence to its material form. It may not be intended to desemiotize the stage, but it increases the chances for the occurrence of desemiotization, encouraging a director to try for a *performance* or the audience to find one where none was intended. The stylized acting tableaux in *Dracula* were vigorously applauded as *performances* by director and actors, and I am not sure whether their performant appeal did not mask their referential function at least for part of the public.

## Restriction

While they pursue different goals, transformational strategies often cause similar or closely related alterations of the textual world. The strategy of restriction is particularly tied to the strategy of reinforcement. Both restriction and reinforcement focus on texts that can yield equivocal readings; and both manipulate possible competing references, supporting some at the expense of others. Occasionally they even converge, since reinforcing one referent can, in extreme cases, entail downgrading all other possible referents, and hence restricting a complex story to a single simplified version. If Mesguich had expanded his reinforcement of a bourgeois image to cover all appearances of Polonius, he would have eliminated incoherences in his performance and restricted a textually complex personality to a coherent but stereotyped bourgeois figure.

There remains that, as a rule, the two strategies seek different aims and use different techniques in manipulating stage signs. Reinforcement accumulates converging signs in order to stress one feature of the textual world, but does not deliberately seek to exclude signs that point to possible competing features. Restriction, in contrast, pays no special attention to signs that support the chosen feature, but seeks a deliberate exclusion of signs that could refer to competing features. If he applied restriction instead of reinforcement to convey a bourgeois image of Polonius, Mesguich would have produced only a few nonverbal signs that refer to bourgeois mentality, say, paternalistic gestures, but he would have drastically eliminated all other nonverbal signs that could suggest other images of Polonius.

Through such exclusions, restriction offers quite an efficient way of clarifying polyphonic or ambiguous texts. It does not target obscurity resulting from a lack of information, and hence requiring a reinforcement of imprecise referents. On the contrary, restriction is applied in priority to texts that have an overabundance of possible referents, and/or possible meanings. The ambiguity that restriction intends to correct rarely derives from the imprecision of the dialogue; it is rather created by precise verbal signs that, on their own, that is, in the absence of additional stage indications, yield precise but competing referents, demanding specific choices. When Hugo shoots Hoederer in *Les Mains sales*, his words can refer to several clear reasons for his action, including jealousy; but it is not clear at all which is the right reason. On the stage, one may want to retain that textual ambiguity; but one can also downgrade some of these reasons through a deliberate avoidance of confirming nonverbal signs. Jealousy, for example, would be discounted if Hugo showed no signs that he is jealous, and the ambiguity would be reduced.

Most restrictive tactics are applied to small units of the dialogue. They serve to clarify minor obscure points of the text. By the same token, however, when they are carried out systematically, they simplify the entire imaginary story world. To that extent, they deprive spectators from freely choosing between various interpretations of the story. It is difficult to assess the impact of such transformations. In general, the resulting loss in meaning is accepted as a small price to pay for any coherent staging. But there are texts where polyvalence plays a major role in the structure of the story. Applied to such texts, restriction may change a major textual meaning.

A restriction that would clarify Hugo's reasons for killing Hoederer would result in such a major modification of meaning. Yet the text would not be fundamentally altered because, after all, it is not Hugo's reason for shooting that is at issue in the play but his reason for letting himself be shot. A better example is provided by Brecht's *The Resistible Rise of Arturo Ui*. With all sorts of ambiguous verbal suggestions, the text draws a parallel between the successful crime career of a Chicago gangster and the rise to political power of Adolf Hitler in Germany. The protagonist is a criminal in both stories, and refers to both specific figures. On the stage, however, one could be tempted to reduce Arturo Ui to only one referential character. If he were to be only a gangster, for example, one would apply restriction and exclude all stage signs—accents, costumes, sets—that could refer to Germany. Or, if Ui were to stand only for Hitler, restriction would remove all nonverbal signs pointing to Chicago. In each case the performance would gain in cohesion and smoothness, but the intended function of the text as a political warning against nazism, its satirical style, and the intricate duality of its story would be totally transformed. In fact, restriction would lead to subversion, a much more radical strategy of transformation.

Texts that rely heavily on ambivalence and/or polyphony are not very numerous. As a rule, there is little risk that a clarifying restriction will turn into subversion. In fact, there are few chances that restriction will cause any serious transformation of textual references since its purpose, in most general terms, is to assist the text in eliminating possible sources of confusion.

## Subversion

In its most general sense, subversion occurs whenever textual referents are contradicted by referents of nonverbal stage signs. Subversion is obvious when a dwarf plays the part of a giant, a night scene takes place in bright daylight, or a wealthy family's drawing room is furnished with rickety chairs. In each case, the nonverbal signs refer to polar opposites of information provided in the text. But subversion is not limited to strict antitheses. In a milder form, it also occurs when, against expectations, nonverbal signs fail to confirm a textual indication because they offer on their own some merely different referents. For example, the average height of an actor suffices to subvert a verbal reference to a giant character, and solid middle-class furniture will effectively undermine the vision of a millionaire's interior.

The scope of subversion can greatly vary. Instead of altering an obvious physical feature of the textual world, as in the examples above, subversion can focus on more subtle targets that, in a given socio-cultural group, are merely considered as probable minor features of a complex referent. On a society matron, for instance, a simple gray dress would be acceptable; but a miniskirt and bobby socks would fall outside the range of acceptability and hence would partly subvert her image. But not totally, nor reliably. Only the context can determine each time how much a partial subversion will transform the total textual world.

More generally, the power of a subversion always depends on many factors. Some stage signs are more effective than others in certain situations. For example, paralinguistic signs are particularly well suited for the subversion of textual emotions. One could be disturbed, and look for rational explanations, if Laertes were garbed as a clown while grieving at his sister's death, but one would be properly scandalized, and question his sanity, if his voice expressed amusement. Another important factor concerns the convergence and/or density of subverting signs. Single and light subversions have but a passing impact on textual referents which, in well-structured stories, always tend to reemerge from their transformation. A rapid vision of a miniskirt and bobby socks on a society matron might shock the audience, but it will be forgotten unless it is prolonged or reinforced with other nonverbal signs, say, painted lips, a shrill laughter, giddy steps. And Mnouchkine could not have successfully transformed the story of Richard II into a story of a Kabuki performance if she had not sustained, almost till the very end, a systematic convergence of subversive costumes, gestures, movements, and sounds. Her subversion was all the more remarkable because, despite its massive application, it never turned into parody.

Any very strong subversion, indeed, always risks generating parody. And parody constitutes perhaps the greatest threat to the text. Even a minor parody, transforming a discrete unit of the text, always endangers the coherence of a performance, suggests a flaw in the imaginary story world. On the other hand, when it is kept carefully from contaminating major textual referents, it can serve as a greatly needed breather of comic relief. In Mesguich's *Hamlet*, the brief appearance of Polonius as a clown, jumping over piles of books while discussing principles of education, was clearly intended to bring about laughter—and be forgotten. The overall avant-garde staging frame enabled Mesguich to reduce a minor parody to the function of an amusing interlude in an otherwise serious production. More traditional performances, sensitive to incoherence, find it more difficult to integrate even minimal forms of parody. Their use of subversion is hence generally limited to safe, small alterations of minor textual references. In fact, subversion rarely occurs in traditional performances, except as a source of humor in comedies.

Total parodies, subverting an entire text, conceivably could attract avant-garde companies. But they do not. Not because they are hard to achieve. On the contrary, they only require a systematic subversion of all major textual referents without much original input by the director. Perhaps this is the reason why they fail to appeal to innovative directors. The few total parodies I remember—very vaguely—were staged by student groups motivated by an iconoclastic animosity toward society and its culture of classics. Parodic subversion offered them an easy way to create surprise, laughter or outrage, suspense, absurdity. Carried out in a more serious spirit, staging contradictions between words and action, a sustained parody can help to illuminate concealed flaws in social reality, and the hypocrisy of public ideologies. But it is a blunt instrument, requiring a steady directorial hand lest it produce risible story worlds that cannot be taken seriously. Like other strategies of transformation, subversion leading to parody must then be used with subtlety; but it can achieve remarkable results.

For example, staged by the Ridiculous Theatre at the Annenberg Theatre, a recent version of *Camille* owed much of its surprising success to a clever handling of a very gross subversion. Adjusting an old melodrama to a sophisticated audience of the 1980s offered a difficult challenge. The English adaptation of Dumas's *La dame aux camélias*, originally written in stilted nineteenth-century French, did a good job of linguistic rejuvenation but it did not much change the melodramatic lines of the story. However, in a bold move, the director—the late Charles Ludlam—undertook to play himself the part of Marguerite Gauthier, a ravishing demimondaine dying of early tuberculosis. Ludlam, a stocky and virile-looking man, brazenly showed his hairy legs as he swirled the skirts of his woman's costume, and occasionally let his contrived woman's voice slip into a deep bass. As an actor, that is, as the primary stage sign standing for the frail and feminine Marguerite, he exemplified an extreme form of subversion. Supported by two other male actors also standing for female characters, this strategy clearly generated a sustained parody, and indeed caused at first a good deal of hilarity in the audience. *Camille* was on the way of turning into a low comedy.

Yet, as the performance moved on, laughter diminished, and died out. Despite a major parodic subversion, all other textual referents, confirmed or lightly reinforced by nonverbal stage signs, gradually asserted their tragic meaning. At the end, a subdued audience watched in silence Marguerite's death, with many handkerchiefs in evidence. Had a young actress acted out seriously the role of Marguerite, the outcome no doubt would have been different. The probable modern response to an improbably sentimental story would have produced the probable transformation of a serious drama into a ridiculous melodrama, perhaps a laughable comedy. Ludlam's gross subversion served as a safety valve: it contained, deviated, and let escape safely all the parodic potential of the text. Laughter was focused on a single feature of the stage, a single incongruity in the imaginary world; and, once that feature or that incongruity became accepted or forgotten, the performance and its story regained the credibility that they had a century earlier. No other strategy, I think, could have achieved such a full recovery of meaning, nor a comparably successful blending of humor and tragedy.

## Diversion: Substituting and Masking Strategies

As it is understood here, *diversion* occurs whenever nonverbal stage signs communicate distinct referents on their own, that is, without any direct relation to the referents of the verbal signs. In that sense, diversion has an autonomous impact on the story world; strictly speaking, it does not confirm, or reinforce, or restrict, or even subvert indications given in the dialogue. It simply adds new features to a probable imaginary world: either a probable world concretized during a literary read-

ing of the text, or the world intended to be evoked in a virtual performance by the means of probable transformations of textual referents.

As a source of autonomous signs, diversion principally relies on the
operation of optional rather than compulsory signs. It manifests the
directorial freedom to place on the stage, during verbal exchanges or
between them, a vast variety of competing nonverbal signs: silent
performers, distracting activities, all sorts of props, startling visual and
sound effects. As a transformational strategy, diversion thus offers
directors a great opportunity for creative innovations and, by the same
token, imaginative *performances*.

Like other strategies, diversion varies in scope. More than others, it
is totally unpredictable. It originates in the free imagination of directors who play with staging resources without consideration for textual
constraints. Many truly surprising stage features, demonstrating a director's originality, are generated by diversion. To that extent, allowing
for a display of exceptional talent, diversion feeds the performant
function. But, since it always employs stage signs, diversion also has a
referential impact. The two functions can work well together. For
example, in Chéreau's production of *La Dispute*, when two old black
retainers sang a Negro spiritual, the audience responded with an appreciation of two *performances*: outstanding singing on the one hand,
and, on the other, a daring directorial inclusion of twentieth-century
music in an eighteenth-century story; but, at the same time, the reference to an exotic continent was successfully concretized by the French
spectators. The world of the black singers substituted for a short while
for the textual world of *La Dispute*'s world, and left its imprint on it.

Whether Chéreau actually planned to transform the textual story
world with a touch of exoticism is irrelevant. Intentionally or not, his
diversion did achieve a marked transformation. But then, any autonomous stage feature introduced by diversion always somehow alters the
concretization of textual referents and sometimes the meaning of the
text. The specific reasons that motivate a diversion determine each
time the nature of the resulting transformation; but there are many
such possible reasons and they are as unpredictable as the concrete
diversions that they generate. It is impossible, therefore, to order
various types of diversionary transformations on the basis of their
contingent aims or results. On the other hand, however, subversions
can be grouped in two large categories corresponding to two different
tactics with which they undermine textual referents: substitution and
masking.

Substitution takes place when referents of autonomous nonverbal
signs, added on the stage by the director, offer a vision of the imaginary
story world that replaces, for a period of time, the vision of the world

inspired by the dialogue. A long diversion may lead to a competition between the two worlds, or to their uneasy superimposition, as in a double film exposure. Thus, when the traditional Comédie Française allowed Robert Hirsch, in the title role of *Les Fourberies de Scapin*, to walk onto the stage dressed in a striped sailor's T-shirt and to turn acrobatic somersaults, a modern image of a waterfront as shown in a Broadway musical combined, but never merged, with the image of seventeenth-century France conveyed by the traditional costumes and wigs of other actors. Taken somewhat farther, and used more deliberately, this strategy of superimposed worlds could culminate in a performance that would refer simultaneously to two very distinct stories: an option that, to my knowledge, avant-garde theatre seems not to have yet fully explored.

Usually, however, substitutions are relatively short, and the overall vision of the textual world emerges little changed by the glimpses of the diversionary world. The scene with black singers in *La Dispute* might have had a small impact on the total performance. But, in Mesguich's *Hamlet*, the incestuous lovemaking of Laertes and Ophelia, shown with provocative body language signs without any dialogue support, failed to alter the overall perception of their roles in Hamlet's story. Nor did Planchon's evocation of a totalitarian society in *Tartuffe*'s last scene project its political meaning, retroactively, on the vision of a seventeenth-century world that was projected by the rest of his production. And no wonder, since diversion in the form of substitution has no direct action on the verbal signs in the dialogue and, leaving them intact, enables them to resume their normal function after a pause comparable to an intermission. At the end of the performance, the textual story world may be slightly modified by substitutions, but its main features remain stable.

The masking diversion seeks, in contrast, to act directly on the verbal signs, to obliterate their textual referents. As it is understood here, masking occurs when autonomous stage signs, by their sheer presence, draw attention away from the dialogue and prevent it from being clearly perceived by the audience. No doubt there are other ways of tampering with the dialogue, some very crude. Words covered by a loud sound, or delivered in an inaudible voice, or indistinctly enunciated, are practically excised from the staged text. But these tactics, however common, come close to violating the basic theatrical convention whereby a text must not be changed on the stage. The masking diversion, on the contrary, strictly complies with the convention, protects the sanctity of the text and the audibility of all its verbal signs. It simply masks them, interposing, between the dialogue and the audience, a competing set of nonverbal stage signs that creates a potential

screen. In other terms, with masking, words are heard but not decoded, while eyes focus on an unrelated action on the stage.

A successful application of masking created much controversy
when Planchon staged Molière's *Georges Dandin* in the 1970s. During
the first scene, Dandin informs his intendant about the dinner he plans
for his in-laws, complains about the way they treat him, and generally
finds fault with his connubial life: a rather long expository exchange
which Planchon's actors delivered very clearly. But he placed them
backstage, while downstage was given to the silent antics of two ser-
vants carrying a huge table board, setting it down, turning it around,
moving it forward and back, turning it around again and again, shaking heads in approval and disapproval, and finally leaving the stage
just before the end of the expository dialogue. Some spectators might
have listened to Dandin's lines; most did not, fascinated by the farcical
stage business. Dandin's verbal references were effectively masked by
comic stage references to the futility, perhaps inanity of human activities. One should also note that Planchon's gambit not only elicited
laughter but was hailed as a director's *performance*, an evidence of
originality.

For, like substitution, masking best succeeds when it is supported
by the magic of the performant function. In order to monopolize the
audience's attention, autonomous stage signs must present a special
interest; and, since they do not contribute directly to the story, that
interest is sustained by the expectation of seeing some exceptional
achievement, hence a *performance*. In Planchon's production, that
achievement was found in a daring staging of a classic, and in the
creation of an extremely funny scene. In Mesguich's staging of *Hamlet*,
the revolving prompter boxes offered a totally unexpected device and
striking visual and sound effects. In the same production, the two
naked Ophelias provided a rewarding satisfaction of the erotic interest—a most effective source of nontheatrical *performances*, an easy and
tempting way for a director to divert the reception of a canonical text.

In either of its two forms, diversion thus manifests two basic tensions in theatre: on the one hand, the tension between the referential
and the performant functions, the competing appeals of an imaginary
story and a real *performance* on the stage; on the other hand, the
constant tension between the text and the performance, the verbal and
nonverbal signs, the creative contributions of author and director. In
that sense, diversion is perhaps the most profoundly theatrical of all
strategies that transform a text into a performance, and the most fertile
source of experimentation. At the cutting edge of theatre change, it
has inspired some of the most memorable performances of the last

decades, and some of the most naive failures, entertaining even the most blasé spectators.

## 6. Reception

### Reception and the Consumer Society

Within the total theatre process, understood as a series of production/reception transformations, the reception of public performances is neither the only form of reception nor the final stage in the process. In fact, as we noted, it generates the production of further texts—reception texts—and these texts in turn are received by various readers, including the producers of dramatic texts and performances. Traditionally, however, and especially since the promotion of the *Rezeptionsaesthetik*, reception of public performances has been considered to be the theatre reception par excellence: the concluding manifestation of theatre. A theatre production, it is argued, is finalized in its performance; that performance is produced for an audience; and hence the production fulfills its function only when it is received by the audience, by concrete spectators. Furthermore, it is also asserted, producers of text and performance anticipate this final reception, and thus orient their production in a way to meet the *horizon of expectations* of spectators—expectations recorded in reception texts. In short, not only the final stage of the theatre process but also its inception cannot be fully grasped without a clear understanding of the public reception.

By this logic, in theory quite persuasive, reception of public performances deserves a special attention. To mark its unique role, I shall in this section refer to it by the general term of *reception*, disregarding now all other instances of reception that take place during the total theatre process. In that restricted sense, as a response to public performances, reception raises however several problems that cast some doubts on its claimed major function.

It is significant, for example, and perhaps disturbing, that the role of reception as a key to understanding theatre has been acknowledged only during the last few decades. For many centuries, production was taken to hold this key position. At first, the meaning of a dramatic text was sought and found in the intentions of its author, like the meaning of the world in God's will and the meaning of history in ambitions of kings. By the end of the nineteenth century, stage directors merely took over the role of authors as personal creators of performances. True, about the same time, the growing interest in social laws undermined the belief in the magic of individual creation, and inspired early forms of sociocriticism. But production remained the source of meaning: "intentional fallacy" was simply replaced by an equally naive deterministic fallacy.

Then, well into the twentieth century, the focus of attention moved from production to the product. As civilization grew more mechanical, and man more dependent on devices that eluded his control and assumed an appearance of autonomy, products were increasingly judged by their performance rather than by their proclaimed purpose. The question became: What did they actually offer to the buyer? On the marketplace of art works, products were tasted and tested for their directly experienced values. Theatre texts and performances, viewed in the spirit of new criticism and structuralism, were expected to yield their own meanings to discerning consumers.

The current interest in reception seems to have emerged when the direct testing of goods was replaced, as mass media expanded, by a growing reliance on their reputation. Today's consumers seem no longer to judge products by their actual performance but by the appeal of their image. Not products but signs of products are now displayed in marketplaces, urging us to buy what we may find desirable rather than what we need. Advertisement, and indeed production, trust in marketing surveys to detect our preferences, and to publicize products with signs that fit our horizon of expectations. In the modern consumer society, the consumer is indeed a king, but a manipulated king whose weaknesses are thoroughly explored and exploited. Hence the development of sciences of signs that serve manipulation: linguistics, rhetoric, poetics, semiotics. Hence the critical attention to the "implicit" or "ideal" reader in literature. Hence, more generally, the *Rezeptionsaesthetik*. Hence also, as a reaction, a growing distrust of signs, leading to recent attempts to deconstruct them, to raise the performant function in theatre above its referential function, to assert the role of wild pulsions of the desiring subject.

These observations are not intended to minimize the interest of reception studies. Critical approaches must not be judged by their cultural source. Their validity is not tied to the particular time when they become popular: it can be traced in past approaches, or be adapted to new conditions. The old-fashioned attention to production has been revived today in forms that focus on the unconscious: individual, cultural, or political. And, while the emergence of the consumer society has highlighted the role of reception in theatre, it did not create it: reception problems have always been acknowledged. There remains that their current fashion raises several interesting questions.

It is somewhat paradoxical, for example, that theatre studies focus on public reception, clearly oriented by consumer taste, at a time when theatre as such manages to resist the pressure of the consumer society, and excludes advertising from the stage. Perhaps the interest in theatre reception studies is somewhat artificial? Perhaps the persuasive logic of the reception theory cannot be easily applied to the concrete theatrical practice? What indeed *is* the real role of reception in the full theatre process? What gains can be expected from studies of that reception? And, in the first place, is there but one reception, a global response to a theatre performance, or are there rather two different forms of reception, generated separately by the performant and the referential functions?

## Reception and the Performant Function

Most theories of theatre, we have seen, are oriented by referential concerns, postulating that reception must meet the goals of storytelling. They expect spectators to learn about human action, purge their emotions, acquire new convictions, take a political action, imitate models of social behaviors, and so forth. By that logic, a performance is successful when the response of the audience corresponds to the intentions of the producers. And an ideal reception occurs when the best possible communication takes place between the stage and the audience, that is, when theatre signs are clearly decoded. From that perspective, reception is strictly limited to referential operations. No significant role is reserved for the performant function.

Other theories, focusing on theatre as a medium for playing games or satisfying individual and social needs, assign a greater role to the impact of performers on the performance. But these theories pay little attention to the goals and problems of public reception. From their perspective, an audience is principally needed only to encourage the performers. Spectators are expected to show some understanding of the story told by the performers, but these referential expectations form only a minimal horizon. It is also important no doubt that spectators be willing to acknowledge outstanding *performances* on the stage, if and when they occur. But these theories attribute no distinct function to such *performances*, assign them no special role within the global reception.

There is a third way of approaching theatre, potentially more appropriate for reception studies. It postulates that public performances can be best understood from the perspective of the audience: its expectations and responses. But what are the goals pursued by spectators? To what extent are they interested in the meaning of signs and/or in *performances*? We shall see below how, in terms of this approach, an audience's expectations can be related to the referential function. It is sufficient to note now that the corresponding reception focuses on semiotic operations. In short, with some exceptions, an approach centered on the audience reserves no major function for the reception of the performant function.

Whatever the perspective, it thus appears that the reception of the performant function is downgraded, if acknowledged at all, as a distinct form of global reception. Which is somewhat surprising since theatre obviously caters to both performant and referential functions and, ideally, a global reception ought to include both types of reception. A serious reception theory ought to examine each type separately, acknowledging its different nature, role, and impact. In fact, we have seen, most available reception texts support that approach. They not only record reactions to story and its meaning, but also praise exceptional achievements on the stage: acting, sets, aesthetic or erotic appeal of performers. Yet this textual evidence has been rarely tied in theoretical works to a distinct reception of *performances*. In studies of global reception, comments about *performances* are treated like comments about story and meaning, without differentiation between reactions to the performant and referential functions. In sum, there is still a great deal of confusion about the role and the reception of *performances*.

Thus *performances* are assumed to participate in the creation of the referential world, to generate meanings in the imaginary story. For example, the success of Olivier's version of *Hamlet* has been traditionally attributed to Olivier's outstanding personality: not only to his performance as actor, but also to a charismatic physical presence that was credited with creating a truly new Hamlet. And so it must have seemed to many spectators thinking back about the performance. In reality, their memory most likely merged two separate processes: one, essentially semiotic, whereby Olivier as a stage sign referred them to a new Hamlet in the story space; and two, a performant experience, whereby Olivier's *performance* as an actor, as an aesthetic and erotic figure, and as a celebrated "star," fulfilled their wish to witness an exceptional event. Delighted by the *performance*, they endowed the new Hamlet with an original personality that might have eluded them, or failed to impress them, if it had been conveyed by a less celebrated actor.

In other terms, the performant function did not participate directly in the referential process; it only assisted in its success. The same observation can be made about all performances where one or several *performances* contribute to *enhance* the global reception. Each time, the performant function merely helps to improve conditions of felicity that affect the outcome of all forms of communication (and not only speech acts). In fact, in that sense, a *performance* on the stage constitutes no doubt the most powerful factor of felicity in theatre, a most effective condition for a successful operation of signs.

Obviously, there are many other conditions of felicity. They are rarely discussed by semioticians because they do not change the coded nature of signs, nor their direct references. But they influence pragmatics of reception. It is well known that most sets of signs, including performances, are received differently under different conditions of time, light, temperature, noise, physical surroundings, human environment. In the case of theatre, the audience is also affected by the comfort of seats, distance from the stage, size and shape of the auditorium, sources of light, visibility. For each of these conditions, learning from experience, spectators develop, consciously or unconsciously, specific horizons of felicity; and their reception of signs varies with the degree to which actual conditions meet these expectations.

Most theatre producers, aware of these problems, try to provide their public with good material conditions. But little theoretical research has been carried out in that area.[8] As a rule, it is assumed that expectations of material felicity are always somehow met; and they cause little further concern. There is no need to discuss them here. In contrast, the role of the *performance* as a major theatrical factor of felicity must not be minimized. For, unlike other sources of felicity, *performances* form an integral part of the performance, are planned by producers, and generate loud forms of public reception.

It is important to be aware, for example, that reception of *performances* is not uniform, and may exert a negative as well as a positive influence on the global reception. And that, regardless of individual variations in responses, spectators can be expected to react differently to nontheatrical and to theatrical *performances*. A nontheatrical *performance*, let us recall, occurs when an achievement on the stage surpasses norms set by achievements outside theatre: quality of paintings, sex appeal of faces or figures, elegance of dresses, display of wealth, reputation of personalities. The pleasure derived from such *performances* promotes a good reception of the imaginary story; but it also makes it more difficult to keep up with that story. For, when the stage is desemiotized by a nontheatrical *performance*, spectators are mentally transported into the space of their real-life experiences, outside the two spaces proper to theatre: the stage and the story world. They see real people, real dresses, real paintings, rather than actors, costumes, and sets, or characters in their imaginary surroundings. The dividing line between reality and theatre, postulated by the theatrical pact, is momentarily erased. Such lapses into reality obviously perturb the conditions of referential reception. Unless, of course, as shall be seen shortly, spectators have reasons to erase the separation between the real world and the story world.

In most cases, the impact of nontheatrical *performances* on the referential function is thus both favorable and damaging, and cannot be clearly assessed. In contrast, a good reception of properly theatrical *performances*—great acting, bold staging, striking designs—involves theatre signs that always operate on the stage; and hence it always helps to improve conditions of referential reception. Audiences are eager to witness such *performances*; and, when they occur, their reception is smoothly inserted into the shuttle movement of attention between the stage and the story world. A theatrical *performance* can thus be expected to have a positive influence on the global reception.

There is another difference between the two types of *performances*: their reception expresses appreciation of stage features that have different degrees of precision. Theatrical *performances*, as we shall see, reward a limited range of stage features. Horizons of expectations for nontheatrical *performances* are, in contrast, limitless; in theory, any discrete feature of the real world could be shown on the stage in a superior form. Practically, of course, only features related to actors, costumes, props, and sets are highlighted as *performances* in reception texts. One could perhaps determine what specific categories of *performances* are favored in given cultures, and, within each category, what particular features are preferred at various times. It could be shown, for example, that spectators in the west have been more responsive, over several centuries, to the appeal of attractive actresses than to the appeal of handsome male performers; but also that the focus of their erotic interest has moved from a daring décolleté to a provocative face, from delicate ankles to shapely legs to bared bodies.

A systematic survey of such horizons of expectations could help to explain shifts in staging strategies that rely on nontheatrical *performances*. It would contribute information to the history of theatre staging. Some of these strategies, however, seem to reflect cultural changes that have no direct relation to the expectations of audiences. The display of opulent furniture, or dazzling light effects, became a potential source of *performances* only when furniture and electricity made their first appearances on the stage. More generally, to the extent that nontheatrical expectations always reflect cultural interests, their horizons reveal more about the evolution of a society's taste, customs, or ideology, than about the dynamics of staging. In fact, one might argue, any serious survey of nontheatrical *performances* belongs in cultural studies rather than in theatre studies.

This observation is particularly valid for studies of *performances* that occurred before the invention of photography. For centuries reception texts offered no precise data about nontheatrical *performances*. Occasional references to the exceptional sex appeal of a performer, or the beauty of a costume, give no detailed information from which to deduce what were the erotic or aesthetic canons at the time. For an assessment of past staging strategies, then, one is reduced to hypotheses based on the evidence of changing fashions found in general iconography, various narratives, private letters, and archival documents—all sources traditionally studied by historians of culture.

Current research prospects are better but not much more encouraging. For many years now, theatre performances have been faithfully recorded in photographs and films that provide exact and reliable data. For the first time, looking at concrete images, we can *see* what specific types of nontheatrical *performances* might have taken place in individual productions. But not all problems are solved. We still must guess which *performances* actually lead to a favorable reception. In fact, the availability of visual evidence supplies us with a surfeit of possible *performances*, an overabundance of possible nontheatrical achievements. For, promoted by illustrated media, cultural interests expand continuously into new areas, and thus expand the horizons of expectations. At the same time, spectators are stimulated by the consumer culture to price all marketed products, including performances offered on the stage. Taught to look for the best deals everywhere, they expect theatre to provide them with a multiplicity of best achievements. Their reception of nontheatrical *performances* tends thus to be indiscriminate, hasty, and often surprising. By the same token, of course, the significance of their global reception becomes diluted, reducing the interest of reception studies.

Reception of properly theatrical *performances* offers fewer problems. It acknowledges superior achievements in very precise features of staging: acting, directing, designing. Also, it is based on relatively clear notions of competence that a *performance* must surpass: notions firmly grounded in concrete experiences of theatre supported by familiarity with reception texts. True, norms of competence are never very stable, and horizons of *performances* always change. But, at a given time, in a given social group, most spectators can be assumed to expect the same type of *probable performances*, highlighted in *probable* reception texts. For example, these texts clearly document that the transition from realistic to symbolic staging in early twentieth-century France, or from emotional to controlled acting in German theatre in Brecht's time, was generally expected and accepted.

The reception of theatrical *performances*, evidenced in reliable documents, can thus throw a revealing light on the history of staging styles. Ideally, it could even suggest the emergence of new norms set by a repeated occurrence of similar new *performances*. Systematic reception studies could thus contribute to the goals of the *Rezeptionsaesthetik*, generating a new history of theatre performances. For, contrary to records of nontheatrical *performances*, always problematic, most records of exceptional theatrical achievements focus on exact staging features; and, at least today, when they fail to be sufficiently detailed, they can be supplemented with photographic or cinematic evidence.

Of course, not all theatre performances are reviewed in reception texts, and not all reception texts mention theatrical *performances*. The actual reception of the performant function will always somewhat elude historians of theatre. Also, reception texts usually convey the horizon of expectations of professional critics who, for one reason or another, are likely to deviate from the actual reception by real audiences, and hence from real expectations. But these are perils of all reception studies. A more important reservation concerns the ability of reception texts, past or present, to assess the true role played by *performances* in theatre reception. Because the performant function is still a source of confusion, the impact of *performances* is often overestimated, underestimated, or misunderstood, leading to a distorted view of the global perception. One can only wish that, in the future, better informed texts might inspire historians to raise studies of *performance* reception to a level comparable to the level already reached by studies of referential reception.

## Referential Reception

### Concretization in Theatre

The semiotic process underlying all forms of referential reception, and hence also the reception of public performances, has been identified earlier as *concretization*. We have seen how readers of a text, whether literary or theatrical, must draw on their own experiences in order to concretize, in their minds, concepts conveyed by verbal signs. To that extent, reception of a text always involves enriching referential concepts with a number of concrete properties supplied by the reader. These properties mainly concern physical appearances of people and places, or, more generally, all of what Roman Ingarden has called areas of *indeterminacy*: features that verbal signs fail to communicate and that readers must imagine on their own with varying attention to details.

The audience of a theatre performance, in contrast, rarely needs to supply additional properties in order to concretize physical appearances. Most appearances are fully communicated by performance signs: spectators perceive the story world as a mirror image of the stage, with all its needed concrete physical features. Properties that are supplied by spectators on their own only concern that which cannot be shown on the stage: ideas, emotions, motivations, but also places and events that are merely mentioned. These theatrical areas of indeterminacy do not affect the primary visualization of the story world. The mental vision of characters and action demands attention to what takes place on the stage but no additional effort. Many spectators, we noted earlier, are satisfied with such a minimal theatrical reception. Many others, however, also want to understand hidden reasons for a character's action, to find explanations for the story's events, to deduce its meaning. Commentary signs may help them, but a full mental concretization of a meaning will always require adding many supplementary properties to the story world: a complex and often problematic task.

The main problem concerns the source of these additional properties. We have seen that spectators find them in their vision of their own real world, and then project them on the imaginary world. But are these private visions totally individual, and hence unpredictable? It is preferable to assume, from the sociosemiotic perspective, that such visions are largely shared in a given group of spectators, and that they generate similar *probable* concretizations that lead to a probable group reception. Also, again for sociosemiotic purposes, it is convenient to locate the source of the shared vision in the *social context*, that is, in various factors that combine to generate ideologies. But the notion of a social context, however popular it may be,[9] is itself quite complex and often misleading.

Let us consider a relatively neutral production of *Hamlet* in today's upper-bourgeois social context. Concretizing Hamlet's world will require, on a most elementary level, enriching direct references of stage signs, including words, with a number of additional factual properties, that is, with information. One may expect, today, that most spectators will know where Denmark, Sweden, and Poland are located; what was in "past times" the role of a king; why people carried swords; and why young ladies could be sent to a nunnery. To that extent, most modern spectators share a certain "audience's competence": the minimal knowledge needed to concretize various features of the story world that are neither "shown" on the stage nor "explained" in the text. Each given social context may be expected to determine the limits of its audience's competence, or, rather, to set a variable range of limits corresponding to various levels of competence.

But even on each level it is difficult to define the exact limits of audience's competence. What level of competence—elementary? average? superior?—would involve, for upper-bourgeois spectators, the knowledge of dynastic rules in medieval Denmark and/or Elizabethan

England? Or knowledge of past and current beliefs in ghosts? Which level would require familiarity with theatre productions in Shakespeare's time, or today? Or information about Wittenberg University? Or ideas about power relations between parents and children during the decline of feudalism? One could easily expand the list of such questions. Any complex theatre performance contains many "latent" references, and it is hazardous to determine, without the assistance of surveys that are as yet in a far future, which set of factual information corresponds to which level of competence at a given time and for a given performance. Still, the concept is interesting because it deals with relatively objective factors. True, even factual knowledge has ideological connotations, but, as a source of concretization, it clearly involves simpler problems than does ideology. And a shared global social context includes much factual knowledge.

The impact of ideology on concretization is more subtle. It principally bears on subjective areas of indeterminacy, those that factual competence cannot easily concretize. A high level of knowledge of Hamlet's world suffices to explain some hidden but simple reasons for Hamlet's behavior: his secret ambitions, deep fears or desires, perhaps temperamental shortcomings. But, if they want to clarify more complex features of Hamlet's psychology, spectators must apply their own notions of psychology, based on prevailing ideas in their group. And, even in relatively homogeneous groups, no uniform ideology informs notions about psychology; no consensus guarantees that all spectators will believe in the Oedipus complex. Nor can one expect, even in a small group, that a single dominant ideology will impose unanimous views about political, social, or philosophical issues. At best, one can only detect ideological trends, generating several probable ideological concretizations. But even that relative probability becomes problematic whenever the area to concretize is narrowed down to issues that involve very personal ideological choices and presuppositions.

It is likely, for example, or even probable, that an upper-bourgeois modern audience, given proper staging encouragement, will have no trouble concretizing an Oedipal Hamlet. It is possible that a majority of spectators will be satisfied with this vision. But it is also possible that some conservative spectators, looking for deeper meanings, will carry out a further concretization of Hamlet's society where the display of a Freudian complex, viewed as a sign of loss of values, would be reinforced by other decadent features that manifest a general moral disintegration. Other spectators, motivated by left-wing ideology, may prefer to concretize the Oedipal Hamlet as a revolutionary who breaks the incest taboo but also, more generally, challenges all political and social rules. One may even suppose that for some spectators, interested in the symbolic function of art, an Oedipal version of *Hamlet* will generate the concretization of a theatrical world wherein staged Freudian complexes, and other deep troubles, are perceived as stylized forms of behavior that serve to express and neutralize conflicting psychic structures.

These concretizations are not mutually exclusive. They can overlap and, within the same group of spectators, combine with other concretizations, influenced by other ideological factors. The notion of a probable concretization becomes impractical on the level of such highly individualized responses. One should also note that a strong staging, with persuasive commentary signs, often manages to convey successfully its own ideology to a receptive audience. In such cases, spectators are compelled to elaborate a concretization that may not correspond to their own ideological preferences. Their response will then depend on the strength of their ideological commitment and on personal temperament. Thus, an upper-bourgeois French audience, captivated by a "faithful" staging of a Paul Claudel drama, will probably concretize, without much resistance, a world illustrating the value of Catholic faith. But individual reactions can vary. Catholic spectators, perhaps most Christian spectators, despite some possible reservations, will probably approve the spirit of the staging, and their concretization will be enhanced with the glow of truth. Atheists, in contrast, will probably respond with disapproval, and, depending on their personal feelings of tolerance, that is, on an unpredictable ideological factor, they will either dismiss their concretizations as misrepresentations of truth, to be best forgotten, or store them in their memories as an informative vision of a regrettable illusion.

In sum, in the absence of very detailed reception texts, it is hard to determine what are the precise features of a probable concretization, and to relate these features to ideologies found in the social context. Of course, these are pragmatic concerns: they do not invalidate the role of concretization as the central process of referential reception. The fact remains, however, that in theory as well as in practice, both concretization and referential reception involve complicated mental operations. When spectators draw references from their personal experience, or from their personal vision of the real world, and project them on the story world, they always somehow transform the vision of that world as it is communicated on the stage, and, hence, always somehow recreate and restructure that world: a complex, arduous, frustrating, and finally gratuitous activity that demands an expenditure of mental energy. One may then ask: what moves spectators to carry out that activity? Is it a necessary part of the theatrical experience? Or does concretization, especially in the form of restructuring, satisfy some special human need?

## Restructuring Imaginary Worlds: Play in the Gap

Obviously, there are many reasons why spectators are drawn to theatre: to learn about themselves and the world, to benefit from emotional purges, to participate in rituals, to watch reenacted social games, to experience a magic communion with performing artists, to be amused or entertained, but also to demonstrate group solidarity, to meet demands of cultural status, to support local charities, to please spouses or friends. All of these reasons interact, overlap, compete, and sometimes counteract each other. Anything related to theatre is always complex, including audiences and their motivations. Yet, a theory of theatre must bring an order to complexity, and single out those features of theatrical experience that can be clearly ordered. Hence my basic hypothesis about sociosemiotic sources of theatrical production; hence also, in the same reductive spirit, my somewhat different hypothesis about psychological sources of reception, that is, about the need that spectators satisfy when they attend a theatre performance. In terms of this hypothesis, as shall be seen presently, it is the general need to restructure fictional worlds that is satisfied in theatre.

Both of my hypotheses assume that a story world is always fictional. The production hypothesis, as was noted earlier, postulates that authors and directors exploit the freedom in fiction, and its convenient disguises, to propose unconscious solutions for social tensions that are felt but not yet conceptualized: more about it in Part IV. But spectators, involved in the reception of theatre fiction, must be motivated by other reasons than those of its producers. Spectators face an already given world—the imaginary story world—and, hence, cannot produce a new fiction on their own: they do not use the magic of free creation to solve unconscious problems. On the other hand, we have seen, the given imaginary world is always incomplete and unstable; and, in the process of concretizing it, spectators must restructure it in their mind. That restructuring, we also saw, has no practical consequences for the spectators. It is a gratuitous activity that finds its main reward in its own process: in other terms, it is a game. For games, by their function, have no direct impact on real life. True, games can be taken as seriously as real life, or real life as lightly as games, but such exceptions are obvious dysfunctions of the game principle.[10]

Like any game, then, restructuring in theatre involves no risk in real life. Furthermore, it is enjoyable. For, when they freely restructure an imaginary world, spectators draw pleasure from exercising the same mental faculty that, in the real world, enables them to structure and restructure reality, that is, to organize their environment. As Piaget demonstrated, this structuring is an essential human activity, satisfying a drive as basic as the sexual drive.[11] Yet, while normally gratified by structuring activities, the drive to structure, like the sexual drive, may be frustrated and then will decline without disappearing. A critical phase is notably reached when new structures collide with previously established structures. Ideally, the integration of such new structures in a coherent total network, that is, in an orderly vision of the world, calls for a thorough restructuring of old structures: an effort that is particularly painful when the old structures have become rigid. Sooner or later, in order to avoid such painful restructuring, most adults thus learn to live with conflicting structures and to block out contradictions. The price is a gradual withering of their structuring activity.

Yet withering of structuring activity does not entail the disappearance of the structuring drive. In fact, checked in real life, that drive can still be pleasantly satisfied when one plays a game. And there are many available games. Players involved in a game of fiction can structure and restructure imaginary worlds defined by arbitrary rules: they draw from that process as much gratification as if they were dealing with their real world, but they know that their game structures do not risk colliding with their structured notions about their real lives. There are many types of fiction worlds that provide that experience, each with its own special rules. In theatre, spectators satisfy their structuring need when they carry out the needed theatrical concretization. My hypothesis is then that the structuring drive, gratified in the process of concretizing, motivates spectators to seek a theatre experience, determines the nature of their responses, and hence underlies the operation of the referential reception.

By the same logic, a successful reception takes place when the structuring activity is truly gratifying: when concretization stimulates the mind but is not excessively laborious. Thus, on the one hand, the staged story world must not coincide exactly with the real world; when they concretize it with features drawn from their reality, spectators must create new structures in order to satisfy their structuring drive. On the other hand, that world cannot be really alien: spectators must be able to concretize it with restructuring strategies that they have learned in their lives. No doubt, most performances usually meet both requirements, since any theatre world contains a mixture of familiar and unfamiliar features. But the effort needed to concretize that world depends on the magnitude of the gap between features referring to reality and to fiction: the larger the gap, the more pleasurable, but also the more difficult the restructuring activity.

In theory, one could thus posit that, for any staging, there exists an ideal gap between reality and fiction. Practically, however, it is impossible to measure that gap, or to predict what it could be. The problem stems in part from variations in the way that audiences structure their reality, and in part from variations in staging practices. For example, French bourgeois today, attending a Molière play, may be expected to find fewer features to restructure than industrial workers. But staging can reduce the gap for an audience of workers and increase it for an audience of bourgeois. Staging can also play with the gap when different performances of a dramatic text are produced for the same audience: the scope of restructuring will change as the story world changes. An ideal gap can thus never be defined. And, for the same reasons, it is also difficult to assess the magnitude of a concrete gap. Any given audience structures its reality in many ways, and even its probable structures elude a precise analysis; there is no reliable method with which to measure how much a given staging increases, or reduces, the play in the gap.

Yet the notion of the gap is practical. It helps to explain how we determine the final meaning of a dramatic text or a performance (see Part II, section 4). One meaning, we noted, can be defined as our vision of the real world that needs a minimal transformation to coincide with our vision of the story world. That transformation, we also noted, depends on the degree of similarity between ideologies that structure the two visions. The notion of the gap enables us now to add that ideological analogies are not alone at work: a right balance between familiar and unfamiliar factual features can also help reduce the transformations needed to bring the two world visions together. A change in the scope of the gap may thus change our vision of the real world that is closest to the story world, that is, it may change for us the meaning of the story world.

The notion of the gap also helps clarify the somewhat confused concept of theatre as *entertainment*. True, all good theatre performances always entertain to the extent that they provide an intellectual, emotional, or sensual stimulation. But so do other types of public events, or various media forms, artistic or not. In that sense, entertainment is an almost meaningless notion. Spectators who claim that they go to theatre in order to be entertained rather than to be emotionally moved, or made to think, have a more specific meaning in mind.[12] They seek an experience that does not seriously involve their emotions or ideas: one that does not endanger their perception of real life. In that restricted sense, entertainment implies a distraction, a diversion, a Pascalian "divertissement": a temporary escape from existential projects or worries.

Some performances are particularly suitable for this type of entertainment: light musicals and comedies. The question is: How do they
work? Their secret is often attributed to the type of stories they tell, to
their happy end. But the story as such has a very minor influence on
the escape mechanism: in many cases, it is very familiar, and hence not
apt to distract from reality. The magic of entertainment must be sought
rather in the structures of the imaginary world, and, in particular, in a
careful determination of the gap between fictional and real structures.
Which is not easy to do. Two contrasted strategies will illustrate paradoxes and traps that are involved even in the simplest types of gaps.

The first strategy—production of very wide gaps—discourages
spectators from satisfying their structuring drive. To that extent, it has
negative effects on the audience's expectation. Unable to relate to
glimpses of an overly alien world, spectators give up trying to understand it, renounce concretization. By the same occasion, they deny it
any possible real meaning. Their reception endows it with a shimmer-
ing appearance of sheer fancy: a series of disconnected images that
cannot be related to real-life experience. On the other hand, however,
a truly passive audience can be expected, like children, to be fascinated
by the seduction of clearly fictional images. Akin to fairy tales, these
images exert a magic hold on attention, diverting it from real-life
problems. In short, they entertain at no expense of structuring energy:
a good deal for consumers of culture. A successful musical like *Cats*
provides this type of entertainment. But then, downgrading the operations of the referential function and relying on the visual appeal of the
performant function, *Cats* barely qualifies as theatre.

The second strategy—production of minimal gaps—has more
subtle effects, but is equally well adapted to the consumer culture. It
follows the policy of offering the best possible deal: meeting a need at
the cheapest price. Thus a minimal gap, requiring a minimal effort,
provides but a minimal satisfaction of the structuring drive, but does
not block it. As they face imaginary worlds containing familiar structures, but also a few obscure spots, spectators are invited to concretize
them safely, at a very low expense of mental energy and, one assumes,
without much emotional involvement. Furthermore, since such worlds
resemble each other to the extent that they all look like the real world,
each new concretization requires less effort: only names, places, and
contingent events are new. The pleasure of restructuring is naturally
reduced. But this repetitive nature of reception, supported by uniform
styles of staging, has its own appeal: it meets the desire for repetition
that Freud places among basic human drives. As the restructuring
activity fades, and repetitions multiply, spectators gradually give up
forging connections to their real world, and substitute connections to

previous similar theatre worlds. Distracted from their real lives, they are entertained by a purely theatrical experience. Watching a Mike Nichols play, they are pleased because it meets their expectation of restructuring once again the familiar structures of Mike Nichols's worlds. They also enjoy, of course, competent and sometimes outstanding performances: great staging, good actors, clever sets.

This variant of entertainment, one may observe, serves very well a function of theatre that is particularly pertinent to sociocriticism: confirmation and promotion of the prevailing view of the world. True, *all* entertainments, as defined here, serve that end by turning people away from problems of the real world, and hence from the perception of flaws in its ideology. But performances with minimized gaps, and hence minimal concretizations, also have an *active* role in promoting socially accepted ideas about life and society. Spectators who might have some doubts are reassured when they observe, over and over again, that characters with whom they identify trust in these ideas, and are eventually rewarded for their faith. Furthermore, these reassuring characters offer exemplary models: for, however familiar their situations, actions, emotions, and words, they are enhanced with great acting and smooth staging. The audience feels uplifted when it restructures in its own image, without much thinking, a glamorous version of the shared notions of human and social reality.

One could claim that both strategies—excessive and minimal gaps—dominate in truly popular forms of theatre, or at least those that are reputed to be good entertainment. Thus the past success of the Grand Guignol theatre could be explained by the wide gap between its improbably gruesome world and the rather tame world of early twentieth-century French society: spectators could enjoy blood and terror because they did not feel threatened. Today, blood and terror are a part of real city life; and the gap would have been uncomfortably reduced if the Grand Guignol had survived. But it closed down after World War II: it was no longer entertaining. In contrast, the popularity of penny gaff shows in London pubs, where the line between performers and spectators was very thin, could be attributed to a minimization of the gap and the appeal of repetitions. And penny gaff shows disappeared when the gap increased in scope.

But popular theatre is still little known. Is it only or mainly entertainment? Or does it express the need for group communion? Does it serve ritual functions? Or is it always a form of rebellion, or a safety valve channeling popular discontent through modern forms of carnival? It certainly often conveys conservative views of dominant groups. There is still much confusion about popular theatre: about its stated goals and its actual function. And there are very few genuine reception texts to check the various theories. Serious research is thus much needed in that area. Meantime, it is safer not to speculate about the nature of truly popular reception.

## What Reception Data and Texts?

In fact, much research is still needed about all types of reception. We still lack appropriate data, especially reliable reception texts. To be able to assess any given reception, one obviously first needs evidence of that reception: a concrete manifestation of the way in which spectators respond to a public performance. And there are only two possible types of such evidence: either the reception itself, as it is experienced, directly or indirectly, at the time it actually takes place; or a record of that reception, usually made at some time after it took place. Both types of data are still very problematic.

First, direct observation: it must be carried from within the audience, that is, by a spectator. In theory, all spectators experience a performance from the beginning until the end, and hence have the possibility of assessing directly their own responses. True, some spectators, for various reasons, have no reaction at all, turning their attention away from the stage. Also true, other spectators may be involved so intensely in the story that they become unaware of their own reaction to the story world: they can only record their response to the performance after it is over. The ideal observer is a spectator who is prepared to watch his or her own reactions, to formulate and modify them intermittently during the entire performance, and to record them during that time.

In fact, the most interesting records we have about reception are based on the observations of such spectators. Of course, they are inevitably subjective. But some objectivity can be added when spectators/observers are able to watch not only their own responses but also the responses of other spectators: faint or loud expressions of approval, dismay, joy, horror, and so forth, or verbal comments. Most appraisals of performances I have offered here rely on such observations, noted down sometimes during the production or immediately after it, and eventually transcribed into this text. There are other and better reconstitutions of this type by Patrice Pavis or Michel Corvin.[13]

Yet, however interesting, valuable, and indispensable they may be as reception texts, such records are not very reliable as evidence of real reception, even limited to one individual: partly because they are always simplified and/or distorted in the transcription; partly because they are affected by contingent conditions of reception, say, by all sorts of noises; partly because a watchful observer is not an average spectator but a professional theatre critic or scholar, influenced by professional concerns. The resulting reception texts are always problematic. And all these reasons to question an observer's account of his or her own reception also undermine that observer's account of the reception of other spectators.

Hence the temptation to turn to a scientific assessment of reception. In theory, a camera that records facial expressions and the movement of eyes as they focus on various stage features, or an appliance that measures the rhythm of breathing, blood pressure, muscular contractions, can provide some indication of a spectator's interest in specific characters or events of the story. But a reception deduced from such general reactions would be very general indeed, accounting for very elementary and mainly emotional responses. It would be hardly able to distinguish between the reception of referential and performant features of the performance. Besides, the technology needed for such a study has not yet been perfected. Practically, then, an objective study of direct reception is still elusive.

Not much more promising are the prospects of objective studies of reception carried out some time after the performance. Some experiments have been carried out in that area, notably in Holland: attempts at retrieving an audience's reception by the means of a detailed questionnaire or with the help of segmented projections of video recordings of the performance.[14] It is possible that a more systematic exploration of that approach may yield valuable—and perhaps surprising— reception data. The subjective factor present in individual observations can indeed be suppressed by studying entire audiences. But the temporal gap between the actual reception and its study cannot be eliminated. The reception data will always refer to a reconstituted reception, affected by memory tricks, by an unconscious reorganization of the performance in terms of its outcome, by the influence of the conditions of the experiment.

The same shortcomings undermine the value of all written reception texts. As noted above, they are problematic because they are never totally spontaneous, disinterested, reliable. Reviews in newspapers and commercial periodicals are written to please the public of the given publication. Receptions recorded in letters, memoirs, novels, or scholarly articles and books also are consciously or unconsciously slated to amuse, interest, or impress their readers. At best, they can be taken to offer an honest reconstitution of a reconstructed reception, that is, a global response to a performance, ordered and simplified by the stylistic or ideological requirements of a literary expression.

Furthermore, the most informative of these reception texts are written by a small minority of spectators, and cannot claim to convey the reactions of actual audiences. True, this elitist origin does not affect their ability to shape the dominant horizons of expectations. Both consumers and producers of theatre rely on media reviews to determine what a dramatic text or a performance should be. In fact, the prestige of professional reviewers adds weight to their judgments. But are dominant horizons effectively dominant? Do they play a major role in a medium wherein the ideology of small groups often has a major influence on the choice of texts and staging styles? Can they account for the emergence of the avant-garde, and the dynamic evolution of theatre that ignores rules and expectations? The impact of reception on production is not a very well-known process. From a sociosemiotic perspective, changes in production, reception, and horizons of expectations constitute but surface manifestations of more fundamental changes in social conditions and ideologies.

## Notes

1. In properly literary narratives a similar distinction can be made between writings that mainly tell *what* is happening, satisfying the interests of a relatively simple public that enjoys epics or dime novels, and writings that explain *why* things are happening, bringing up psychological, sociological, or philosophical reasons that correspond to the concerns of a more sophisticated audience. This distinction operates regardless of the individual talents of the narrators. However, preference for one or the other type of story is certainly influenced by technical, economic, and social factors.

2. See the discussion of *Les Mains sales* below and my essay, "*Les Mains sales* ou La clôture du verbe," in *Sartre et la mise en scène*, ed. M. Issacharoff and J.-C. Vilquin (Paris: Klincksick, 1982), pp. 68–82.

3. See my essay, "Vers le mathématexte au théâtre: en codant Godot," in *Sémiologie de la représentation*, ed. A. Helbo (Bruxelles: Complexe, 1975), pp. 42–60.

4. See *Les voies de la création théâtrale*, vol. 1 (Paris: CNRS, 1970).

5. At the University of Pennsylvania, from 1982 to 1989, in a theory of theatre class attended by theatre majors. Altogether close to sixty students were instructed to justify, by ideological reasons, their ideal staging of *Godot*. Only one student seemed to be moved by a mainly personal concern, proposing a staging that stressed abuses of parental authority.

6. See, for example, Paul Ekman, Wallace Friesen, and Sonia Ancoli, "Facial Signs of Emotional Experience," *Journal of Personality and Social Psychology* 39, no. 6 (1980), pp. 1125–34. Ekman, associated with other scholars, is continuing research in that area, and several other more detailed reports are available.

7. See Tadeusz Kowzan, "Signe zéro de la parole," *Degrés* 31 (Summer 1982), pp. a–a16.

8. See, for example, Ed Tan and Henry Schoenmakers, "'Good Guy Bad Guy' Effect in Political Theatre," in *Semiotics of Drama and Theatre*, ed. Herta Schmid and Aloysius Van Kesteren (Amsterdam: John Benjamins, 1984), pp.

467–508. It is significant that the reported experimental study was focused on political interpretation, and that its observation of the influence of physical conditions of reception was only dictated by methodological concerns. I must add that literary scholarship also seems little interested in physical conditions of reading.

9. First formulated by Jan Mukařovský, the theory of the "social context" has been recently further developed by Patrice Pavis, who integrates in it Ingarden's "concretization" as well as Lacan's considerations on the function of signifiers. Pavis's own scheme is quite detailed, and seems practical, but it presents some semiotic problems due to an occasional confusion between signifiers, signifieds, and referents. Cf. Patrice Pavis, *Voix et images de la scène. Vers une sémiologie de la réception*, 2nd ed. (Lille: Presses Universitaires de Lille, 1985), pp. 245–68.

10. The two types of dysfunction are well known. Games taken too seriously are a common occurrence in sport, to the point that a special category of professionals whose incomes depend on their performance had to form institutions in order to distinguish them from amateurs, i.e., true sportsmen who do not take money when they play games. The appeal of poker, based on monetary interests, testifies to a similar dysfunction in card games. Inversely, the very term "playboys" discloses the perception that some people do not take life seriously enough, are not properly practical or professional. Of course, there are problems with the notion of gratuituous games opposed to pragmatic life. There is no call here to outline a theory of games. Let me simply suggest that gratuituous activities, however playful, obviously have a positive or negative impact on our lives, but that this impact cannot be quantified, whereas the impact of practical activities can always be measured as a quantity: money, time, possessions.

11. See Jean Piaget, *Biologie et connaissance* (Paris: Gallimard [Idées], 1967), passim.

12. Thus a 1984 French survey shows that an overwhelming majority of theatre spectators claim that they attend theatre to be entertained (98%), to find an escape from their real lives (64%). But then only 2% of the French go to the theatre more than four times a year, representing no doubt the sophisticated spectators, while 8% two to four times, and 6% once, leaving 84 % who never go to the theatre. See *Télérama*, no. 1785 (31 March–6 April 1984), pp. 4–11.

13. See Patrice Pavis, *Voix et images de la scène. Vers une sémiologie de la réception*, pp. 187–95; Michel Corvin, "Sémiologie et spectacle: *George Dandin* (mise en scène de D. Benoin)," in *Sémiologie et théâtre. Organon 80* (Lyon: CERTC, 1980), pp. 93–152; and Michel Corvin, *Molière et ses metteurs en scène pour une analyse de la représentation* (Lyon: Presses Universitaires de Lyon, 1985), passim. All three texts are illustrated with photographs.

14. For the former, rather successful, see Ed Tan and Henry Schoenmakers, "'Good Guy Bad Guy' Effect in Political Theatre." The latter, reported orally by Aloysius Van Kesteren, seem more problematic.

# IV: Playwrights, Directors, Actors, and Their Work

## 1. "Authors" and the Production of Dramatic Texts

The series of transformations that define theatre as a total process begins, by convention, with the production of a text. In reality, any textual production is preceded by many other transformational activities, involving ways in which producers of texts transform their personal experiences into ideas about life and art. And personal experiences involve encounters with cultural notions that result themselves from a constant process of ideological transformations. Notions about society, for example, or, more specifically, about theatre and its horizons of expectations, derive from transformed receptions of social or theatre texts, transmitted orally or in media. But these early phases in the theatrical process leave few distinct traces. In contrast, the production of a dramatic text offers a concrete first basis, a solid starting point.

A sociosemiotic study of theatre, then, must require first a clear grasp of how that production takes place. But it is also important to understand how much textual production can influence further theatrical transformations, that is, what authority is granted to texts that result from production. The corresponding two questions are: What factors present at the time of production inspire the meaning of dramatic texts? And what factors account for the control exerted by that meaning over succeeding theatrical processes? In both cases, a special role is played by the producer, first viewed as a creative "author" of the text and then as its authoritative "owner."

## Absent, Mediating, Involved, and Dead Authors

To be sure, producers of texts do not need to be individual "authors," identified by their name and endowed, in Michel Foucault's sense, with variable powers over their discourse.[1] The authorial function, we noted, can be carried out in theatre by directors and actors together, by anonymous groups, or by a slowly evolving popular tradition. These variations, however, have a minor impact on production processes. True, in the case of collective authors, a text cannot be normally attributed to personal problems of an individual author. But social problems affect groups as well as individuals, and hence may be expected to inspire the same type of production whatever the exact identity of the authors. Indeed, from a sociocritical perspective, the generation of a dramatic text is not determined by the specific personality of producers but by the specific nature of their society. More about it later.

On the other hand, the actual identity of producers has a major influence on the power attributed to their texts. For example, individual authors enjoy today more prestige than collective authors and, as a rule, their intentions are given a greater consideration. However not all individual authors are equally respected as producers, and individual authority, always unstable, depends on changes in cultural factors. The division between individual and collective identities, while certainly useful, is too general to account for such fluctuations. It is preferable to group all authors in four other categories of identity—categories that correspond more directly to the degrees of authority granted to the meaning of their texts.

Two of these categories are little affected by changes in social conditions. The first covers various types of *absent* authors, that is, authors who cannot be identified. It is a vast category that includes modern producers of collective works, legendary and/or successive producers of texts transmitted by oral tradition, and anonymous or forgotten playwrights. Their authorial function, severed from a concrete personal authority, is always inevitably diluted. As a result, absent authors rarely exert any direct power on the treatment of their texts. True, in some instances, ritual conventions or traditional practices may be granted a stable authority: the textual messages of the Ramlila, the Oberammergau passion play, or medieval farces are usually closely respected. As a rule, however, in most modern societies, the productions of absent authors can be expected to open a space of free transformations. It is somewhat paradoxical, in an age of innovations, that this freedom is rather timidly exploited. It would seem that the absence of authority is not always acknowledged in the reception of traditional texts. And contemporary collective productions, claiming to have no single author, are nevertheless attributed to a specific individual, generally the director, as happened to the Théâtre du Soleil's collective *L'Age d'or* which is usually mentioned as Mnouchkine's text.

The second category of authors with little power over their production groups various mediators between an initial text and the dramatic text to be staged. All translators belong in that category, even when they sharply modify the foreign texts. Thus, in eighteenth-century France, authors who rewrote and, indeed, massacred Shakespeare's plays, had no real authority over the resulting hybrid textual meanings. Today, most *mediating* authors draw their theatre texts from texts first produced in a different medium: novels, historical documents, or films. Responsibility for the adapted dramatic text is generally shared between the original and the mediating author, but in varying proportions. The scope of transformations, but also the prestige of a name, exert a major influence. When Camus adapted a Dostoevski novel, both authors were made equally responsible for its staged version. On the other hand, although J. L. Charrière actually wrote the text of the *Mahabharata* staged by Peter Brook, the play is generally regarded as Brook's production, and the contributions of both Charrière and the original Indian epic are practically dismissed. In most cases, the real power of mediating authors over the future of their text is in fact minimal. At best, they may try to influence the first staging of their adaptation, hoping to match the direct influence that certain living playwrights exert on the first performance of their original works.

Such living playwrights compose a third category: authors who are granted a considerable authority over their textual meaning because, during their lifetimes, they are actively *involved* in the staging of their texts. Clearly not all living authors belong in that category. Many refrain, in fact, from any intervention in the staging and reception process, limiting their theatrical activity to the production of texts. In that sense, they rarely wield greater authority than dead authors, and can be assimilated to them and grouped with them in the next category. Of course, *all* living authors sooner or later become dead authors. The properly distinct category of involved authors has thus an always fluid composition. It is continuously depleted but also renewed with new living authors anxious to protect their texts. But their authority can only exert an ephemeral control. There remains that they directly affect the staging of new plays, the activity that, with the revival of old plays, forms the basic mission of theatre.

The actual power of involved authors expresses the intensity of their involvement. In that sense, it depends no doubt on various unpredictable individual factors: temperament, practical interests, status.

It is likely, however, that it also reflects the nature of three goals that are usually claimed to motivate textual production: self-expression, communication, and pragmatic rewards, each one involving a different attitude toward the staging of the text. An author may sincerely believe, like a romantic poet, that writing a dramatic text fulfills his or her personal destiny, dictated by a higher power or by an unique personal talent. Such an author will fiercely protest against any alteration of the text on the stage. Other authors, more oriented toward the aims of communication, may believe that their texts offer society an important value, whether ideological or aesthetic. These authors will also try to protect their textual intentions against possible distortions, relying on extensive staging directions and commentary like Bernard Shaw, or, like the normally withdrawn Samuel Beckett, intervening in actual stage rehearsals. Such authors, however, are usually amenable to minor changes that fit with the main thrust of the text, allowing for some staging invention. There remain pragmatic authors, mainly interested in the success of their texts. In contrast with the other types, they are willing, ready, and eager to welcome any directorial transformation of their textual meaning as long as it enhances the appeal of the resulting performance, and hence increases financial rewards or prestige. In fact, some pragmatic authors, in order to put all chances on their side, write their texts for specific directors and/or actors reputed for their popularity: Jules Romains wrote the very successful *Knock* to be staged and performed by Louis Jouvet.

In most cases, of course, involved authors seem to display all three attitudes, while leaning toward the one that best corresponds to their temperamental inclination. But social factors also influence their choice of goals. Self-expression surely exerts a special appeal in a society, or in a social group, where creative individuals feel estranged from public life and seek identity in the solipsist pursuit of a personal art. This artistic individualism has few chances to occur in a dynamic and well-integrated society that promotes satisfaction of cultural as well as material goals; it rather springs up when, excluded from public affairs, creative individuals feel that society also thwarts their cultural aspirations. The thrust of romanticism in early nineteenth-century France, but also some bohemian trends in the American 1920s, reflect this rejection of mainstream values by individuals who, secure in their means, cannot find a meaningful role in a culture dominated by conformism and/or materialism. To a certain degree, the postwar prosperity of the period between 1950 and 1970 lead to a comparable emergence of marginal theatre groups, inspired by the creative impulses of collective authors, directors, and actors.

Though it rejects social values, self-expression can then be expected, for practical reasons, to thrive in uniform societies that are stable enough to support individual artistic dissent. In contrast, a society torn by political or social strife, with powerful groups dissenting from the dominant culture, produces authors who want to communicate their ideas in order to promote dissent. Most modern "committed" authors—from Sartre to Miller to Megan Terry—emerged in such times of ideological turmoil. As a rule, their commitment results from a clear polarization of positions due to the appeal of a powerful partisan "cause." However, when dissenting groups fragment into multiple subgroups, or "groupuscules," with manifold militant programs but no unified platform, ideological commitment tends to yield to the appeal of wild self-expression, or the two attitudes are brought together, as in early productions of the Living Theatre or Arrabal's plays.

Like self-expression, the pragmatic attitude also benefits from stability and prosperity: a wealthy society enables authors to gain financial and social rewards. More important, however, is the sway that, in a general climate of prosperity, material values hold over creative individuals. When they are made to believe that success is a major value, and indeed can be obtained, potential authors prefer to be successful rather than to express a personal truth. A consumer oriented society furthers such beliefs, especially in the absence of competing "causes." At the present time, it would seem that the pragmatic attitude is gaining ground. It dominates mainstream theatre on Broadway, in London, or in Paris; but it also can be detected in the evolution of the increasingly institutionalized avant-garde.

The last, and most important, category groups *dead* authors: those individual authors who, at a specific time in the past, wrote a dramatic text, released it to potential directors, and, after death, lost any personal control over its future staging. In that sense dead authors are the ideal agents of a clearly distinct authorial function. Dead authors are also ideal authors to the extent that, sooner or later, all authors fall into that category, and those of their texts that survive, or are revived, are viewed as texts of dead authors. And, since theatre always involves new stagings of old texts, and the repertory of these texts always grows, dead authors provide the most stable model of ideal authorship. In contrast, however, the authority granted to their texts is never very stable. It is influenced by variable sociocultural factors that also affect the authority of living authors, though to a lesser extent.

## Variations in Authorial Authority

The first of these variables concerns *the prestige of literary texts*. Since the nineteenth century, we have seen, drama as literature has been competing with drama as theatre, dramatic texts often reaching a larger audience than stage productions. At the same time, a growing number of professional writers, including playwrights, have been gaining high visibility and prestige. The power of the printed word, supported by the impact of staged texts, accrued thus in the twentieth century to enhance the authority of dramatic authors and their texts. But litera- ture was not always granted great prestige. And it seems today to have been replaced by other genres and media as the main source of infor- mation and ideological persuasion. With the advent of mass produced press, radio, television, and film, the power of literary texts is under- mined by the power of new media, especially images. The leading role of the dramatic author is taken over by "personalities" more directly associated with the visual form of theatre, that is, with the perform- ance: actors, directors, producers. A dead author's text may still be celebrated for its literary value by critics and students of literature, but, when it enters the staging process, it tends to be subordinated, by producers and consumers of theatre, to the concerns of the perform- ance.

Second variable: the *status of proprietary rights*. Whether the notion of proprietary rights is strictly bourgeois, or a natural human concept that the bourgeois society has made into a basic feature of its ideology, is not at issue here. It is enough to observe that, before the emergence of Greek, Roman, and modern bourgeoisie (in the last case, before feudalism declined) ownership was attributed to a group or a king rather than granted in sacred trust to an individual. There is no doubt indeed that the valorization of proprietary rights is closely tied to the rise of the bourgeois individual, who was expected to promote and defend individual interests that were inherited by direct descendants. The most important individual interests were rights to titles, land, or material possessions, and they received strong legal protection. Less concrete, and rewarded in the form of reputation, were rights to authorship, which were more difficult to enforce, but which profited from the general respect for individual property. When, however, writing literature became a profitable profession, notably at the end of the nineteenth century, moral authorship rights were reinforced with legal protection of the income they generated, even for a certain time after the death of the writer. Dead authors, including playwrights, perceived as posthumous owners of their texts, thus retained their authority over the future of these texts, sources of material gains for legal heirs but also sources of meaning for all potential readers.

Today proprietary rights still form the backbone of social struc- ture, and authorship is still revered by most people as the property of the author. True, at various times and especially since 1950, many

dissenting groups have opposed bourgeois ideology and tried to minimize the value of proprietary rights. In the field of theatre, they
advocated, with diverse success, the practice of collective authorship
and, denying any rights to dead authors, the freedom to transform
their texts. Some of the most exciting theatre experiences came from
these groups. But their influence remains marginal and unstable. The
authority of dead authors ultimately will depend on the survival or
decline of the entire ideology of bourgeois individualism.

A third variable concerns *the attitude toward the past*. This factor
involves the way a society looks at its tradition and its monuments, its
history and its great men. Of course, in any complex society, some
groups will dissent from the dominant culture. In the 1960s, students
promoting contemporary "relevance" fought to reform teaching that
relied on traditional programs. And, in seventeenth-century France,
the celebrated "querelle des anciens et des modernes" originated in the
claim that living writers were at least equal to the great "classic" writers.
As a rule, however, tradition prevails, appropriating successive gains of
modernity. Supporters of literary traditions successfully appeal to a
filial respect for cultural heritage (we are what our past made us); to
patriotism (the greatness of a nation rests on its great authors); and to
the golden rule of time-testing (a living writer may be forgotten, but
the survival of "classics" demonstrates their excellence). Furthermore,
as their works are read in schools, and performed on reputed stages,
the authors of "classics" become the symbols of past and traditions and,
as such, heroic figures to be studied and respected. These are powerful
arguments. They work particularly well in social groups that have
reasons to preserve the status quo, that is, to maintain a traditional
ideology.

Conversely, in groups committed to radical change, most of these
arguments are downgraded, and the traditional respect for an un-
touchable author is undermined. Texts of dead authors may be revived, but for the purpose of yielding new meanings: freed from an
obsolete authorial authority, they are taken over by the agents of
change, by living directors and actors. In extreme cases, even new
authors are granted only a temporary authority, with no claims to
traditional status in the future; and they must share that limited authority with the producers of performances. In fact, the very notion of
an author's text is subverted. Reduced to the status of a "dramatic text,"
it is subordinated to the concerns of the "theatrical text," the text of all
signs displayed on the stage. Much of the current avant-garde theatre,
as well as modern theatre criticism, testifies to such a radical commitment to change.

It is tempting to attribute that commitment to a general subversive leaning of artists and intellectuals. Many of them seem indeed to distrust tradition and display ambiguous feelings toward a past that both feeds inspiration and must be overcome. But even in these circles the attitudes fluctuate, and not always in harmony with the general evolution of ideology. It is significant, in that sense, that the spirit of change is now gaining in the mainstream society while many artists and intellectuals are turning toward traditional values. Does this mean that the attitude toward the past has no stable relation to any particular social group? Let us rather say that this attitude reflects many changing factors. And keep in mind that it forms but one of the variables that affect the authority of dead authors over their texts.

The last variable that must be mentioned concerns the way in which theatre is perceived: *as art or as communication*. At its origins, by its ritual function, theatre was essentially a ceremonial form of a mythical communication between human beings and superior powers: no individual author was involved. With Aristotle, however, and the emergence of theatre as a form of art, the author as an artist was granted a creative role in theatrical processes. Viewed in that role, the individual author becomes the inspired creator of an art that expresses a general truth. Performers only implement the author's vision, and hence can only be expected to follow its meaning. Furthermore, as was earlier discussed, the traditional concept of theatre as art postulates that it has a permanent core: the unchanging verbal text. By that logic, the meaning of that text has priority in the theatrical process; and the author of the text, as the source of that meaning, has a permanent authority over its future artistic manifestations.

By and large, theatre is still acknowledged to be an artistic form. But the notion of art has become problematic. Besides, theatre is viewed today rather as a form of communication. More specifically: as a special version of a speech act, whereby a performance communicates its signs not only, or mainly, to convey information but to bring about a certain reaction on the part of the audience. From that perspective, of course, the permanent textual core, and authorial control over its meaning, appear to be secondary. As is the case for rituals, the roles of text and author are played by specific conditions of the transaction between the stage and the audience, that is, by the performance, and by general cultural and social conditions that affect the outcome of that transaction. Hence the priority assigned to the director, who manages the performance, and to actors, who are the concrete producers of speech acts and thus directly influence the audience. The author's text becomes flexible material that must be molded in order to achieve the goals of the performance.

Yet the speech act theory does not fully explain how theatre operates as a communication. The form of the text, that is, its art, still is valued by spectators for its own sake, and the meaning as such still plays a major role in reception. The author's ideas are still interpreted and discussed, at least when the performed text has a clearly identified individual author. But the author's sacred status as creator of art is over. Even acknowledged dramatic geniuses, say, Shakespeare or Molière, while often "faithfully" performed, are deprived of any stable control over the meaning of their texts.

In fact, none of the four variables is stable. But, though they fluctuate, they remain interrelated. Thus respect for literature, art, and tradition clearly reflects an ideology that upholds proprietary rights. No wonder then that authorial authority grew in harmony with the development of the bourgeois society. But that society is now undergoing severe changes. Mass media, mechanized daily activities, computers, multinational economy—all these manifestations of the "future shock" are increasingly subverting beliefs in individual proprietary rights, stable traditions, art as an unique creation, and the preeminence of literature. It is quite conceivable that both author and text may lose, in a not distant future, the privileged position to which they still cling in the theatrical process.

## Production of the Text

### A Short Statement on Theory and Method

From a sociocritical perspective, the production of a dramatic text does not significantly differ from the production of a narrative fiction. True, a play is not a novel, and playwrights and novelists write under different constraints; but this difference mainly affects forms. Nor are all plays equally creative: "hacks" imitate "great" authors. But, matters of form set aside, the production of such imitations mirrors the production of their models, and needs no special explanation. Regardless of formal variations, in short, a dramatic text operates as does any fiction: it tells a story that is not taken to be true, that is, that does not fully coincide with our representation of History, although it may contain many of its features. The same sociocritical questions can thus be raised about plays, novels, or films: *Why* do they tell fictions, and what social factors explain *why* they tell a particular fiction rather than any other?

A full answer would require an extended discussion of theories of fiction, from Plato and Aristotle to Taine, Marx, Freud, Lukacs, Goldmann, Jameson, and so on. I attempted to outline in the Introduction the main directions of these approaches, including the notions of mediation and unconscious projection, and my own reasons to supplement them with the concept of "semiotic malaise." It may be helpful, however, to review now my main theoretical premises in the form of seven postulates.

1. Sensitive writers share with their group an unconscious feeling of malaise created by social disturbances that elude identification, that is, by emerging problems that cannot be conceptualized because the ideology of the time, and hence the historical discourse, are as yet unable to perceive their existence.

2. A sensitive writer, in an unconscious response to that feeling of malaise, unconsciously disguises the disturbing problem in a fictional story, similar to a "freudian dream," and, as happens in such a dream, solves it in its disguised form.

3. A fiction, indeed, can operate like a dream because it does not need to conform to the "true" logic of reality; and its space of freedom, wide open to the projection of unconscious desires, enables it to acknowledge, in a disguised form, the existence of problems ignored by History or repressed by individuals—that is, to fulfill what I take to be the special function of fiction.

4. Problems that thus inspire, and inform, fictional stories result from a tension between, on the one hand, rapid changes in society and, on the other, an ideology that lags behind, lacking the proper signs to identify these changes—a tension that creates a "semiotic malaise" because changing features of reality slip from under existing semiotic codes and signs.

5. An analysis of fictional structures can reveal, under surface disguises, significant structural flaws—incoherences or conflicts—that correspond to the unconscious tensions that fiction attempts to resolve.

6. Unconscious surface disguises, as in a dream, are always somehow related to the problems they mask, and this close connection—or similarity—helps to identify the specific semiotic tensions that generate structural flaws in the story.

7. Once identified, the semiotic malaise can then be attributed to social or cultural changes that are recorded by History at some later date, or to changes not yet acknowledged but that can be proposed as hypotheses leading to a rewriting of History.

These postulates must be variously related, and applied, to different types of fiction. In a dramatic text, centered on dialogue, one expects to find deep structures in the fragmentation of the story into discrete units (acts, scenes), and in the resolution of conflicts that, with various degrees of disguise, are defined by characters in their own words.

## Illustration: Corneille's *Le Cid*

Few dramatic texts are as well known as *Le Cid*: generations of students of French literature had to read and study it. Its story takes place in medieval Spain, but Corneille wrote it in 1636–1637, when Richelieu was striving to turn France into a modern state, with all political power vested in the king. On the surface, the story appears coherent, supported by several symmetrical structures. The mainspring of the plot, as critics and teachers would point out, is a dramatic choice between love and duty, or passion and honor, or even virtue and vice. Rodrigue loves Chimène but, to avenge an insult to his father, he must challenge and kill Chimène's father; and, conversely, while Chimène loves Rodrigue, she must press for his execution in order to avenge her own father: a supposedly heroic double dilemma. In fact, for Rodrigue, the choice is easy: by the end of act 1, he concludes that his honor demands setting "duty" above love. Chimène also has no problem choosing duty: however torn she is, she keeps asking for Rodrigue's head and, when he is pardoned, still refuses to marry him. At the end, the king enforces the marriage: the lovers will be happily reunited.

This surface "happy ending," isolated from other features of the plot, to be discussed below, discloses, however, a first structural flaw. Rodrigue's matrimonial reward comes *after* a conclusive demonstration of his sense of duty, that is, after he kills Chimène's father, but Chimène is denied the satisfaction of *her* sense of duty: her forced marriage demands that she give up honor for love. In other terms, Rodrigue is consistently honorable but Chimène is not; and if she is not, then the king is not either, since he dictates her final choice. Yet they are all praised for their decisions: a contradictory judgment. But there is more. The stable sense of honor can be viewed as Rodrigue's innate quality, a feature of his *être* (essence), whereas Chimène and the king only display signs of honor as a contingent part of their *paraître* (appearance). The seventeenth-century French writers struggled a lot to reconcile these two notions, notably in hybrid forms of "*gloire*" and "merit," but here they are sharply contrasted and yet evenly endorsed. An underlying tension is clearly at work, undermining the sense of "honor." Conceived as "duty" to one's family, specifically to the father, honor as an ideal value is both affirmed (Rodrigue) and negated (Chimène, the king), and its ability to refer to a concrete behavior is implicitly questioned. Visibly two competing meanings of honor inform the deep structures of the story, reflecting the influence of other values or other concepts of "duty."

The "happy ending" in fact suggests the nature of one other value:

duty to the state. It is the king, embodying the state power, who orders Chimène to give up her revenge; and when she obeys, she trades duty to her father for duty to her king as head of state. A shift of authority from father to king is not uncommon; but, in this case, the greater value of duty to the king is also stressed by the king's own notion of duty which informs the second major feature of the story: Rodrigue's crime and redemption.

The problem is that, as was often noted, by killing Chimène's father, Rodrigue deprives the kingdom of its strongest defender in a time of foreign danger: a serious crime against the welfare of the state.[2] Actually, Chimène's father himself, when he risks his life in accepting Rodrigue's challenge, acts against the interests and explicit orders of the king. His death may thus be viewed as a punishment for setting personal honor above duty to the state. By that logic, of course, Rodrigue should also be dealt an exemplary death. But—another structural flaw—the king procrastinates for no good reason. Time elapses and young Rodrigue, on his own initiative, rallies Spanish troops and crushes a night assault by a Moorish army. By the same token, he demonstrates that he can replace Chimène's father as defender of the kingdom. He is then forgiven and rewarded with power (and Chimène) by a delighted king. His earlier sin against duty to the state is redeemed by an unexpected heroic discharge of that same duty: on the surface, the story remains coherent.

A closer analysis reveals, however, that Rodrigue's heroism is not motivated by a sense of duty to the state. It rather results from a feeling of despair and an exalted notion of personal "gloire." He leads the fight against the Moors as a reckless individual, not by the order of the king nor in any official capacity. In fact, his action is a form of insubordination, confirming that his first loyalty is to private concerns: his father's or his own honor. If "honor" means indeed duty to the state, as the king makes clear, then Rodrigue's honorable *être* is flawed, since it only generates duty to family. Both terms, "honor" and "duty," are thus revealed to be ambiguous; they are obsolete signs that cannot refer with precision to a concrete behavior: a symptom of semiotic malaise.

Let us then forget about honor, duty, and "gloire," and focus on Rodrigue's actual behavior. In all its manifestations, even when they conflict, it clearly refers to a concept that is never mentioned in the text: individualism. From the onset, we have seen, he acts as an exemplary lover; and while he accepts losing his beloved, he never gives up his love and eventually sees it rewarded. But love is not only a passion: since its first textual appearance in *Tristan et Yseut*, it has served in Western literature as an unconscious disguise for individualism—an unidentifiable source of antisocial acts that ideology cannot explain.

Indeed, all passionate love, including Rodrigue's, stands for an absolute value for a single individual; it cannot be shared and is only understood by society when it is translated into a social institution: marriage. By giving Chimène to Rodrigue, the king channels love, and hence individualism, into an acceptable and responsible direction: as a happily married lover, that is, as a tamed individualist, Rodrigue can be integrated into the social order and serve the state.

No doubt he first gives up his love for the sake of family duty. But this choice does not affect his individualistic stance: it merely subordinates a wild form of individualism to a more traditional one. For, while more understandable than passion, loyalty to the paterfamilias is firmly rooted in bourgeois individualism. It manifests the priority of private interests over public welfare, the will to keep personal profit in one's family. Alien to the feudal mentality, this individualistic family loyalty becomes increasingly respectable as the middle class takes over the power in the modern state. In Corneille's society, and in Rodrigue's fictional world, it is already integrated as an acceptable value, shared also by nobility. True, its bourgeois origins are not acknowledged. Nor, in Rodrigue's case, is the tie between his individualism and his duty to his father spelled out. But that tie informs the censure of his family honor, too individualistic to serve the duty to the state.

Individualism thus provides the key to Rodrigue's problematic behavior. When one substitutes individualism for love, "honor," "duty," and "gloire," the tangled structure of Rodrigue's censure and reward reveals, under its semiotic confusion, a wishful—though unconscious—solution of a malaise related to individualism: malaise created when bourgeois dynamism was harnessed in the service of French monarchy. It is now well known that traditional nobility, both of Sword and Gown, viewed with alarm the growing number of talented commoners entrusted with powerful offices and raised to noble rank. The seventeenth-century ideology could explain, as exceptional scandals, a few such violations of order, but it had no concepts to account for its concerted subversion carried out with the complicity of the state. The notion of the preeminence of individual worth, whatever the social origin, was widely accepted only a century later, and the bourgeois dominance acknowledged only after 1789. Meantime, however, individualism was changing the social fabric, with disturbing effects that, in the absence of appropriate signs, were neither clearly grasped nor identified as such.

Fiction, on the other hand, could freely express the unconscious feeling of malaise, and, under unconscious disguises, it could seek to resolve it. Rodrigue's story proposes such a solution, and—by my hypothesis—can be explained by the social conditions that inspired it.

Corneille's unconscious project was intended, from that perspective, to show and justify the process by which, in his time, the modern state must, all at once, acknowledge the dynamism of bourgeois individualism breaking through traditional order, recognize the danger of its self-oriented power, control and harness its force, and reward it by gratifying the individual Eros. Thus Rodrigue: a wild individual, censured for his family loyalty, threatened with death when he harms public welfare; then, when he proves to be useful, enrolled in the service of the king, given a revokable power, and promised a satisfaction of his sexual desire.

This rapid account offers a social reading of *Le Cid* that is neither strikingly original nor necessarily the best. It certainly is overly simple. But it could be reinforced by a converging analysis of other problematic characters: Rodrigue's father and the Infante. And a stronger confirmation can be derived from the notoriously flawed dramatic form of the text. It was the first Corneille tragedy supposed to apply a strict rule of classical tragedy: the unities of time, place, and action. Yet there are major problems. The Infante story challenges the unity of action; and the unity of time, while formally preserved, relies on a sequence of events that strain credulity: within the required twenty-four hours, the reader is asked to believe, Rodrigue meets his father, soliloquizes, challenges and kills Chimène's father, raises an army and defeats the Moors, returns for his trial, and wins another duel. It is significant, in terms of my reading, that these flaws point to a problem that Corneille had trouble solving: how to force his dynamic talent, displayed in his earlier plays, to serve new rigid "classical" conventions; a problem that mirrors—unconsciously—the arduous channeling of bourgeois dynamism into the rigid social conventions of the state.

A more extensive examination could narrow down the historical time when Richelieu's policies, and other social factors, generated the specific deep structures of *Le Cid*. I prefer to conclude this section with a hypothesis about the more general reasons that turned *Le Cid* into a "classic"—reasons that may explain why a socially determined literary text keeps its appeal in a changing society. For dramatic texts, we have seen, the answer partly lies in conditions of transformability, especially ambiguity, that promote innovative transformations of these texts on the stage (see Part III, section 3). But "classics" also remain popular in their original literary form, identical for all readers. Ambiguity again no doubt plays a role here, since it facilitates attributing new meanings to old texts. My hypothesis concerns another feature that has less relevance for theatre but more for classical literature: universality.

Literary themes that have a universal appeal are well known: love and hatred, fear and hope, anxiety and ambition, and so forth. The question is: How are they introduced into a fiction that seeks to solve, with unconscious disguises, contingent social problems that lack universal appeal? I should like to suggest that the answer lies in the process that generates these disguises. More exactly, in the close relation— semantic proximity—between the unconscious real problem and its mask. Thus, in *Le Cid*, a disturbing bourgeois individualism that cannot be identified yet as such, is variously disguised as love, family honor, and personal "gloire": all notions that, in contrast with loyalty to the state, are closely related to individualism. Two of these notions have only a relative interest, limited to a certain type of society: "gloire" and family honor. Love, however, especially when it is crossed by social authority (family, group, or state), is among the most universal themes. And no wonder: it expresses, in a particularly moving form, a total— and yet harmless—dedication to an absolute individual value, a most private truth, an emotion that cannot be reasoned. Indeed, in a crossed love story, whatever its setting, the universal appeal does not lie in the resolution of a real problem disguised as love, but in the resolution of the problem of love, severed from the problem it disguises.

Yet, let us repeat, the recourse to such a universal disguise requires that the historical problem be very close to the disguising universal. Bourgeois individualism, masked as love, meets that condition in *Le Cid*. But this is not always the case. Many dramatic texts originate in malaises, and in semiotic lags, caused by problems that, at the time of textual production, do not closely relate to universal disguises. Thus rapid shifts in the distribution of wealth, in the late nineteenth century, generated few "classic" dramatic texts, although they did so in seventeenth-century France, as in Molière's *Le Bourgeois gentilhomme*. My hypothesis concerning the sources of universality must account for these variations. Let us then say that, in the last analysis, the universal appeal of a text depends not only on the disguised form of an unconscious problem, but also on conditions that influence the unconscious choice of a more or less universal disguise.

These conditions reflect social conditions. Thus dynamic societies, when they reach a high plateau of development, cultural as well as political, tend to formulate their explicit values in terms of universals valid for all times and all people. They are blind to changes that may undermine their ideology and, refusing to acknowledge semiotic lags, they seek to disguise them in the form of values endowed with permanence. In such societies, for example, in seventeenth-century France, fictional stories that express a concealed malaise have a good chance to become "classics," that is, to choose their disguises among familiar universals. In contrast, societies marked by rapid change, and hence sensitive to the fragility of values, find it more arduous to relate their unconscious problems to reliable universals; and they produce fewer "classics." This may be very well the case today. True, some recent dramatic texts, say, Beckett's *Waiting for Godot*, have been hailed as instant modern classics; but one may wonder whether this reputation is truly based on their literary universality, which remains to be demonstrated, or on their success as "transformable" texts, that is, on the widespread appeal of their different performances, which offer their own particular disguises often far removed from their textual sources.

## 2. Directors and Society

### "Absent" and "Collective" Directors

In several respects, the directorial function is diametrically opposed to the authorial function. The author supplies a permanent concrete feature of theatre—the text; the directors's contribution, the performance, is ephemeral, tenuous, and difficult to grasp. The author's text, once published, has an autonomous life; the director's performance constantly needs to be given new life by performers. And the authorial function was always acknowledged as a distinct feature of theatre, whereas a distinct directorial function was recognized as such only in the nineteenth century. Thus Aristotle dwells on textual production and alludes to acting, but says nothing about staging. Even today the role of a director is more problematic than the role of the author. And yet, as agents of the theatrical process, directors can be grouped in nearly the same categories as authors, each category entailing a different relation to their social situation.

A first category groups *absent* directors: all those agents of the directorial function who cannot be identified, usually because that function is not clearly tied to distinct individuals. Instead, the proper directorial activity, staging, is carried out by theatre conventions, more or less explicit. Such conventions openly rule most ritualized forms of theatre where, today as in the past, custom prescribes a strict style of acting, movements, sets and props, costumes, sound effects, and so forth. The Japanese *No*, Punch and Judy shows, and tragedies in ancient Greece and seventeenth-century France clearly belong in that group. But the same approach to staging can also be detected in modern performances whenever individual directors, for reasons to be discussed later, prefer to rely on conventions rather than on their own invention.

Most conventions can be explained by their specific origins, but these origins are generally forgotten, and with them the initial reason for the convention. A performance staged by an absent director rather relies on conventions qua conventions, that is, on formal rules specifying what classes of stage signs are appropriate for given classes of textual topics, regardless of differences between individual texts. This does not mean that the directorial function is eliminated: verbal references are always transformed on the stage, and conventional masks can modify textual meaning as dramatically as can individual facial expressions. In fact, when conventions direct the staging, stage signs are particularly powerful: because they are conventional, and hence familiar, they communicate their references without ambiguity to an audience that has learned to expect them and to accept their authority.

There follows that even avant-garde performances, when they are staged in the spirit of absent directorship, display several ritual features. They stress participation in shared signs, meanings, and aesthetic experiences, and offer a festive occasion for social communion. By the same token, they draw the attention to the skills of performers: in a performance staged by conventions, indeed, the only source of gratifying surprise is a superior *performance*. As a rule, then, in the absence of active directors, bringing in their individual referential concerns, a conventional staging tends to focus on the performant function. And, at the same time, it tends to refer to repetitive and conservative values. In that sense, it satisfies the human hunger for repetitions, amply demonstrated by formulaic media (and explained by Freud). Each new performance thus combines a great deal of similar references with a pinch of a performant difference. No wonder then that, somewhat paradoxically, modern directors who model themselves on absent directors are great favorites of the public. Whether theatre is thus served is not at issue here.

It is important, however, to determine under what conditions staging by convention is favored over staging by the will of directors. There is no question that a staging based on conventions needs the support of a large body of codes, theatrical and cultural, that are shared by performers and spectators. It is generally believed that "primitive" rituals relied on such common codes. It can be assumed also that, in the late Middle Ages, most social groups also shared codes that inspired efficient staging conventions. Thus as the lower-class public of French "soties," or Fools' plays, watched comedians identified only as "The World" or "The People," they understood the specific notions to which the roles referred, even though all comedians were similarly costumed as Fools. And there are reasons to think that the alarming "Gens Nouveaux," more enigmatic to us, were clearly understood to stand for ambitious bourgeois who, at that time, shocking the common people attached to traditions, began to replace nobility in power positions.

This conservatism, incidentally, does not fit well with theories that view the common people as a source of subversion;[3] it rather testifies to its basic trust in social order and its signs.

In modern society, in order to rely on rules of conventions, directors must assume that such shared codes operate in the social group of their potential spectators. By the end of the nineteenth century, one group of this type had clearly emerged: a relatively homogeneous upper middle class with a modicum of cultural aspirations. It still fuels the mainstream of theatrical activity. Staging conventions satisfy its shared referential expectations, while the predictable performances are spiced with occasional surprising *performances*. The text to be staged is not necessarily a classic, nor need it be staged in classical style. In New York, London, or Paris today, the bourgeois audiences have a good knowledge of basic Freudian codes, and can be expected to understand an Oedipal performance of *Hamlet*. However, in revived classics as well as in new plays, staging by convention usually conveys conservative messages. The repetitiousness of such shows, notably middle-class comedies, holds a mirror to a public that is reassured to see its reflection in always the same images.

The category of *collective* directors includes all those performers who, while clearly identifiable as individuals, collaborate in *group* stagings, combining personal contributions. Such collective staging is mainly a modern practice, though it might have originated in the tradition of anonymous staging by medieval companies. To a certain extent, of course, all performances are always staged by a collective directorship, since any staging involves contributions by actors, technicians, or even spectators through a feedback effect. Even most forceful directors need to yield to the strong preferences of their performers and audiences. But such forms of cooperation are contingent, and hardly affect the overall orientation of staging. In contrast, in companies with real collective directorship, the totality of staging decisions originate in the entire performing group—a group purposefully formed to carry out a common staging policy, expressing a common ideological commitment.

It is also true that, in well-integrated collectives, a single coordinator eventually fits together the various individual suggestions and often gives a personal slant to the collective staging. Furthermore, that coordinating function is often entrusted to an individual with personal authority: a charismatic leader who inspires the performing group. Julian Beck and Judith Malina certainly dominated the collective of the Living Theatre, and a similar role is played today by Eugenio Barba, Peter Brook, and Arianne Mnouchkine. But even the best-known coordinators are supposed to be merely an extension of the collective

company. The final staging is given, and must be taken, as a manifestation of the collective will, regardless of compromises that might have
been required.

It is not clear how such a collective will might have operated in
earlier ages of theatre. In modern theatre, however, staging by consensus clearly generates both strength and perils. When the directorial
function is shared by a group, everybody is actively involved in staging
decisions; and actors, designers, or technicians think less about their
individual concerns than about a common search for the best collective
performance. In theory, "collective" performers should thus invest in
their joint activity as much energy as "professional" performers invest
in their careers. At its best, as shown by the Living Theatre, collective
staging indeed becomes a total commitment, a style of living, a communion of inner selves. In fact, the dedication of collective companies
has become exemplary. And few traditional companies have as yet
matched their dynamism, intransigence, and experimental daring.

But collective staging has also its problems. Individual contributions, even when they are coordinated, lack a natural cohesion. They
inspire original and forceful performances, but rarely display the
power of a single focus generated by a strong "concept." For a "concept" always starts with a reductive interpretation of a text, and requires a strict subordination of staging to that initial vision. It demands
both a clear formulation of the "concept" and a tight control over its
implementation: conditions that are better met by individual directors
than by a group. Collective staging, even at its best, risks leading to
referential dispersion.

There are two major approaches for minimizing that danger. The
best current collectives, notably those mentioned above, openly stress
the performant function as a compensation for the referential dispersion. Multiplying displays of acting skills, astonishing resources of
naked human bodies, colorful costumes, gracious or striking postures,
exotic music, faces made up like masks, or, somewhat unexpectedly,
drab sets, minimal props and simple outfits, the collective staging
promotes individual talents of performers, satisfies their performing
needs, and keeps the attention of a public dazzled with a variety of
*performances*. To that extent, "shows" staged by collective directors exploit the performant function as systematically as "shows" staged by
absent directors; they are more daring, however, and target a more
sophisticated audience.

The risk of dispersion is also checked by a shared ideology that
keeps the group together and increases the cohesion of staging. Any
modern theatre collective, indeed, is always potentially unstable. It is
an "unnatural" amalgamate of the functions of director, performer,

staff, and sometimes author. It can be bonded together, however, by an ideology that guards it against functional fragmentation and checks a coordinator's transformation into a director. In the absence of ideology, as in the case of many student groups, collective staging is usually limited to a few productions. In contrast, serious collectives normally show a distinctly ideological profile, though it often is limited to a general anticonformist and subversive stance. Thus inspired, collective directors tend to aggregate in marginal groups wherein they debate their opposition to what they perceive to be the values of the Establishment: tradition, authority, proprietary rights, bourgeois norms, social inequality, dehumanization. They gravitate toward radical positions but avoid definite political ties; or they seek artistic truth in a mystical liberation of repressed human emotions. In either form, their commitment lacks solidity; but it suffices to stabilize and focus their collective staging.

As an outlet for a marginal ideology, collective staging is thus largely tied to the emergence and survival of marginal groups. Obviously, no monolithic society furthers the formation of dissenting collectives. But not all divided societies encourage it equally. A sharp political polarization leaves but a small place for marginal groups. A moderately fragmented society, wherein the vision of the world breaks into several well-defined views, favors instead the emergence of individual directors who capture and advocate the values of the competing groups. The formation of collectives requires a more advanced stage of the disintegration of the social fabric: the creation of "holes" within the network of traditional values, and the resulting search for new, elusive, but always different values. During the 1960s, theatre collectives multiplied: together with flower children and utopian communes, they participated in the exploration of new forms and signs of social life.

Such cultural crises are rare. Semiotic malaises, we noted, instead develop progressively, leading to a gradual reduction of the ideological lag. The pace of change during the 1960s was perhaps too rapid for such an adjustment; neither socialist nor capitalist ideology could explain the causes of the malaise; and all sorts of marginal movements were born. Since then, the causes of the crisis have been diagnosed: the same mechanization of life, development of mass media, and loss of direct control over the environment that was mentioned earlier. Adjusted ideologies dissipate today the semiotic malaise and create new, clear lines of social polarization. The time is not propitious for the survival of marginal groups, nor for a revival of collective staging.

Indeed, nurtured by the semiotic malaise, collective staging had a very short period of vitality—about a decade. Its decline partly reflected a general adaptation to cultural changes, but it was accelerated by economic factors. For, in order to survive, theatre collectives need a very special public: sophisticated, daring, somewhat marginal but also sufficiently wealthy to provide material support for experiments on the stage. In other terms, collective staging best develops in a well-to-do intellectual middle class that can tolerate the formation of its own artistic fringe. The diverging fortunes of the Living Theatre and the Théâtre du Soleil show what can happen when the economic conditions of that group deteriorate: The Living Theatre could not adjust to the recession of the 1970s and, losing the support of a small but affluent public, decided to disband rather than to change its style; on the other hand, a decade later, Mnouchkine's company took in its stride the sudden collapse of the "glorious thirty year expansion" in France, tuned down its subversive tone, and expanded its audience to include conservative layers of Parisian bourgeoisie. The paradox of collective theatre is that its survival depends on the generosity of the same bourgeois society that it finds to be ideologically bankrupt.

## Individual Directors: Tensions and Strategies

The last category groups *individual* directors: those directors who, as individuals, are effectively responsible for the staging viewed as their personal creation. That dominant role of individual directors, let us repeat, was rarely recognized before the nineteenth century. In earlier societies, the directorial function was carried out either by conventions or by authors/actors such as, for example, Molière or Shakespeare. What caused the change? One could try to attribute it to the social and cultural upheavals of the eighteenth century, but that hypothesis cannot be substantiated. Not more enlightening is the theory that directors emerged when performance was split from text, and directors were needed to bring them together.[4] It is more likely that the progress of historic research in the nineteenth century increased the awareness of the differences between the past and the present, between the old meaning of classics and a meaning appealing to living spectators; and directors became entrusted with bridging that gap. One must also take into account the new composition of mainstream theatre audiences: definitely middle class, but a middle class divided along political lines. To appeal to opposing ideologies, canonical dramatic texts had to be transformed in different ways by strongly committed directors.

None of these observations accounts for the creative role played by directors in staging new plays. That role, I believe, must be related to a general crisis of individualism, seeking an outlet in artistic achievement. Initially a subversive bourgeois value, individual success was still promoted by ideology—you cannot keep a good man down!—but it turned into a frustrating ideal when the bourgeoisie, intent on protecting its new hegemony, deprived success of its sense of individualistic achievement. Material success became a socially approved goal rather than a means to affirm personal differences. In contrast, creative art offered a safe form of dissent from pragmatic norms, and a field where excellence could express truly individual talent. Disgruntled bourgeois who turned to aesthetic pursuit were no doubt few, but concentrated in centers of culture—Paris, New York, London, Berlin—which were also the centers of theatrical life. The renaissance of theatre at the turn of the century, from symbolism to surrealism, owes much to its roots in a frustrated bourgeois individualism that was turning to art; and directors, carried by the general movement, asserted their will to be as creative as other artists, that is, to be free to stage their personal visions of the world. One may add that their striving to change the meaning of text was dramatically assisted by the discovery of the magic power of electricity: a technical breakthrough in the art of staging. The role of directors as prime movers in theatre eventually benefited also from many other developments: the prestige of film directors, expansion of mass media that focus on personalities, consolidation of the star system, growing interest in box-office profits secured by experienced directors, and so forth. At the present, the controlling position of directors seems to be stable.

But it is not an easy position. Control over the performance no doubt satisfies a director's ego, and certainly adds power and prestige to the directorial role. But it is a problematic role, generating several tensions. The most constant derives from two directorial activities that are always competing: interpretation and creation. They are not incompatible, but demand a subtle dosage of priorities. The director is responsible for the choice of priorities, yet has no ready guidelines. And the choices are many, ranging from a minimal interpretation of the textual meaning to a free creation of a new meaning. Furthermore, any choice always depends on a multiplicity of unstable factors: personal temperament, individual perception of the directorial function, cultural fashion. True, like collective directors, individual directors are also influenced, in a more reliable manner, by general social conditions. In a society strongly polarized between political issues, directors are likely to be committed to an ideological interpretation of texts; when society is atomized, and the semiotic malaise spreads to ideologies, directors can be expected to seek a solipsistic refuge, together with other artists, in personal free creation. But these are extreme situations. In times of normalcy, directors work in relatively static societies, where interpretation and creation have a comparable appeal.

The proper dosage of priorities is also elusive because, between the two contrasted positions, concrete options usually involve a mix of interpretation and creation. In fact, it is always risky to try to assess their exact dosage in any given staging; and even a mere impression of a general orientation may change from audience to audience, depending on how well informed or sophisticated it is. All performances I have discussed here were certainly both interpretations and creations, though I principally stressed what I perceived to be creation: a matter of personal judgment. Then, of course, some performances have no available text. When Armand Gatti staged his adjustable shows in an old factory in Amsterdam, was he creating a meaning or interpreting a meaning given beforehand?

In most cases, then, the tension between interpretation and creation cannot be grasped with precision. It is likely that few directors are clearly aware of all its implications. Yet, consciously or instinctively, all directors always resolve that tension when they make their staging choices. And these choices are capital not only for the success of a given performance, but also for the director's self-definition as a director and, more generally, as a concrete confirmation of the directorial power. For, in terms of power, each staging reenacts another tension that always undermines a director's role: the tension between, on the one hand, an effective control over staging processes and, on the other hand, a total loss of control over a completed staging.

In its strict sense, indeed, the directorial function is limited to the crucial but ephemeral time when directors actually work on the staging; they have no impact on a text that is given to them before the staging process, nor on the way that performers execute their staging decisions after they are finalized. In theory, and in reality, directors are absent from the final theatrical production; and their contribution can only be found, or rather detected, in the traces it leaves in the performance—traces that, as we shall see, are also problematic. Even the slightest decision they make during the staging process thus fully affects their evanescent art, and engages their total responsibility as artists.

But what is exactly a director's art? What is precisely involved in staging decisions? Both interpretation and creation deal with changes in meaning, and to that extent directors compete with authors (but do not produce permanent texts). They sometimes develop and impose "concepts" in order to convey a specific meaning; at other times, they follow their inspiration in a search for multiple dispersed meanings. In either case, however, their precise contribution always concerns the choice and organization of stage signs. But stage signs, by their nature, generate themselves a tension between directors and performers. For there are many different staging signs, most quite complex, and the directorial control over most of them must be shared. For example, it is hard to distinguish, in facial expressions, intonations, or gestures, the separate contributions of directors and actors; or what a set or a costume owes to the director and the designer. In that sense, all features on the stage are always produced in collaboration. Which means in turn that directors never can fully control the production of their signs; and yet the responsibility for these signs is the main goal of their function.

This tension is more acute in theatre than in other live performing arts: music, opera, ballet, and mine. Orchestra conductors also direct the production of signs, but they are performers themselves, and their presence endows them with a constant control over other performers. Besides, while they are responsible for changes in performances, their contributions affect the limited range of musical signs and rarely lead to significant transformations of meaning. Opera is more like theatre in that it involves a stage with acting performers. But, as a rule, music plays there a more important role than staging, and the directorial function carries less prestige than in theatre.[5] Ballet and mime similarly stress their own systems of signs—dance, acrobatics, and stylized mimicry; and are oriented to the performant function more than to referential meanings. Some of their "directors," especially in avant-garde productions, share with their performers the responsibility for the production of signs, and no doubt experience the same tension as theatre directors. But this type of performance, as well as other hybrid forms, are in fact marginal forms of theatre.[6] Besides, in such forms, the directorial function is often split between directors and performers, leading to continuous supervision and revision of stage signs.

In traditional theatre, in contrast, performers on stage are always on their own. However strict their initial coaching by directors, their actual performance is always unpredictable; it varies from day to day, reflecting changes in mood, surges of personal inspiration, and responses of the audience. On the opening night, or after a short period of adjustment, often in provincial towns, a director's contribution is normally over (although Kantor in Poland keeps directing on the stage). To mark the performances with their vision, and claim it as truly their own, directors must rely on staging instructions that will be carried out in their absence. Their success as directors thus hinges on the memory, goodwill, and talents of other people. In short, with each new show, they stake their future, their self-esteem, and their reputation on decisions that they can neither change nor enforce. It is a hard responsibility to bear. And it generates a number of defensive strategies.

The most popular is to minimize personal responsibility. Invoking "professionalism," directors can give up their freedom as artists and, in a spirit of existentialist "bad faith," model their work on a dominant tradition of staging. Like the "absent" directors discussed above, but by their own choice, they rely on safe conventions: conventions accepted by producers and consumers of theatre. Periods of cultural unrest do not favor that strategy because rapidly changing conventions offer few reliable models. In contrast, stable social groups, such as the middle-class public of Broadway comedies, approve and support conventional staging. The contribution of "professional" directors should not be downgraded: they do not renew theatrical forms but maintain in good health the mainstream theatre.

A second strategy leads to various ways of sharing individual responsibility. In extreme cases, it leads directors—Peter Brook, Grotowski, or Mnouchkine—to promote "collective" staging in their own companies: they unload their responsibility on performers and staff. There is another variant, more pragmatic and perhaps cynical, chosen freely or imposed: shelving responsibility on an outside power. Thus, in state-controlled theatres, directors do not claim to be totally free; even when they are innovative, they do not need to identify with their staging. Of course, many state theatres actually encourage experimentation, offering no alibi for potential failures. In commercial theatres, the role of controlling authority is played by producers or "angels," who are made responsible for those features of staging that fail to meet a director's concept of creative freedom. A third variant is more idealistic, appealing to directors committed to a cause. The outside control is granted to an ideology, or sometimes to a militant group embodying that ideology. Individual staging freedom and, hence, responsibility, are partly given up; but a gratifying identification with the cause compensates identification with the directorial function. Besides, as we have noted, ideological directors generally feel justified in breaking theatre conventions and, hence, are inclined to create new forms. True, they rarely have access to truly commercial stages, but, at times of ideological unrest, they find enthusiastic support in the public of experimental theatres.

In contrast with the two others, the third strategy relies on the affirmation of individual freedom and responsibility. It is evidenced by ambitious directors, to some degree conceited, who identify with their creation and find in it their full self-realization. They believe they can master their destiny as artists; and, hence, that a powerful personal staging, however ephemeral, will leave on their art a permanent mark of their individual talent. Instead of following the public taste, they want to mold their public, with strong and perhaps sensational strikes. The nature of that public is relatively irrelevant to their goals: starting with small theatres, they expect eventually to reach vast audiences—and some of them do, when commercial interests, state authorities, or cultural institutions are drawn to their success. To be sure, they need a relatively free society, but its specific nature does not seem to have a great impact on the appeal, and hence material conditions, of the most gifted among these directors. The growing power of mass media seems to guarantee that they—and the theatre they inspire—will have a bright future.

Yet even most self-confident directors are not in full control of their self-realization in art. They know that staging is always somewhat alienated in the performance, and that a performance, in turn, can only be preserved in alienating forms: memory, written accounts, photographs, video recordings. Aware that their creations have no future, directors must accept that their creative acts have meaning only in the present. But they also know that, even during its own process, staging is not entirely free: it depends on the nature of texts, on staging traditions, and on performers. Truly ambitious directors are thus logically inclined to reduce the influence of these factors.

The influence of texts can be easily controlled. Directors who want to assert their independence as artists and produce their own original meanings, need but to choose creation over interpretation: by that simple decision, all claims of textual meanings are effectively discounted. On the other hand, staging traditions exert a more insidious pressure. To a large extent, they are assimilated by directors and form an integrated part of their inspiration. Yet many independent directors, intent on demonstrating their creative power, find original ways of subverting at least some traditions. Theatre owes them the successive invention of "realistic" "symbolic," "abstract" and "minimal" staging styles; and, more recently, the discovery of the "gestus" and the spectacular potential of the body, breaking the traditional focus on the word. Piscator's introduction of film on the stage formed another break with tradition, now followed by the introduction of multimedia staging. There are no indications that such innovations will stop or slow down.

Controlling the autonomous input of performers is obviously more difficult. Yet directors who want to be the sole masters of their creations are logically also tempted to be masters of their performers. In contrast to directors willing to share staging with a collective, they wish for absolute power and authority of their directives. In its extreme form, that ambition lead Gordon Craig to formulate his notorious concept of puppet-actors: performers reduced to their material function as staging signs, and hence deprived of their human function as producers of signs. Craig's theory was clearly not intended to have practical applications. But it still informs the model of a master-director who forces performers to be disciplined and obedient, and who nevertheless manages to gain their respect.[7]

A successful master-director provides in that sense the ideal incarnation of the free director. From such masters-directors, once they are established, the public expects exceptional performances, even at the expense of theatrical conventions. In his celebrated collage of Arrabal texts, performed as *Le Cimetière des voitures*, Garcia multiplied subversive moves: a misleading title, a jumbled story, an incoherent assemblage of meanings, erotic nudity, scenes of torture, a stage extending into the audience, baroque parades and songs, and the nearly mechanical perfection of his performers. In the early 1970s, even shocked Parisian spectators, impressed by his reputation, applauded Garcia's *performance*. Today masters-directors work under less favorable conditions. They still are respected because they are stars, but the power that derives from reputation also benefits stars among performers. And successful performers always tend to resist the authority of a master-director.

## 3. Actors and Their Paradoxes

It is somewhat paradoxical to conclude a study of theatre—rather than to begin it—with the most popular theatrical figure: the actor. No doubt, in the process of production from text to stage, actors come last; and a theoretical study must follow that order. But the real role of actors in theatre is much more important than their functional place: in the public eye, they truly embody theatre, are identified with it. And no wonder since, among all people involved in theatre, actors are certainly the most *visible*. Authors, directors, designers, technicians—and the growing paratheatrical staff involved in financing, producing, marketing, and booking plays—are physically *absent* at the time of the performance. Besides, while most of their functions are as indispensable as the acting function, they do not need to be carried out by distinctly identified individuals. Tradition, collectives, or actors themselves can replace authors or directors. But no one can substitute for actors.[8] Nor can any feature of the stage match their dominant role. Even when their visible presence is reduced to a head on top of a jar, or a fluorescent mouth on a dark stage, the audience is aware that real actors are speaking, and gives its attention to their words. In short, there can be no theatre without actors. Better: without actors, and their indomitable will to act, there would be no theatre. True, at various times, theatre satisfied various social needs and was tolerated, supported, or even promoted by society; but at other times it was censured, and its survival in folkloric or amateur forms would not have been possible without a constant supply of new and eager actors.

## Actors and Social Subversion

It is not the place here to review the ups and downs of this fascinating affair between actors and theatre; others have done it, and some from a sociological perspective.[9] One point, however, deserves to be stressed: for centuries, in the West, the visibility of actors as individuals on the stage was closely matched by their visibility as individuals in the society. Set apart by their style of living, they were viewed as an alien tribe whose loose morals and mores, displayed openly, were judged to be both reprehensible and seductive, and hence dangerous. Obviously, this only concerns professional actors. Amateurs are rarely identified by their society as actors; and their occasional participation in amateur performances, or in ritual shows, seems rather to enhance their normal social status. Thus, while professional actresses had a dreadful reputation in seventeenth-century France, high-born young ladies supervised by Mme de Maintenon were greatly honored to act in Racine's tragedies written and performed for Louis XIV. Participating today in the Oberammergau passion play, or in Arizona's Yaqui Indian Easter ritual, and a fortiori in urban and suburban amateur groups or in school productions, carries a similar distinction sans opprobrium.

It is also true that many professional actors never conformed to their stereotyped image, lived respectable if not respected lives, or achieved celebrity and social status. Yet, like all others, they were suspected of moral turpitude and, in old France, denied the right to have a Christian burial. For the censure of actors was not simply caused by their assumed wanton mores; other people were also debauched, and not always discreet. But only actors enacted, on public stages, sinful passions much worse than their own weaknesses, and hence more dangerous as models to imitate. Since Plato, indeed, the censure of actors as agents of corruption has been based on the fear of iconic magic: the power of live performers to move spectators, like voyeurs, to an emotional communion that stimulates imitation. Actors themselves, in their personal life, were suspected of being the first victims of the contagious example set by them in their professional roles. It is significant that, even within the theatre world, actors were also singled out, no doubt for similar reasons, as the main source of its general unsavory moral reputation; authors, directors, and staff rarely escaped criticism but, in their own opinion as well as in the public eye, they seem to have been deemed to be more moral than actors.

In the past, then, the dual visibility of actors, on the stage and in society, converged to promote a clearly subversive image. They were distrusted even when they served conservative social functions. Today the situation is more complex. Public visibility of most actors as private individuals has decreased. And their corresponding subversive image has become problematic, even contradictory. In many ways it no longer fits well with the perception of reality. True, it still may reflect the living style of many stars, especially when their success in cinema draws mass media's attention to scandals in their personal lives. But these are exceptions, perhaps envied but not imitated. A certain anticonformism is also still popular among avant-garde groups, and perhaps aspiring young actors, but its appeal is limited and not very obvious in an overall permissive society. The great majority of professional actors appear to be leading a respectable existence. Their private lives may be somewhat unstable, but not as a necessary outcome of their profession; it seems rather to follow the relaxed codes of all "arty" communities.

Even their handling of professional matters is increasingly oriented by businesslike forms of mainstream "professionalism." In a world of professional schools and professional unions, professional journals, agents, contracts, billings, reviews, interviews, photographs, promotional appearances, they are encouraged to protect their professional interests as actors and their material interests as private individuals. And these interests in turn depend on the preservation of a stable and affluent society. No longer disturbing agents of subversion, professional actors increasingly must play an essentially conservative social role.

And yet—and yet!—their image still elicits suspicion. To become an actor is still viewed, with alarm, commiseration, or sympathy, as an act of idealistic rebellion: against parents, material values, social pragmatism. The subversion thus implied clearly contradicts the conservative role that actors play in society: a paradoxical situation. It is important to try to understand its sources, that is, to explain the persistence of a subversive image that has little grounding in reality.

It is unlikely that this image derives, as it did in the past, from the fear that actors on the stage might corrupt public morality. For today's theatre is quite tame: conservative plays greatly outnumber subversive plays; passion and eroticism are no longer very shocking. It would rather seem that the subversive image reflects a distrust of acting as such. Acting indeed, as a form of play, is not a serious activity. Furthermore, acting is also suspect because, under the cover of play, it transgresses the rules of order. Actors on the stage have always been envied, but also criticized, for living vicariously, and yet in public, many different lives and many different social roles. Like Harlequin, whose checkered costume sets him apart from stable social groups, suggesting that he moves freely across them, actors move from role to role, experiencing and demonstrating their freedom to cross all conventional barriers erected by society. And not only once a year, like carnival performers, but in a continuous subversion of social organization. Their personal lives between performances may seem to be peaceful; underneath, however, they are suspected of harboring an unruly disposition nurtured by their subversive switching of roles on the stage. Their very existence, and professional presence, thus suffice to disturb social complacency, whatever the specific nature of their society.

At least, this is my hypothesis. If it is correct, then professional actors today, and in a foreseeable future, will retain their subversive image regardless of their increasingly more conforming behavior. But that paradox operates only in the domain of public opinion. From the perspective of actors, their function in society, as public and private individuals, involves no contradiction. Dealing with business matters, and at home, they display the same proper signs of conservative professionalism. There remains to be seen whether on the stage, that is, when they are involved in acting and staging, they also play a conservative role in the theatrical processes, or support subversion of traditional performing styles.

## Actors and Staging Styles

The main function of actors is acting on the stage. Strictly speaking, then, their approaches to their function correspond to their approaches to acting. Obviously, different actors believe in different approaches to acting—from Diderot's dispassionate display of learned signs to Stanislavski's emotional identification with the character. These approaches, in turn, involve actors in concrete choices between various training methods and acting styles. Much has been written about these choices, and how they ought to be implemented to improve acting skills. But special acting techniques, as well as techniques of writing and staging, fall outside the boundaries of this study. There is no point either in discussing here to what extent most actors are really committed to their profession. Discounting true amateurs, it can be assumed that all actors take acting to be a very serious activity: they dedicate their lives to it and can be expected to perform it to their best ability.

But the function of actors in not limited to actual acting. It also involves them in the overall staging process: they collaborate with directors in the production of stage signs. We shall see below how this participation in staging involves their dual role as signs and producers of signs, and how it directs their contact with the audience. First, however, it is important to grasp a more fundamental impact of actors as codirectors: the influence they have on the choice of staging styles, and hence on the choice between tradition and change. We have seen that the choice between the interpretation of textual meanings and the creation of new meanings is decided by directors. But the choice between a conservative respect for traditional styles and a subversive introduction of new styles requires the assent of actors, directly concerned by the style of acting.

And for many reasons, as staging partners, most actors can be expected to have a clearly conservative influence. Their commitment to their profession certainly promotes respect for traditions. Investing their lives in acting for a public, actors have little to gain and much to risk in taking part in experimentation. They know that, all other things being equal, a performance is most likely to be a public success when it relies on thoroughly tested staging and acting styles, expected and appreciated by the audiences. And success—for actors—means more than passing popularity or applause gratifying the ego: it brings financial gains and enhances the reputation they need for further gains. True, success also can be achieved with experimentation, especially when an actor's or a director's name suffices to draw vast audiences. But few actors can count on such a drawing power. Also true, actors in avant-garde companies, or in companies dedicated to an ideology, willingly engage in subversive staging innovations. But they are on the fringe of theatre. For practical reasons, then, actors are surely justified when they rely on tradition in all its forms: safe texts, safe staging, and safe styles of acting.

This conservative orientation also benefits from a recent emergence of the "organization man" as the model of success. Increasingly, in all types of organizations, hence also in theatre, the ability to please, rather than talent, originality, or power, appears to be rewarded. In a theatre production, actors work with a complex group of direct and indirect producers; and, except for stars, they must avoid conflicts, seeking agreement on the basis of reliable, traditional, conservative conventions. But even stars must please their large audiences and the consumers of media: a vast and hence conservative public. So even they eschew upsetting or disorienting signs on the stage, and reach into a trusted "bag of tricks" to provide the desired entertainment. Mainstream theatre, it was noted, encourages repetitions and relegates surprises to the performant function; in fact, most popular performances rarely rise above the level of traditional "bags of tricks."

One might object that actors are not only motivated by practical, or professional, considerations, but also by an idealistic, and irrepressible, drive to seek self-expression in acting. And it is difficult to deal with subjective motivations. But self-expression is not necessarily tied to a subversive attitude toward acting styles. Rather, like most individual ideals, self-expression tends to be defined in the form of fixed goals, resisting rapid change. When they learn how to express themselves, actors elaborate personal styles of acting, based on personal talent and values; eventually, they create their own traditions. They invest too much effort in that process to let it be voided by the appeal of change. No doubt individual attitudes may vary. Some actors are more adventurous than others, and develop a less protective attitude toward their own acting tradition. But, as a rule, the impulse toward self-expression reinforces rather than subverts a conservative leaning generated by pragmatic concerns. Indeed, whatever their reputation, most professional actors today can be expected to be as conservative on the stage as they are in society. A small number, associated with avant-garde movements, try hard—on the margin—to change staging forms, but the majority contribute to their stability, directly or indirectly.

## Actors as Signs and Producers of Signs

The actual influence of actors on the staging cannot be easily determined. It clearly depends on their relation with the director, who is either more or less willing to share responsibility for the performance. It also depends on the temperament of the actors, who are either more or less willing to defend their own acting styles. They act, at the same time, as extensions of the directorial will and as autonomous artists. This double role creates a tension that is shared by all of the producers of stage signs. Set and costume designers, for example, also follow directorial directives while implementing them with their own creation. Yet, in many ways, this tension has particularly dramatic effects on actors. In the first place, it never subsides. Signs produced by actors have no stable form, as do sets or costumes: they must be constantly reproduced during each performance. Second, these signs are extremely complex. It is difficult to account for the specific features displayed by an actor as a primary sign, and it is even more difficult to determine what features combine at a given moment to operate as a cultural sign—a problem discussed in Part II. Finally, we shall see, only actors participate in theatrical semiosis both as *signs* and as *producers of signs*. All these factors increase the tension: it is always present, it always shifts its focus, and it always involves two different semiotic functions. The last point deserves special attention.

As signs, we recall, actors stand on the stage for their mirror image in the story world. In order to function as signs, they must display features that refer to imaginary characters. Some of these features—the basic attributes of the body—are chosen by directors during the casting process. But gestures, postures, intonations, expressions must be produced by actors when they are acting. The resulting complex signs are initially conceived by directors, and to that extent actors as signs are indeed directorial signs. But these signs can function only when acting actors give them a concrete form on the stage, and to that extent actors as signs are produced by the actors themselves. This dual role enables actors to have a personal impact on their function as signs and hence on a performance's meaning: an impact that is never fixed in advance, and for which actors must bear the responsibility during each performance.

But actors also share in the production of signs other than themselves. They are needed to release the meaning of symbolic stage signs that subvert iconicity: slabs manage to stand for beds or chairs only when actors lie or sit on them. Better, gestures can produce signs out of nothing: performing in Thornton Wilder's *Our Town*, skilled actors manage to have an empty stage refer to a house, a door, a piece of furniture. But even standard iconic stage signs can be modified by acting: an ornamental sword acquires a different meaning when an actor views it with alarm as a weapon. In fact, some semioticians of theatre have claimed that this deictic power constitutes a major function of acting, needed to show exactly what is taking place, as well as when and where.[10] In most cases, however, deixis plays a minor role on the stage.

It is enough to note that actors on the stage not only produce themselves as signs but also, as actor/signs, produce or modify other signs around them; and that this double production is directly perceived and assessed by the audience. No wonder then that actors, more often than directors, are praised for the success of a performance or blamed for its failure: they are judged to be "good" or "bad" actors rather than "well-directed" or "poorly directed" actors. They know that their reputation based on such judgments is often unfair, that their performance partly reflects decisions of directors; but, while on the stage, they also know that they are on their own, and endowed with an extraordinary semiotic and performant power. That knowledge no doubt stimulates their will to leave their own mark on the performance.

They are also aware, however, that directorial instructions are not the only constraints that check their freedom. The human body has limited possibilities and, despite avant-garde progress in expanding them, there are limits that cannot be breached. The freedom of actors can be exercised only within these limits. All the more important, then, becomes the training—and mastery—of those features of face and body that can be controlled. For each actor they form a personal repertory of signs that he or she is able to display on the stage. This repertory grows with experience, but always remains personal, limited to individual expressions and gestures. And it is from that pool of personal physical resources that actors select their signs.

But that selection, that is, actual acting, is also marked by a tension. We recall that actors on the stage, solicited by the referential as well as the performant functions, always carry out two parallel and yet competing activities: production of signs and display of performing skills. Both activities make use of the same physical resources: facial or body features, quality of voice. True, the shape of an ironic smile or of an apologetic gesture, produced as a sign, is partly dictated by the general coded shape of such a smile or gesture. But it is always also determined by the individual shape of an actor's smile or gesture. On the one hand, then, in order to produce effective signs, actors must strive to form coded shapes and diversify them as subtly as needed to meet referential demands. On the other hand, as individual performers, identified by distinct physical features, they are tempted to form, without change, only those personal shapes that have become familiar to the public.

These competing goals of acting are always reconciled on the stage, but preference may be shown for one or the other. The two extreme positions are captured in the French observation that good actors, dedicated to the production of referential signs, "se mettent dans la peau du personnage" (identify with individual characters), but great actors, dedicated to the promotion of their own performant persona, "mettent le personnage dans leur peau" (identify all characters with themselves). Most actors no doubt fall between the two models. They want to be good actors, and refer effectively to characters, but they are also interested in repeating their own gestures and expressions. Moving from character to character, they are tempted to produce their own signs rather than to switch each time to the production of different signs. Usually, the tension leads to a compromise, for actors want to play roles, or they would not be actors; and so they limit repetition to the features of their personal styles with which they want to impress the audience.

## Actors and the Audience

It is only when they face the audience that actors resolve all their tensions. Their production of signs may be influenced, as we have seen, by their philosophy of staging, rather conservative, by their claim to artistic freedom, somewhat subversive, and by their stake in their reputation as performers. These influences affect actors in various degrees at different stages of the theatrical process. Preference for conservative staging styles, for example, plays a major role during the early phases of staging; on the other hand, the assimilation of acting to creative art—a product of cultural conditions—shapes an actor's personality before the staging begins. Some influences may converge, others may compete. Their final reconciliation takes place on the opening night of the performance. At that time, however, actors are obliged to take under consideration one additional factor: the reaction of the public.

It bears repeating: theatre is a form of live communication, and hence always involves a constant interaction between senders and receivers of signs.[11] In that sense, as in many others, theatre differs from cinema, which only involves a one-way transmission of signs. And, within theatre, the two-way communication specifically concerns the actors. In contrast with the author of a dramatic text, who never observes the reactions of individual readers, or the director who can observe an audience's reactions but cannot respond to them, actors are in contact with the public, and both perceive their reactions and respond to them. Furthermore, that communication cannot be broken off during the performance. Actors are always expected to discharge all of their acting obligations on the stage. Strictly speaking, spectators have more freedom: they can leave the theatre, or withdraw into slumber or dreams; but this behavior also constitutes a form of communication, albeit rarely perceptible from the stage. Besides, it is limited to a small part of the audience. As a rule, actors and spectators are forced to communicate during the entire performance.

Their communication no doubt is affected by the conditions in which it takes place. We noted the impact that the physical features of the auditorium may have on the reception of signs by the audience. Similar physical features influence the reception signs sent by the audience. For example, actors rarely *see* the audience, and hence perceive few visual signs, if any. On the other hand, they can hear sounded signs: voices, laughter, hisses, foot-stamping, applause, and so forth. For several reasons, they are in fact compelled to watch for these signs, to assess their meaning, and thus to monitor the success of their contribution to theatre as communication: a complex project.

For actors, indeed, theatre communication is not limited to a single goal. When they display referential signs, they certainly aim at telling a story; but they also want to elicit a response from the audience: an emotional reaction, an expansion or change of ideas, a determination to improve the world. At the same time, hoping for a theatrical *performance*, most actors want to be applauded for their acting skills. That applause is also pursued by actors who are reputed for their personal seduction, or their public personality, and who seek a confirmation of their continued appeal. The ritual aspect of theatre, binding together actors and their public in an enclosed ceremonial space, generates its own goals. Actors know that they must sustain the magic communion that transforms a performance into a community rite; and they watch for signs of a breakdown in order to restore the communion with adjusted acting. They also are aware that theatre, like circus, involves a ritual challenge to its performers; that a performance always includes a degree of suspense; that spectators are—unconsciously?—thrilled by the prospect of an artist's failure: a cat tamer maimed by a lion, an acrobat falling down, an actor missing cues; and that their professional, and individual, pride as actors needs public acknowledgment that they meet the challenge.

The range of signs that the public can use to communicate its reactions to actors is less limited than one might think. Some signs are very loud and, within specific cultural groups, very clear: applause, whistling, foot-stamping, and standing up express approval; hisses, boos, and snickers express disapproval. Sobbing and sniffling usually refer to distress, and laughter stands for amusement or happiness. Private conversations, or snores, or creaking seats, are less perceptible but quite reliable signs of lack of interest or boredom. And highly emotional audiences often offer, and indeed shout, precise verbal comments on the story told by the actors or on their performance. To be sure, even these obvious signs may have different meanings depending on circumstances. Laughter heard during a tragic scene is a sign of derision, and hence failure. Applause that interrupts a crucial action signals an appreciation of a *performance* but a failing in the storytelling. Then there are signs that always must be interpreted because they are ambiguous. Glacial silence, for example, could mean disapproval, or indifference, or, on the contrary, a passionate involvement in the story. In that sense, the most ambiguous signs, but also the most usual, are sent by an audience that is divided, and whose various sounds compete for the attention of actors.

Reading an audience's signs is thus both easy and difficult: they are always there but they fluctuate in power and in clarity. Even seasoned actors may fail to understand them correctly. But the real problem lies in formulating appropriate responses and communicating them on the stage. To a certain extent actors must display the same flexibility as people engaged in live communication in everyday situations: they must adapt their verbal and body language signs to changing signs of their interlocutors. The commedia dell'arte has raised this flexibility to the level of principle, demanding from its performers that they change words, gestures, and movements to suit the reactions of specific audiences. Similar basic adjustments are occasionally made in avant-garde staging, particularly when it provides for an interaction between actors and the public as, say, in *Dionysus in 69* or *Orlando Furioso*. In most cases, the permanence of the dramatic text, the linear logic of the story, the strict design of a staging, and the unpredictable nature of reactions shown by the audience limit the scope of such adjustments. But they always can be made by actors who feel that the performance is not fully meeting its goals, and that a change in acting is needed as a corrective action.

Thus, in a Washington, D.C., performance of Genet's *The Blacks*, staged by a black company for a white audience in the early 1960s, an actress was instructed to step out of her textual role, hand her knitting to a male spectator, and, when he handed it back, make the provocative comment: "This is damn white of you!" But, on the night I saw the play, the spectator—perhaps warned by newspaper reports—refused to give back the knitting. Everything froze for several tense minutes, then the actress shrugged and resumed her story lines. The performance *had* to go on, and the verbal signs that the actress was to insert in response to a visual sign of the audience, that is, its disturbing whiteness, had to be sacrificed.

Yet the intention of the black company was recovered by a spontaneous adjustment of its acting. The ironic comment was supposed to convey a sense of racial tension that was inscribed in Genet's text, but it risked being lost in a conventional performance. The Washington audience, principally interested in the theatrical values of the play, needed to be jolted in order to understand its ideological violence. The improvised long and tense freeze, creating an atmosphere of open conflict, achieved that goal as well if not better than the planned ironic comment. The actors discharged their roles as adjusters of signs, displaying their ability to adapt their adjustments to an unpredictable change in the audience's reactions. In other terms, taking over from the author *and* from the director, they demonstrated that they were, as actors, ultimately responsible for the meaning of the performance.

Any new performance, however repetitive, opens thus a space of freedom where actors, however well-rehearsed, can always improvise their production of signs. True, when the staging does not change, as is usually the case, successive performances show but minute alterations. These alterations are rarely quite the same in each show because acting always somewhat changes. On the other hand, they do not vary much from one show to another because audiences also vary little, and actors do not need to make dramatic adjustments. As a rule, it is sufficient to modify the intensity of signs without changing their meaning. When the audience fails to laugh as loudly as it should, or does not laugh at all, actors try to make their faces look funnier, or exaggerate their funny intonations, but seldom switch the type of their signs. Sometimes they add new stage business, but rarely without warning their partners. Ideally, they seek to turn a given performance into the best possible performance for the given audience; but they do not create a truly different performance. And the spectators are aware of this mild scope of change. Few people attend more than one performance of the same theatrical production. They come to see live actors, they want to be thrilled by their acting, but they have no special interest in watching the same actors, or even their substitutes, in the same play. Yet they will return to the same play staged by a different director—the guiding spirit of a performance's originality.

The paradox of actors can thus be summed up as a discrepancy between their central role in the implementation of theatre communication and their marginal role in the determination of that communication. They monopolize the phatic function: show after show, they strive to please and seduce the public through live close contact. They know that no message can go through without their production of signs, and that this production requires a constant adjustment that they must make on their own. They also know that, each time they go on the stage, their entire raison d'être is at stake at the same time as the performance. They expect to be appreciated, admired, desired for their acting achievement. And yet, their work as actors only affects the quality of the performance, not its general nature. They control neither the dramatic text nor the staging that shapes the ideas and forms of a performance. They live for a brief appearance on the stage, and for their public image, but they leave little behind them. They produce no permanent art, no meaning of their own that can inspire future artists. When they are acting, in fact, they always substitute for other people—characters, authors, directors—and they execute the projects of these "others" rather than their own. They feel they are creative individuals, but they are mainly perceived, by themselves as well as by others, in their role as actors.

## Notes

1. Michel Foucault, "What Is an Author," in Michel Foucault, *Language, Counter-Memory, Practice*, trans. D. F. Bouchard and S. Simon, ed. D. F. Bouchard (Ithaca, N.Y.: Cornell University Press, 1977).

2. It is rather clear, in addition, that a private duel is also viewed as being illegal, and hence that even the challenge must be censored. This point must have been very obvious to the French spectators, especially among the nobility, who resented the strict measures taken by Richelieu to put an end to dueling in France.

3. So much for illusions, inspired by Bakhtin's carnival theory, that popular or folkloric art media, including theatre, are subversive in nature. The "soties," at any rate, clearly were intended to defend the social status quo.

4. See Bernard Dort, *Théâtre réel* (Paris: Seuil, 1971), pp. 55–56.

5. Obviously, an exceptional staging, usually directed by a reputed theatre director, may carry as much weight as the musical performance. Thus the "French" Bayreuth version of Wagner's *Ring* owed its distinct character, and success, as much to Patrice Chéreau's staging as to Pierre Boulez's musical direction.

6. In this category would fall productions of reputed, somewhat traditional, but difficult to classify groups such as the Warsaw Mime Theatre, a combination of mime, ballet, and theatre; and, of course, the Peking Opera. But also many experiments of the extreme avant-garde, such as *Quarantaine*, which Le Plan K created in Mexico in 1980 before moving it to its central space in La Raffinerie in Brussels.

7. Among recent directors, Giorgio Strehler no doubt best represents that type today. His control over actors is as legendary as his control over all features of the staging.

8. Puppets, or other mechanical devices, can replace actors in certain cases, but they are clearly conceived and perceived to be conventional substitutes for actors, tied to them by their human voices and stylized gestures produced by human agents. For a detailed analysis of semiotic aspects of puppetry see Jiři Veltruský, "Puppetry and Acting," in *Semiotica* 47¼, (1983), pp. 69–122.

9. The best known is no doubt Jean Duvignaud's *L'Acteur* (Paris, Gallimard, 1965). But there are many serious studies of the history of theatre, actors, and publics, and most of them contain detailed bibliographies.

10. See Alessandro Serpieri, "Ipotesi teorica di segmentazione del testo teatrale" in *Come comunica il teatro: dal testo alla scena* (Milan: Il Formichiere, 1978), pp. 11–54. See also Keir Elam, *The Semiotics of Theatre and Drama* (London and New York: Methuen, 1980), pp. 138–48. One notes that they relate the operation of the deixis to the elusive problem of the segmentation of the performance.

11. There is no need here to refute, once again, Georges Mounin's hasty claim that theatre is not real communication. Ruffini, Pavis, Elam, de Marinis, Helbo, and many others have clearly established that, during a performance, signs are sent from the stage to the audience, with various intentions; and that they generate various responses, some of which take the form of signs sent from the audience to the stage, generating in turn a new cycle of communication.

# Bibliography

This is not an exhaustive bibliography of sociosemiotics of theatre. Readers interested in basic works on the theory of theatre, sociocriticism, and semiotics are referred to any of the many available bibliographies in these fields. I have only listed, among texts that I had consulted, those that I have quoted, those that I have found particularly stimulating, and those that may throw further light on the points with which I am dealing.

Alter, Jean. "Vers le mathématexte au théâtre: en codant Godot." In *Sémiologie de la représentation*, ed. André Helbo, pp. 42–60. Bruxelles: Complexe, 1975.

———. "From Text to Performance: Semiotics of Theatricality." *Poetics Today* 2, no. 3 (Spring 1981), pp. 113–140.

———. "*Les Mains sales* ou La clôture du verbe." In *Sartre et la mise en scène*, ed. M. Issacharoff and J.-C. Vilquin, pp. 68–82. Paris, Klincksieck, 1982.

———. "Performance and "Performance': On the Margins of Theatre Semiotics." *Degrés*, no. 30 (Spring 1982), pp. d–d14.

———. "Meaning and Theatre: Reassigning Performance Signs." In *Semiotica Acta* (1985 SSA Conference), pp. 86–96. Lanham, Md.: American University Press, 1986

———. "Waiting for the Referent, Waiting for Godot: On Referring in Theatre." *On Referring in Literature*, pp. 42–66. Bloomington: Indiana University Press, 1987.

———. "Reception of Performance in Theatre." *Polish Art Studies* 9 (1988), pp. 88–101.

Aristotle. *Poetics*. Everyman's Library. London and New York: Dent & Dutton, 1943 (1934).

Barba, Eugenio. "Anthropologie théâtrale." *Degrés*, no. 29 (Winter 1982),pp. g–ˋg30.

———. *The Dilated Body*, followed by *The Gospel According to Oxyrhincus*. Rome: Zeami Libri, 1985.

Barry, Jackson. *Dramatic Structure*. Berkeley: University of California Press, 1970.

Barthes, Roland. *Essais critiques*. Paris: Seuil (Points), 1964.

Bassnett-McGuire, Susan. "An Introduction to Theatre Semiotics." *Theatre Quarterly 38* 10 (1980), pp. 47–53.

Beckerman, Bernard. *Dynamics of Drama: Theory and Method of Analysis*, new ed. New York: Drama Book Specialists, 1979.

Biner, Pierre. *The Living Theatre*. New York: Avon Books, 1973 (1970).

Bogatyrev, Petr. "Semiotics of Folk Theatre." In *Semiotics of Art: Prague School Contributions*, ed. L. Matejka and I. R. Titunik, pp. 32–50. Cambridge, Mass.: MIT Press, 1976.

Borie, Monique. "Théâtre et anthropologie: l'usage de l'autre culture." *Degrés*, no. 32 (Fall 1982), pp. b–b8.

Bouissac, Paul. *Circus and Culture: A Semiotic Approach*. Bloomington and London: Indiana University Press, 1976.

Brach-Czaina, Jolanta. "The Individuation Process in the Post-theatrical Activity of Grotowski." In *Polish Art Studies, Past and Present*, no. 3, pp. 143–65. Wrocław, Ossolineum, 1982.

Brook, Peter. *The Empty Space*. New York; Atheneum, 1981.

Buczynska-Garewicz, Hanna. "Sign and Dialog," *AJS* 2, no. 1–2 (1983), pp. 27–43.

Burns, E. and T. Burns. *Sociology of Literature and Drama*. Harmondsworth: Penguin, 1973.

Caillois, Roger. *Les jeux et les hommes*. Paris: Gallimard (Les Idées), 1967.

Carlson, Marvin. "Semiotics and Nonsemiotics in Performance," *Semiotica* (1983), pp. 671–76.

———. *Theories of the Theater: A Historical and Critical Survey from the Greeks to the Present*. Ithaca, N.Y.: Cornell University Press, 1984.

———. "Theater as Event," *Semiotica*, 56¾, (1985), pp. 309–14.

Cary, Joseph. "Futurism and the French *Théâtre d'Avant-Garde*." In *Total Theatre: A Critical Anthology*, ed. E. T. Kirby, pp. 99–114, New York: Dutton, 1969.

Caune, Jean. *La dramatisation*. Lourain: Cahiers théâtre Lourain, 1981.

Champigny, Robert. *Le genre dramatique. Essai*. Monte-Carlo: Editions Regain, 1965.

Chauduri, Una. "Seeing, Saying, Knowing: Hamlet and the Tenuous Project of Drama Semiotics." *New Orleans Review* 11, ¾ (Fall/Winter 1984), pp. 119–27.

Cole, David. *The Theatrical Event. A Mythos, A Vocabulary, A Perspective*. Middletown, Conn. Wesleyan University Press, 1975.

Copferman, Emile. *Vers un théâtre différent*. Paris: Maspero, 1976.

Coppieters, Frank. "Performance and Perception." *Poetics Today* 2, no. 3 (Spring 1981), pp. 35–48.

Corvin, Michel. "Sémiologie et spectacle: *George Dandin* (mise en scène de D. Benoin)." In *Sémiologie et théâtre. Organon 80*, pp. 93–152.

———. "La rédondance du signe dans le fonctionnement théâtral." *Degrés*, no. 13 (Spring 1980), pp. c–c23.

———. *Molière et ses metteurs en scène: pour une analyse de la représentation*. Lyon: Presses Universitaires de Lyon, 1985.

Deely, John, ed.*Semiotica 85* (Lanham, Md.: University Press of America, 1986).

*Degrés.* "Sémiologie du spectacle. Modèles théoriques." No. 29, Winter 1982. (acta of 1981 AISS-IASPA Conference).

———. "Sémiologie du spectacle. Performance/Représentation." No. 30, Spring 1982. (acta of 1981 AISS-IASPA Conference).

———. "Sémiologie du spectacle. Réception." No. 31, Summer 1982. (acta of 1981 AISS-IASPA Conference)

———. "Sémiologie du spectacle. Sens et culture." No. 32, Fall 1982. (acta of 1981 AISS-IASPA conference).

De Kuyper, Eric and Emile Poppe. "Pour une sémiotique du spectaculaire." *Degrés*, no. 15 (1978).

Demarcy, Richard. *Eléments d'une sociologie du spectacle.* Paris: 10/18, 1973.

De Marinis, Marco. "Vers une pragmatique de la communication théâtrale." *Versus 30* (Sep.–Dec. 1981), pp. 71–86.

———. *Semiotica del Teatro: l'analysi testuale dello spettacolo.* Milano: Bompiani, 1982.

———. "Toward a Cognitive Semiotic of Theatrical Emotions," *Versus 41* (May–August 1985), pp. 5–20.

Descotes, Maurice. *Le public de théâtre et son histoire.* Paris: PUF, 1964.

De Toro, Fernando. *Semiotica del teatro. Del texto a la puesta en escena.* Buenos Aires: Editorial Galerna, 1987.

Dichy, Albert. "Objets, acteurs, personnages dans le discours scénique." *Littérature*, no. 43, (Oct. 1981), pp. 89–99.

Dinu, Mihai. "Contribution à l'étude mathématique du théâtre." *Revue roumaine de mathématiques pures et appliquées* 15, no. 1 (1970); pp. 521–543.

Dort, Bernard. *Théâtre réel.* Paris: Seuil, 1971.

———. "Du 'bon sport.'" *Le Monde*, 28 Dec 1980, p. 8.

*Double Page.* "Théâtre du Soleil: Shakespeare." Paris: SNEP, 1982.

Ducrot, Oswald and Tzvetan Todorov. *Dictionnaire encyclopédique des sciences du language.* Paris: Seuil, 1972.

Durand, Régis. "Sémiologie et relations dans le champ du spectaculaire." *Degrés*, no. 29 (Winter 1982), pp. d–d5.

Duvignaud, Jean. *L'Acteur. Esquisse d'une sociologie du comédien.* Paris: Gallimard (Bibliothèque des Idées), 1965.

———. *Sociologie du théâtre. Essais sur les ombres collectives.* Paris: PUF, 1965.

———, ed. *La relation théâtrale.* Lille: Presses Universitaires de Lille, 1980.

Eco, Umberto. *A Theory of Semiotics.* Bloomington: Indiana University Press, 1976.

———. "Semiotics of Theatrical Performance." *The Drama Review* 21, no. 2 (March 1977), pp. 107–17.

Ekman, Paul, Wallace Friesen, and Sonia Ancoli. "Facial Signs of Emotional Experience." *Journal of Personality and Social Psychology* 39, no. 6 (1980), pp. 1125–34.

Elam, Keir. *The Semiotics of Theatre and Drama.* London and New York: Methuen, 1980.

———. "Much Ado About Doing Things With Words (and Other Means):

Some Problems in the Pragmatics of Theatre and Drama." In *Performing Texts*, ed. M. Issacharoff and R. Jones, pp. 39–58. Philadelphia: University of Pennsylvania Press, 1988.

Ertel, Evelyne. "Eléments pour une sémiologie du théâtre." *Travail Théâtral* 28/29 (1977); pp. 121–50.

———. "Vers une analyse sémiologique de la représentation." *Travail Théâtral* 32/33 (1979), pp. 164–72.

Fischer-Lichte, Erika. *Semiotik des Theater*. 3 vols. Tübingen: Gunter Narr, 1983.

———, ed. *Das Drama und seine Inszenierung*. Tübingen: Max Niemeyer, 1985.

Foucault, Michel. "What is an Author?" In *Language, Counter-Memory, Practice*, trans. D. F. Bouchard and S. Simon, ed. D. F. Bouchard. Ithaca, N.Y.: Cornell University Press, 1977.

Gasparro, Rosalba. *Il testo e l'immaginario: Argomenti di semiotica teatrale*. Palermo: ILA Palma, 1983.

Glowinski, Michal. "On concretization." *Roman Ingarden and Contemporary Polish Aesthetics: Essays*, ed. Piotr Graff and Slaw Krzemien-Ojak, pp. 33–45. Warsaw: PWN, 1975.

Goffman, Erving. *Frame Analysis*. New York: Harper, 1974.

Gossman, Lionel. "The Signs of Theatre." *Theatre Research International* 2, no. 1 (Oct. 1976).

Graff, Piotr, and Slaw Krzemien-Ojak, eds. *Roman Ingarden and Contemporary Polish Aesthetics: Essays*. Warsaw: PWN, 1975.

Greimas, A. J. *Sémantique structurale*. Paris: Larousse. 1966.

Green, André. *Hamlet et **Hamlet**. Une interprétation psychanalytique de la représentation*. Paris: Balland, 1982.

Grotowski, Jerzy. *Toward a Poor Theatre*. New York: Simon & Schuster, 1968.

Helbo, André. *Les mots et les gestes. Essai sur le théâtre*. Lille: Presses Universitaires de Lille, 1983.

———. ed. *Sémiologie de la représentation*. Bruxelles: Compléxe, 1975.

———, ed. *Approches de l'opéra*. Paris: Didier Erudition, 1986.

Helbo, André, J. D. Johansen, P. Davis, and A. Ubersfeld, eds. *Théâtre: modes d'approche*. Bruxelles: Editions labor, 1987.

Hess-Luttich, Ernest. *Zeichen und Schichten in Drama und Theater: Gerhardt Hauptmanns "Ratten"*. Berlin: Erich Schmidt, 1985.

———, ed. *Multimedial Communications*. Vol. 2, *Theatre Semiotics*. Tübingen: Gunter Narr, 1982.

Honzl, Jindrich. "Dynamics of the Sign in the Theatre." In *Semiotics of Art: Prague School Contributions*, ed. L. Matejka and I. R. Titunik, pp. 74–93. Cambridge, Mass.: MIT Press, 1976.

Hotier, Hugues. *Signes du cirque: approche sémiologique*. Bruxelles: AISS-IASPA, 1984.

Huizinga, Johan. *Homo Ludens*. Boston: Beacon Press, 1955.

Ingarden, Roman. *The Literary Work of Art. An Investigation on the Borderlines of Ontology, Logic and Theory of Literature*. Evanston, Ill.: Northwestern University Press, 1973 (1931).

————. *The Cognition of the Literary Work of Art*. Evanston, Ill.: Northwestern University Press, 1973 (1935).

*Interazione, Dialogo, Convenzioni*. Il caso del testo drammatico. Bologna: CLUEB, 1983.

Iser, Wolfgang. "Aspects génériques de la réception." *Poétique* 39 (1979), pp. 253–362.

Issacharoff, Michael. "Texte théâtral et didascalecture." *MLN* 96 (May 1981), pp. 809–23.

————. *Le spectacle du discours*. Paris: Corti, 1985.

Issacharoff, Michael and R. Jones, eds. *Performing Texts*. Philadelphia: University of Pennsylvania Press, 1988.

Jauss, Hans Robert. "La jouissance esthétique. Les expériences fondamentales de la poiesis, de l'aesthesis et de la catharsis." *Poétique* 39 (Sept. 1979), pp. 261–74.

Kirby, Ernest Theodore. *Ur-Drama: The Origins of Theatre*. New York: New York University Press, 1972.

————, ed. *Total Theatre: A Critical Anthology*. New York: Dutton, 1969.

Kowalewicz, Kazimierz. "Problemy socjologii teatru." *Studia Sociologiczne*. 3, no. 66 (1977), pp. 251–76.

————. "O odbiorze widowiska teatralnego." *Przeglad Sociologiczny* 33, pp 89–102.

Kowzan, Tadeusz. *Littérature et spectacle*. The Hague: Mouton, 1975.

————. "Le texte et son interprétation théâtrale," *Semiotica* 33, ¾ (1981), pp. 201–10.

————. "Signe zéro de la parole." *Degrés*, no. 3 (Summer 1982), pp. a–a16.

————. "Aristote, théoricien de l'art du spectacle." In *Théâtre de toujours d'Aristote à Kalisky*, ed. G. Debusscher and A. Van Crugten, pp. 24–30. Bruxelles: Editions de l'Université de Bruxelles, 1983.

Laborit, Henri. "Le geste et la parole. Le théâtre vu dans l'optique de la biologie des comportements." *Degrés*, no. 29 (Winter 1982), pp. b–b24.

*Les voies de la création théâtrale*. Vols. 1–11. Paris: CNRS, 1970–83.

Lotman, Jurij. "Semiotyka Sceny," trans. B. Zylko. *Dialog* 29, no. 11 (Nov. 1984), pp. 87–103.

Marcus, Salomon. "Semiotics of Theatre: A Mathematical Linguistic Approach." *Revue Roumaine de Linguistique* 25, no. 3 (1980), pp. 161–89.

Marinetti, F. T. "Futurism and the Theatre." In *Total Theatre*, ed. E. T. Kirby, pp. 89–95. New York: Dutton, 1969.

Matejka, L, ed. *Sound, Sign and Meaning*. Ann Arbor, Mich.: Slavic Contributions, 1976.

Matejka, L., and I. R. Titunik, eds. *Semiotics of Art: Prague School Contributions*. Cambridge, Mass.: MIT Press, 1976.

Mauron, Charles. *Phèdre*. Paris: Corti, 1968.

Moholy-Nagy, L. "Theatre, Circus, Variety." In *Total Theatre*, ed. E. T. Kirby, pp. 114–25. New York: Dutton, 1969.

Mounin, George. "La communication théâtrale," *Introduction à la sémiologie*. Paris: Minuit, 1970.

Nadin, Mihai. "Signs Functioning in Performance." *The Drama Review* 84 (Dec. 1979), pp. 105–20.

Nagler, A. M. *A Source Book in Theatrical History*. New York: Dover, 1959 (1952).

Ogden, C. K. and I. A. Richards, *The Meaning of Meaning*. 8th ed. New York: Harcourt, Brace, 1956.

Osinsky. Zbigniew. *Grotowski and His Laboratory*. New York: PAJ Publications, 1985.

Pavis, Patrice. *Problèmes de sémiologie théâtrale*. Montréal: Presses de l'Université du Québec, 1976.

———. *Voix et images de la scène. Vers une sémiologie de la réception*. 2d ed. Lille: Presses Universitaires de Lille, 1985.

———. *Marivaux à l'épreuve de la scène*. Paris: Publications de la Sorbonne, 1986.

———. *Dictionnaire du théâtre: termes et concepts de l'analyse théâtrale*. 2nd edition. Paris: Editions sociales, 1987.

Peckham, Morse. *Man's Rage for Chaos: Biology, Behavior and the Arts*. New York: Schocken Books, 1967.

Pelc, Jerzy. *Wstep do Semiotyki*. Warszawa: Wiedza Powszechna, 1982.

Piaget, Jean. *Biologie et connaissance*. Paris: Gallimard (Idées), 1967.

*Poetics Today*. Drama, Theater, Performance: A Semiotic Perspective. Vol. 2, no. 3 (Spring 1981).

Prieto, Luis. *Messages et signaux*. Paris: PUF, 1966.

Pronko, Leonard C. "Kabuki and the Elizabethan Theatre." In *Total Theatre*, ed. E. T. Kirby, pp. 187–96. New York: Dutton, 1969.

Roubine, Jean-Jacques. *Théâtre et mise en scène: 1880–1980*. Paris: PUF, 1980.

Rozik Eli. "Theatre as a Language: A Semiotic Approach." *Semiotica* 45½ (1983), pp. 65–87.

Ruffini, Franco. "Semiotica del teatro: ricognizione degli studi." *Biblioteca teatrale* 9 (1974), pp. 34–81.

———. *Semiotica del testo: l'esempio teatro*. Roma: Bulzoni, 1978.

Ryan, Marie-Laure. "Fiction, Non-Factuals and the Principle of Minimal Departure." *Poetics* 8 (1980).

Schechner, Richard. *Essays on Performance Theory, 1970–1976*. New York: Drama Book Specialists, 1977.

———. *Between Theater and Anthropology*. Philadelphia: University of Pennsylvania Press, 1985.

Scherer, Jacques. *La dramaturgie classique en France*. Paris: Nizet, 1970.

Schmid, Herta, and Aloysius Van Kesteren, eds. *Semiotics of Drama and Theatre*: Amsterdam: John Benjamins, 1984.

Searle, John. "The Logic of Fictional Discourse." *New Literary History*, no. 6 (1975a), pp. 319–32.

*Semiologie et théâtre. Organon 80*. Lyon: CERTC, 1980.

Serpieri, Alessandro. *Come comunica il teatro: dal testo alla scena*. Milan: Il Formichiere, 1978.

Shank, Theodore. *The Art of Dramatic Art*. New York: Dell Publishing, 1972 (1969).

Sinko, Grzegorz. *Opis przedstawienia teatralnego*. Problem semiotyczny. Wrocław: Ossolineum, 1982.

———. *Postać sceniczna i jej premiany w teatrze XX wieku*. Wrocaw: Ossolineum, 1988.

Slawinska, Irena. *Wspólczesna refleksja o teatrze*. Krakow: Wydawnictwo Literackie, 1979.

Souriau, Etienne. *Les deux cent mille situations dramatiques*. Paris: Flammarion, 1950.

Spariosu, Mikai. "Literature and Play: A Socio-cultural Approach." *Degrés*, no. 32 (Fall 1982), pp. k–k11.

Stierle, Karlheinz. "Réception et fiction." *Poétique*, no. 39 (Sept 1979), 299–320.

Tan, Ed and Henry Schoenmaker. "'Good Guy Bad Guy' Effect in Political Theatre." In *Semiotics of Drama and Theatre*, ed. Herta Schmid and Aloysius Van Kesteren, pp. 467–508. Amsterdam: John Benjamins, 1984.

*Télérama*. No. 1785, March 31–April 6, 1984.

Tomaselli, Keyan. "The Semiotics of Alternative Theatre in South Africa." *Critical Arts*. 2, no. 1 (1981), pp. 14–33.

Tomasino, Renato. *La forma del teatro. Analisi e storia delle pratiche di spettacolo*. Palermo: Acquario, 1984.

Turner, Victor. *From Ritual to Theatre: The Human Seriousness of Play*. New York: Performance Arts Journal Press, 1982.

Ubersfeld, Anne. *Lire le théâtre*. Paris: Editions sociales, 1978.

———. *L'Ecole du spectateur*. *Lire le théâtre* 2. Paris: Editions sociales, 1981.

Van Kesteren, Aloysius. "Explicit Theory Versus Implicit Theory II: Ideology of a Theatre Group." In *Zeichen und Realitat*, ed. Klaus Oehler. Tübingen: Stauffenburg, 1984.

———. "Fundamentals in Theatre Research." In *Semiotics of Drama and Theatre*, ed. Herta Schmid and Aloysius Van Kesteren, pp. 19–63. Amsterdam: John Benjamins, 1984.

Van Zyl, John. "Towards a Socio-Semiotics of Performance." *Semiotic Scene*, 2 no. 2 (April 1979), pp. 99–111.

Veillon, O. R., ed. *Antoine Vitez: Toutes les mises en scène*. Paris: Jean-Cyrille Godefroy, 1981.

Veinstein, André. *La mise en scène théâtrale et sa condition esthétique*. Paris: Flammarion, 1968.

Veltruský, Jiří. "Puppetry and Acting." *Semiotica* 47¼ (1983), pp. 69–122.

———. "Drama as Literature and Performance." In *Das Drama und seine Inszenierung*, ed. E. Fischer-Lichte, pp. 12–21. Tübingen: Max Niemeyer, 1985.

Warning, Rainer. "Pour une pragmatique du discours fictionnel." *Poétique* 39 (Sep. 1979), pp. 320–37.

Williams, Raymond. *Drama in Performance*. London: Penguin Books (Pelican Books), 1972 (1968).

Yamaguchi, Masao. "Theatrical Space in Japan, a Semiotic Approach." *Japan and America: A Journal of Cultural Studies* 1, no. 1 (1984), pp. 1–8.

# Index

Entries in this index refer to: (1) key theoretical notions; (2) selected dramatic texts, identified by title and/or author; (3) specific concrete performances, identified by director's name and/or title of play; and (4) theoreticians and critics who are *discussed* in the text. No entries are provided for authors, directors, actors, theoreticians, critics, and works that are merely mentioned in the text or in notes.